Minnesota
Bike Atlas

Seventh Edition

Published by
Hostelling International USA–Minnesota Council
and the Twin Cities Bicycling Club

Bike Atlas Disclaimer

Please take advantage of the excellent routes offered in this Atlas. The routes were developed to showcase bicycle-friendly secondary roadways and area bike trails. The Twin Cities Bicycling Club and Hostelling International USA – Minnesota Council cannot be held responsible for changing road conditions or road closures. Keep in mind that the amount of traffic you encounter is largely dependent upon the time of day and day of week that you choose to ride.

Always ride responsibly and lawfully.

Address inquires to:
Permissions, Hostelling International USA–Minnesota,
622 Selby Ave, St. Paul, Minnesota 55104

ISBN - 13: 9780971026612 Paperback

Printed in the United States of America

Table of Contents

PHOTOGRAPHER © 2007 ROB MANN

THE TWIN CITIES AREA IS A GREAT PLACE TO RIDE

Do you know of any really great places to ride your bike?

We do. We're the Twin Cities Bicycling Club (TCBC), the largest recreational cycling club in Minnesota. We've been hosting organized club rides in the Minneapolis/St. Paul area and beyond for over thirty years. At last count, we were 1500 members strong. And we ride virtually every day of the year. This 7th edition of the Minnesota Bike Atlas, a joint production of TCBC and The Minnesota Council of Hostelling International USA, is a collection of some of our favorite routes. We're confident some of them will become your favorites, too.

Why are we so sure you'll find your new favorite route in this book? We believe the cyclists who live in the area and love to ride are the best source of information about great places to ride. TCBC's volunteer Ride Leaders designed these routes. We pored over bike and trail maps, explored the nooks and crannies of parks and neighborhoods on our bikes, and documented these routes. We know every smooth stretch of blacktop, challenging hill, winding park trail, remote- but-beautiful county road and creative shortcut through neighborhood streets. We even know the convenience stores en route with the best selection of snacks and sport drinks. We designed and refined these routes for TCBC and road-tested them with club riders. We invite you to experience some of our favorite routes and we're happy to share them with you!

You'll need four things to make the most of this book. First, make sure you're capable of and comfortable with the features of the route you choose to ride. A brief description of the route (e.g., distance, terrain, roads or trails) is provided on the map legend to help you know what kind of ride you're in for.

Second, you need to have a reliable bicycle. If you haven't done so lately, take your bike into your local bike shop and have it looked over by a mechanic. Nothing stops a good ride faster than a busted bike.

Third, have a "Plan B" if something goes wrong. Ride with the tools you need to make basic repairs, such as changing a flat tire. Have a plan if something more unexpected happens; it's always a good idea to bring some money, a cell phone, or a friend along for the ride.

SCENIC RIDES IN WESTERN WISCONSIN

Finally, approach these routes with a sense of adventure. Roads and trails are always changing. For example, the August 2007 I-35W bridge collapse occurred just as we were finalizing the routes that appear in this book. That event changed the Twin Cities in many ways, not the least of which was forcing the closure of a well-traveled stretch of bike path along the Mississippi River near downtown Minneapolis. Until that bridge is rebuilt and the West River Road reopened, cyclists are finding other ways to get where they need to go. You may encounter detours or road changes on any of these routes as construction projects, road repairs, and new developments alter our landscape. With an adventurous spirit, you will easily roll with these changes… in every sense of the word.

Make this Atlas your own. Mark it up. Make notations in the margins. Circle rides you have done. Devise your own rating system. Print copies of the rides and route descriptions off of the CD and take them along with you on the rides. Use the Ride Journal to track your rides, noting the conditions, the weather, great sights along the way, spots for a picnic, etc. In short, make this your Atlas of Minnesota explorations by bicycle.

Have a great ride!

Minnesota Ironman® Bike Ride

MINNESOTA IRONMAN® BICYCLE RIDE IN LAKEVILLE MINNESOTA

HI-Minnesota has been biking since its inception in 1939. We are proud to co-present the 7th Edition of the Minnesota Bike Atlas in association with TCBC.

Introduction:

We are a mission-driven non-profit organization, part of a worldwide network, based around the principle that international travel does the world good by expanding the world view of its citizens through experience and exchange.

Our Mission Statement:

"To develop culturally sensitive world citizens through educational programs, promotion of responsible travel, and positive hostelling experiences."

What We Do:

You may know the Minnesota Council of Hostelling International USA by any of its three major activities:

1. The Minnesota Ironman® Bike Ride, which we have been running for over 40 years, serves as the major fundraiser for our organization.

2. Travel education programming and travel related services (Eurail Pass sales, hostel memberships, professional travel advice) which we offer in our offices at 622 Selby Avenue in St. Paul.

MISSISSIPPI HEADWATERS

MISSISSIPPI HEADWATERS HOSTEL - ITASCA STATE PARK NEAR BEMIDJI

3. The Mississippi Headwaters Hostel, located in Itasca State Park near Bemidji, MN. Our hostel is an excellant destination for groups and invididuals looking for a great place to stay while they explore the headwaters of the Mississippi.

Programs & Services

Visit our office in St. Paul for:

- *Eurail Passes*
- *HI Memberships*
- *Excellent travel advice*
- *Information on local biking*
- *Travel/Educational presentations*

Thinking about Traveling to:

Europe, Australia, South America, Asia? Then join us for a Travelers Circle! Hosted the 3rd Thursday of each month at our St. Paul headquarters, we discuss fascinating travel destinations and savvy travel tips with new speakers each month. Check out our website for details!

Contact:

HI-MN

622 Selby Ave. St. Paul, MN 55104

T: 651.251.1495

E: info@himinnesota.org

W: www.himinnesota.org

www.ironmanbikeride.org

1939 AYH
WEATHER VANE
LOGO

Twin Cities Bicycling Club

PHOTOGRAPHER © 2007 ROB MANN

THE TWIN CITIES HAS SOME OF THE BEST PLACES TO RIDE IN THE COUNTRY - STONE ARCH EXPRESS PAGE 31

A Message from the Authors

The Twin Cities Bicycling Club had its origins in the 1970's as the bicycling arm of Hostelling International - Minnesota Council. TCBC was formally organized in 1993 and we became an independant non-profit organization in 2000.

Today, TCBC is the largest recreational bicycling club in the Minneapolis-St. Paul area and one of the most active bicycling clubs in the United States. TCBC rides are open to members and non-members. We typically appeal to adult cyclists who enjoy group riding but don't want to race. Our rides are on roads or paved trails and we offer fun for all skill levels. Occasionally we offer other events such as family rides and off-road mountain bike rides.

MILEAGE
RECOGNITION
MEDALLION

PHOTOGRAPHER © 2007 SCOTT LARSON

A SPECTACULAR FALL RIDE ON CRUISIN' THE COULEES - PAGE 122

Our Mission Statement:

"To promote safe and effective bicycling and recreational bicycle rides for the Minneapolis-Saint Paul area."

What We Do:

- Organize and lead over 1,800 bike rides throughout the year
- Offer bicycling-related educational seminars
- Promote good bicycling practices on roads and trails
- Ride our bikes a lot!

TCBC Rides are led by our trained volunteer Ride Leaders. At the beginning of each ride, the Ride Leader gives a briefing with an emphasis on safe riding, a description of the route, the level of difficulty and rest stop designations. Ride Leaders check to make sure everyone is wearing a properly fitted helmet, a club rule. To help riders feel comfortable, Ride Leaders also like to introduce new riders to the group.

In addition to all the rides put on by our leaders, TCBC also hosts a number of annual events including our "All-Club" rides on Labor Day and Memorial Day.

OUR FAVORITE
ROAD SIGN

Twin Cities Bicycling Club

ARTISTIC EPICUREAN RIDE

TCBC CLUB JERSEYS 1992 2001 2003 2006

On July 4th of each year we host the "Watermelon Ride" – with both trail and road routes. This event is a favorite for our members and the community. Everyone enjoys the great picnic at the end! WOW (Weekend-On-Wheels), typically scheduled for early August, is an organized weekend ride for club members that happens in various locations around the state and western Wisconsin. Throughout the year, TCBC offers seminars with topics ranging from bicycle advocacy, bike trips, tire changing and bicycle maintenance. And in the winter, our members come together for recognition of their achievements as club riders and volunteers at our annual banquet

Benefits of Membership:

- *TCBC News*, published 10 times per year
- Great website, with up-to-date ride schedule
- TCBC on-line member forums
- Discounts at many local bike shops
- Liability and medical insurance coverage during club rides
- Mileage achievements tracked and recognized

"THE DIPPING OF THE TIRES" – MILLE LACS LAKE - ANNUAL TOUR OF LAKES RIDE

CYCLING TRIPS IN U.S AND EUROPE

JULY 4TH WATERMELON RIDE

Check out our website for additional information and for our complete ride schedule.

Contact:
Twin Cities Bicycling Club
P.O. Box 131086
Roseville, MN 55113

www.bikeTCBC.org

AND WE ALWAYS EAT VERY WELL

RIDE SAFE AND RIDE HAPPY

Cyclists are subject to the same laws as the rest of the vehicles on the road.

ALWAYS!

As is true with many sports, riding a bicycle is an activity where there may be hazards that could result in an injury or even death. Anyone who rides wants to take actions to lessen the chance of getting hurt. In the following pages we give you some basic advice about how to bike safely on streets and trails. There are plenty of good tips, but the best advice is to use common sense and stay alert. Ride strong and share the road. Set an example of safety and respect.

Riding in traffic

When you bike on city streets and country roads you are part of traffic. Cyclists are subject to the same laws as the rest of the vehicles on the road. Obey those laws. Safe drivers don't drive through stop signs or red lights, bicyclists shouldn't either.

When riding with cars, buses and trucks, assume that they don't see you. Even when you are riding safely and obeying traffic laws, others on the road may not be. Many drivers are distracted, having telephone conversations, eating, listening to loud music, talking to passengers, or even reading or watching videos. Add intoxicated or otherwise impaired

drivers to the mix and you might just want to get off your bike and walk. Even a cyclist who is "right" loses when struck by a driver.

Most drivers mean well, but some actually target cyclists for verbal abuse or drive too close, trying to cause an accident. But sometimes a well-meaning driver can be dangerous also. Be careful when that driver stops and waves you through an intersection. Although one considerate driver may be looking out for your safety, do not

BE COURTEOUS AND DON'T CONFRONT DRIVERS FOR ANY REASON

assume that other drivers are behaving in a like matter. Riders have been waved through intersections by one driver then plowed down by another, resulting in injury and death. Bottom line? Give cars and other traffic as wide a berth as safely possible and obey the laws. Ride with common sense.

In addition to obeying traffic laws, make yourself visible. Wear clothing with bright colors and reflective material. Use front and rear lights on your bike in low light conditions.

WHEN RIDING IN A GROUP ALWAYS BE PREDICTABLE AND HOLD YOUR LINE

Make eye contact with drivers. Talk to drivers at lights when stopped next to them. Making drivers aware that they are sharing the road with a person fosters an understanding with drivers as well as riders. Sharing the road applies to drivers and cyclists. Treat drivers with the respect that you expect. Obey the traffic laws as you expect them to.

Finally, don't confront drivers for any reason. Get the license plate number and report it.

Other riders

Over the years, we've seen far more riders brought down by other cyclists than by cars. We see cyclists on trails and streets who behave like some drivers listening to an iPod® or radio, talking on a cell phone, running red lights, cutting in and out of traffic, and generally acting unsafe. Avoid these folks. A distracted rider is a dangerous rider.

Be as careful on trails as you are on roads and streets. Don't ride faster than is safe. Obey speed limits for trails and respect other trail users, such as inline skaters, runners, walkers, pets and other cyclists. When passing others, call out "On your left!" Make sure they hear you. Riding fast on trails isn't wise.

Slow riders who make sudden moves, kids (and adults) who don't know the rules for trails - or even their right from left - can cause accidents and injury.

Riding in a group is fun, social, and safer than solo riding because a group is more visible to drivers and others. Drafting, or following closely behind another cyclist and relying on them to fight the wind, can be fun. It also means more to watch out for and a new set of skills to be mastered.

THE FIRST RULE in group riding: Hold your line. That means you need to ride in a straight line at a steady pace. Zipping back and forth and changing speed forces others to brake and accelerate. It is difficult to ride with someone who is so unpredictable.

THE SECOND RULE: Keep pedaling. Pedal/coast/pedal forces the riders behind you to brake then speed up again.

THE THIRD RULE: Be safe. Point out to others hazards such as potholes, cracks, glass, sand, or debris in the road. Communicate stops, turns, and hazards with hand or verbal signals. Be thoughtful of the skill levels of your fellow riders. *Always choose safety over speed.*

BE SAFE!
Always call out and point to any hazard such as potholes, cracks, glass, sand, or debris in the road.

ANOTHER FAVORITE ROAD SIGN

Cycling Safety

MOST IMPORTANT IS WEARING A PROPERLY FITTED HELMET

TCBC HELMET MIRROR

Mirrors

Mirrors can greatly assist a cyclist in seeing and reacting to traffic. Many different models are available. They fit on helmets, bikes or glasses. Once you ride with a mirror that works for you, you'll wonder how you ever got along without it.

EQUIPMENT SAFETY

Helmets

Wearing a properly fitted helmet is the single most important way to reduce the risk of injury and death inherent in cycling. Your helmet should be snug, level and stable. It should comfortably touch your head all around, but stay in place while sustaining blows or shaking. It should sit as low and level on the head as possible, with the strap snug but not too tight.

TCBC MAP CLIP

Use the pads that came with your helmet to adjust the fit. Use thicker pads where needed, or remove pads at the top of the helmet so it fits low enough. When you look up, the front of helmet should just be visible to your eye.

Adjust the helmet straps so the "Y" of the side straps meets just below your ears. The chin strap should be snug against the chin so when you open your mouth wide you can feel the helmet pull down a little. Using the rear straps and plastic holders, adjust the back of the helmet so it sits level and snug.

For a final check, look in the mirror and shake your head back and forth. Make sure your helmet stays in place and feels comfortable.

CLOTHING APPROPRIATE FOR WEATHER

Clothing

Wear bright and easy-to-see jerseys and jackets. Well-fitted clothing appropriate to the weather keeps a cyclist happy, comfortable and safe. Gloves help your sweaty hands keep their grip, provide cushioning while riding, keep you warm on cooler days and protect your hands in case of a fall.

Bikes

Inspect your bike before every ride. Use the bike "Top 10 Check List" located on page 16 of this Atlas. Pump tires to recommended tire pressure. Make sure you know and understand how to take off wheels and change a tube or tire. Keep your chain lubricated and clean. Repair any broken parts as soon as possible. Don't ride unless you are sure your bike is safe.

CORRECT FIT – SNUG, LEVEL AND STABLE

HELMET SITS LOW ON THE FOREHEAD, JUST ABOVE THE EYEBROW.

HELMET IS LEVEL ACROSS THE TOP OF YOUR HEAD.

CHIN STRAP IS FASTENED TIGHT ENOUGH TO ALLOW ONLY ONE FINGER WIDTH OF SPACE TO SQUEEZE BETWEEN YOUR STRAP AND CHIN.

HELMET SHOULD FIT SNUGLY WITH SIDE STRAPS STRADDLING YOUR EARS AND THE BUCKLES RIGHT BELOW YOUR EARLOBES.

FOR A FINAL CHECK, GENTLY TRY TO ROLL THE HELMET BACK AND FORTH ON THE HEAD. THE HELMET SHOULD NOT MOVE MORE THAN 1/2 INCH IN ANY DIRECTION.

HELMET IS SITTING TOO FAR BACK ON HEAD.

HELMET IS NOT LEVEL ACROSS THE TOP OF HEAD.

CHIN STRAP IS TOO LOOSE AND SIDE STRAPS ARE NOT PROPERLY FITTED AROUND THE EARS.

ADJUSTMENT BUCKLE IS NOT PROPERLY FITTED UNDER EARLOBES.

INCORRECT FIT

IF YOUR HELMET...

saved your head once in a crash, then it did its job, and it's time to retire it to the trash and buy yourself a new one. Cheap insurance.

If your helmet was purchased over five years ago, get an opinion about getting a new one to protect you. If your helmet is over ten years old, you most likley need a new one.

If your helmet makes your head really hot even when the weather isn't really hot, then count the number of vents on your helmet, and go buy yourself a helmet with more vents in it and sweat wicking pads to keep you cooler.

If your helmet gives you a "bad hair day" look, then bring along a great-looking cap to cover your hair after the ride.

You've found a route you want to try... now print your map and you're ready to ride! Wait - not yet. You have plenty of time to do a pre-ride check. We've divided it into two parts: the rider and the bike.

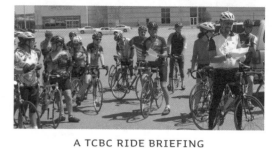

A TCBC RIDE BRIEFING

The Bike's Top Ten Checklist

If you do nothing else for your bike, there are two things you should routinely do. Steps 1 and 2 below will elliminate many common problems and you will be a happy cyclist for many miles.

1. Check tire pressure. Inflate tires to manufacturer's recommended pressure. Look for cuts, bulges and worn spots. Replace tire if needed.

DRIBBLE A SMALL AMOUNT OF LUBE DIRECTLY ONTO BACK OF CHAIN ON THE CASSETTE WHILE TURNING CRANK

2. Clean and lubricate chain. Clean after every ride and apply lubrication if needed. Apply very LITTLE lubrication. No need to soak chain. Just dribble a small amount while turning cranks or apply one drop at a time to rollers on chain only. Do this after a ride and you won't forget or be in too big of a hurry before next ride.

3. Tubes - carry at least one, perhaps two.

4. Patch kit for tubes, just in case you have multiple flats.

5. Air pump that can pump up your tire to required pressure.

6. Tire levers to remove tire from rim.

7. Multi-tool

8. Chain tool and pin (if needed), to fit your chain.

9. Tire boot for temporary patch on a worn or cut tire.

10. Duct tape - you would be surprised how handy it can be. Not a big roll, just enough to use just in case.

The Rider's Top Ten Checklist

1. Helmet - adjusted to fit. Snug, level and stable - and worn every time you ride. *No ifs, ands or buts.*

2. Glasses - shades for a sunny day, clear for when its not. A bug or rock in the eye at 25 MPH isn't fun.

3. Mirror - many riders use a mirror attached to glasses, helmet or bike. Once you start using a mirror, you won't leave home without it.

4. Sunscreen - use a broad-spectrum sunscreen with an SPF of at least 15 on all exposed skin, including the lips, even on cloudy days. Reapply sunscreen frequently.

5. Clothing for biking that is warm/cool/dry enough for route and weather.

6. Understanding of and willingness to follow traffic laws. Pay attention, be courteous and yield right of way on trails, streets and roads.

7. Ride safely and within your abilities. Don't confront motorists, get plate number if you can and report them. Stay cool.

8. Sports drink or water to stay hydrated. Perhaps a snack or power bar.

9. ID, insurance card and money or a credit card.

10. Cell phones are great in an emergency. You can turn them off until you need them. It's not safe to talk and ride at the same time.

| NEW TIRE TUBES | MULTI TOOL | CHAIN TOOL & PIN | TIRE LEVERS | DUCT TAPE | TIRE BOOT | PATCH KIT |

SEAT BAG CONTENTS

TAIL LIGHT

MAP CLIP

HELMET

TIRE PUMP

WATER

TIRE PUMP

EYE PROTECTION

REAR VIEW MIRROR

Things To Do Before Each Ride

• Pump air into your tires before each ride. Find the manufacturer's recommended pressure by reading the PSI on the side of the tire. Never over inflate a tire beyond it's recommended tire pressure.

• Inspect your tires for any deep cuts or cracks and wear. When tires are worn and thin they are more suseptable to flats. Always carry a new spare tube and patch kit and tire changing tools and pump.

• Check that your riding position is comfortable and that your leg is almost fully extended when pedaling. Check that your saddle is level and aligned with frame and that your saddle adjustment clamp and seat post clamp are tight.

• Lubricate your chain and derailleurs after every 40 miles of riding. Make sure all components are clean and free of lube buildup before lubricating. Lubricate your cables at cable stops.

• Check wheel alignment by picking up one end of the bike and spinning the wheel. Make sure the wheel spins true without any wobble or brake drag. Also check spoke tension making sure they are tight. Check the quick release levers to make sure they are tight.

• Always test your brakes by squeezing the brake levers to see if they engage properly. Inspect the pads for wear and check the brake release levers to make sure they are engaged.

• Always wear a properly fitted bike helmet (snug, level and stable). Bring enough water to keep yourself hydrated during a ride (i.e.- one bottle for every 15-20 miles of riding). Dehydration can cause leg cramps and fatigue.

BE PREPARED!

ALWAYS STOCK YOUR SEAT BAG WITH THE ESSENTIALS SHOWN ABOVE.

Metro

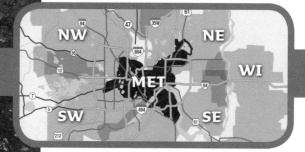

CLUB FAVORITE NEW YEARS DAY
SUMMIT AVE - POLAR BEAR RIDE

RELAX AROUND THE LAKES
GRAND ROUND - PAGE 34

GRAND
ROUNDS

SCENIC BYWAY

MINNEHAHA CREEK TRAIL
CITY EXPLORER - PAGE 36

MENDOTA BRIDGE TRAIL
"U & ME" PAGE 29

HIGH BRIDGE OVERLOOK - STONE ARCH EXPRESS - PAGE 33

Legend: FOOD · WATER · TOILET · FLAT · ROLLING · HILLY · CLIMBS · ROADS · TRAILS · LT TRAFFIC · TRAFFIC · SCENIC · TREATS

Page	Ride	Miles	At Ride Start	Terrain	Highlights
20	SLPing Out	13/26	Food, Water, Toilet	Flat, Trails, LT Traffic	Scenic, Treats
21	Franklin Freezer	21	Food, Water, Toilet	Hilly, Climbs, Roads, Traffic	Scenic
22	Nokomis Out & Back	22	Food, Water, Toilet	Flat, Roads, Trails, Traffic	Scenic
23	Sunrise North	23	Water, Toilet	Rolling, Roads, Trails, Traffic	
24	Great Googly Moogly	23		Flat, Rolling, Roads, Trails, Traffic	
25	Midtown Express	24/27	Water	Flat, Trails, Traffic	Treats
26	Sonny Side Up	24/33	Food, Water, Toilet	Flat, Rolling, Roads, Trails	Treats
27	Pleasant on Pleasant	25	Water, Toilet	Flat, Climbs, Roads, Trails, Traffic	Scenic
28	Thursday Therapy	26/31	Water, Toilet	Flat, Roads, Traffic	
29	U & Me	26	Food, Water, Toilet	Flat, Roads, Traffic	Scenic, Treats
30	Great Buns	26	Food	Flat, Climbs, Roads, Trails	Scenic
31	The Whole Enchilada	26/33		Flat, Climbs, Traffic	
32	Gears Tears & Fears	26/33		Rolling, Climbs, Roads, Traffic	
33	Stone Arch Express	27	Water	Flat, Climbs, Roads, Traffic	
34	Grand Round & Half Round	33/37	Food, Water, Toilet	Rolling, Climbs, Roads, Traffic	Scenic, Treats
35	Winter Warm-Up West	33/39	Food, Water, Toilet	Flat, Climbs, Roads, Traffic	Scenic
36	City Explorer	36	Water, Toilet	Flat, Climbs, Trails, Traffic	Scenic, Treats

Disclaimer: The Twin Cities Bicycling Club, Hostelling International USA – Minnesota Council, and their respective officers, employees, trip leaders and members, and those whose work appears in this Atlas, and those people and establishments who distribute this Atlas, cannot be held responsible for the future condition of any of these routes, or for any injuries or damages sustained or occuring while using these routes.

SLP'ing Out

13 / 26 Miles

Depart from Erik's Bike Shop, NW corner of Minnetonka Blvd (one mile east of 169) and Texas Ave in St Louis Park. This ride is mostly on trails and bicycle lanes.

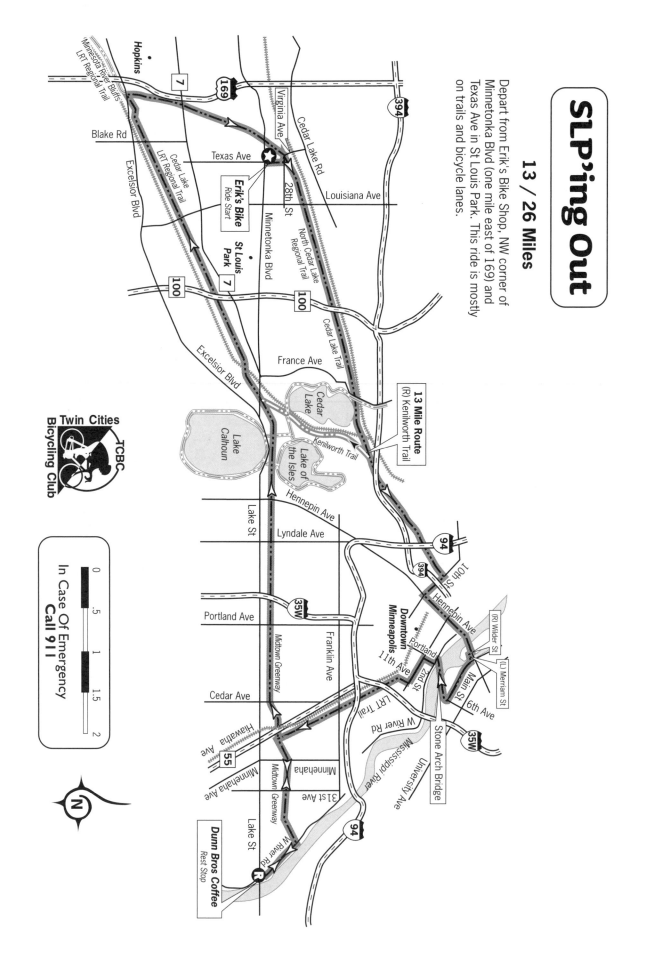

Hopkins

7

169

394

Virginia Ave

Cedar Lake Rd

Blake Rd

Texas Ave

Erik's Bike
Ride Start

28th St

Louisiana Ave

Cedar Lake
LRT Regional Trail

Excelsior Blvd

Minnetonka Blvd

St Louis
Park

7

North Cedar Lake
Regional Trail

100

100

Cedar Lake Trail

Excelsior Blvd

France Ave

Cedar
Lake

13 Mile Route
(R) Kenilworth Trail

Kenilworth Trail

Lake
Calhoun

Lake of
the Isles

Twin Cities
Bicycling Club
TCBC

Hennepin Ave

Lake St

Lyndale Ave

94

394

10th St

Hennepin Ave

Downtown
Minneapolis

(R) Wilder St

(L) Merriam St

Portland

Main St

6th Ave

35W

Portland Ave

Franklin Ave

11th Ave

2nd St

Midtown Greenway

35w

Cedar Ave

Stone Arch Bridge

LRT Trail

W River Rd

University Ave

Mississippi River

Hiawatha Ave

55

Minnehaha Ave

Minnehaha

Midtown Greenway

31st Ave

94

Lake St

W River Rd

Dunn Bros Coffee
Rest Stop

R

In Case Of Emergency
Call 911

0   .5   1   1.5   2

N

20

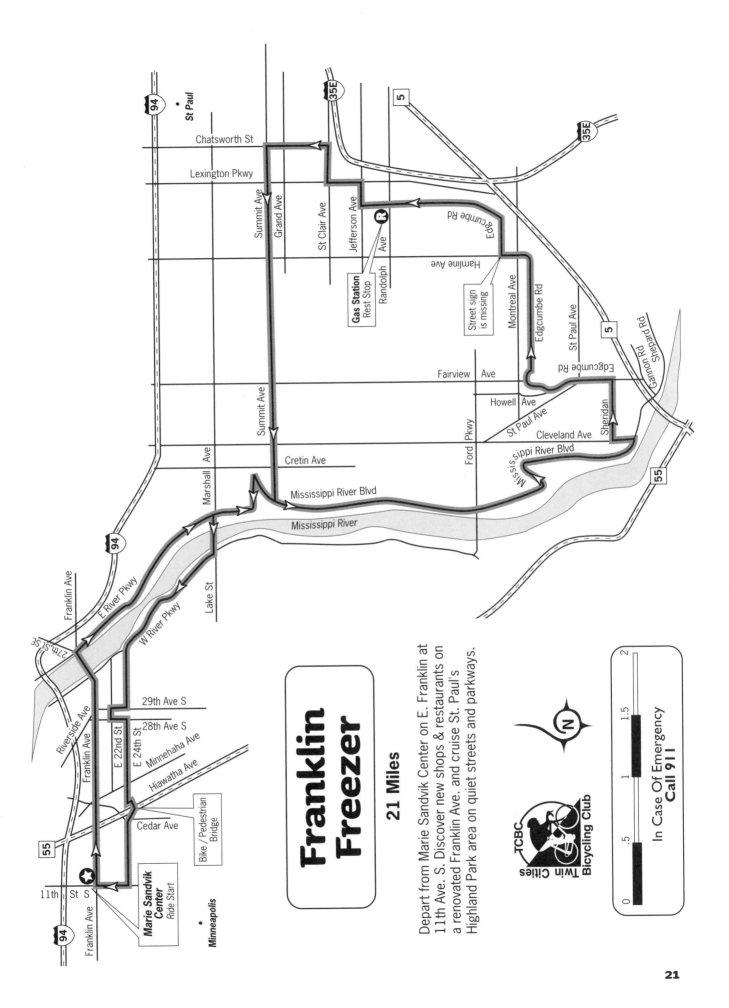

Franklin Freezer

21 Miles

Depart from Marie Sandvik Center on E. Franklin at 11th Ave. S. Discover new shops & restaurants on a renovated Franklin Ave. and cruise St. Paul's Highland Park area on quiet streets and parkways.

In Case Of Emergency
Call 911

Twin Cities
Bicycling Club
TCBC

Marie Sandvik Center
Ride Start

Bike / Pedestrian Bridge

Gas Station
Rest Stop

Street sign is missing

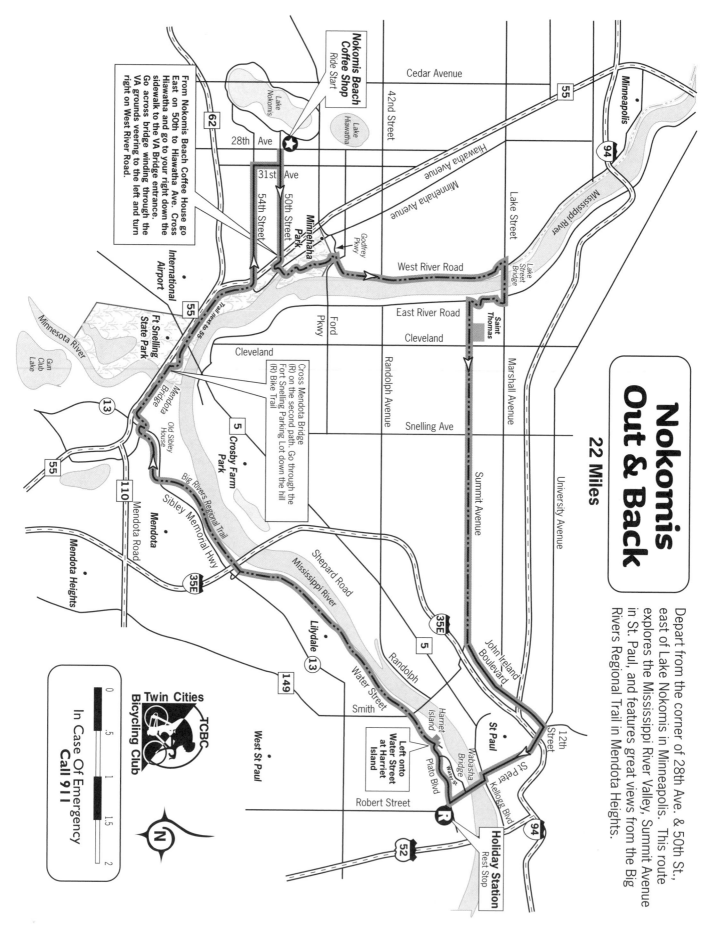

Nokomis Out & Back

22 Miles

Depart from the corner of 28th Ave. & 50th St., east of Lake Nokomis in Minneapolis. This route explores the Mississippi River Valley, Summit Avenue in St. Paul, and features great views from the Big Rivers Regional Trail in Mendota Heights.

Nokomis Beach Coffee Shop
Ride Start

From Nokomis Beach Coffee House go East on 50th to Hiawatha Ave. Cross Hiawatha and go to your right down the sidewalk to the VA Bridge entrance. Go across bridge winding through the VA grounds veering to the left and turn right on West River Road.

Cross Mendota Bridge (R) on the second path. Go through the Fort Snelling Parking Lot down the hill (R) Bike Trail

Left onto Water Street at Harriet Island

Holiday Station
Rest Stop

Cedar Avenue
42nd Street
28th Ave
Lake Nokomis
Lake Hiawatha
31st Ave
54th Street
50th Street
Minnehaha Park
Godfrey Pkwy
Minnehaha Avenue
Hiawatha Avenue
Lake Street
Minneapolis
Mississippi River
West River Road
Lake Street Bridge
East River Road
Cleveland
Saint Thomas
Marshall Avenue
Snelling Ave
University Avenue
Summit Avenue
John Ireland Boulevard
12th Street
St Peter
Kellogg Blvd
Wabasha Bridge
Water St
St Paul
Harriet Island
Plato Blvd
Robert Street
Ford Pkwy
Cleveland
Randolph Avenue
International Airport
Ft Snelling State Park
Trail flex to 55
55
62
Minnesota River
Gun Club Lake
Mendota Bridge
Old Sibley House
13
55
110
Mendota
Mendota Road
Mendota Heights
Sibley Memorial Hwy
Big Rivers Regional Trail
Crosby Farm Park
5
35E
Lilydale
13
149
West St Paul
Mississippi River
Shepard Road
Water Street
Smith
Randolph
5
35E
94
52

Twin Cities Bicycling Club
TCBC

In Case Of Emergency
Call 911

0   .5   1   1.5   2

N

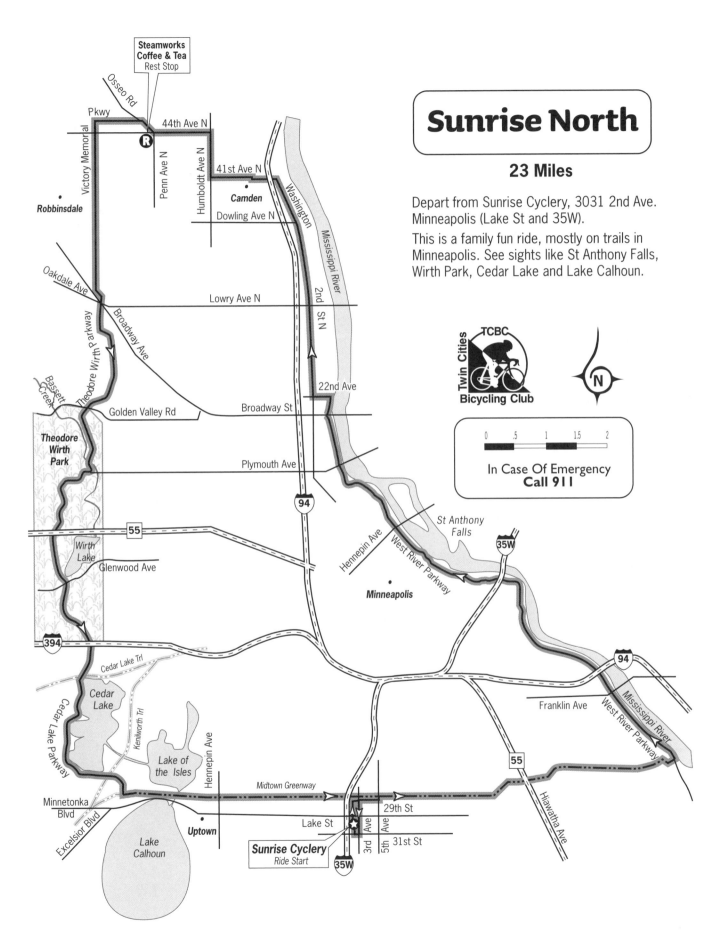

Sunrise North

23 Miles

Depart from Sunrise Cyclery, 3031 2nd Ave. Minneapolis (Lake St and 35W).

This is a family fun ride, mostly on trails in Minneapolis. See sights like St Anthony Falls, Wirth Park, Cedar Lake and Lake Calhoun.

TCBC
Twin Cities Bicycling Club

In Case Of Emergency
Call 911

Steamworks Coffee & Tea
Rest Stop

Osseo Rd
Pkwy
Victory Memorial
44th Ave N
Penn Ave N
Humboldt Ave N
41st Ave N
Camden
Dowling Ave N
Washington
Mississippi River
2nd St N
Robbinsdale
Oakdale Ave
Lowry Ave N
Theodore Wirth Parkway
Broadway Ave
Bassett Creek
Golden Valley Rd
Broadway St
22nd Ave
Theodore Wirth Park
55
Wirth Lake
Plymouth Ave
94
Glenwood Ave
St Anthony Falls
35W
Hennepin Ave
West River Parkway
Minneapolis
394
Cedar Lake Trl
94
Cedar Lake
Kenilworth Trl
Cedar Lake Parkway
Franklin Ave
West River Parkway
Mississippi River
Lake of the Isles
Hennepin Ave
Midtown Greenway
55
Hiawatha Ave
Minnetonka Blvd
Excelsior Blvd
Uptown
Lake St
29th St
3rd Ave
5th Ave
31st St
Lake Calhoun
Sunrise Cyclery Ride Start
35W

23

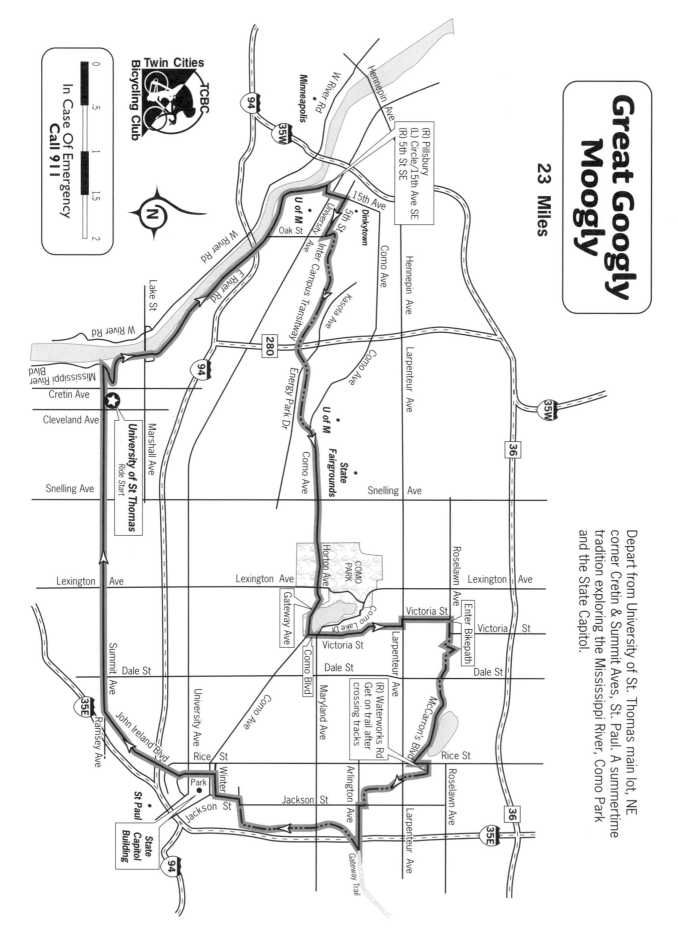

Great Googly Moogly

23 Miles

Depart from University of St. Thomas main lot, NE corner Cretin & Summit Aves, St. Paul. A summertime tradition exploring the Mississippi River, Como Park and the State Capitol.

Twin Cities Bicycling Club — TCBC

In Case Of Emergency
Call 911

0   .5   1   1.5   2

(R) Pillsbury
(L) Circle/15th Ave SE
(R) 5th St SE

University of St Thomas
Ride Start

Enter Bikepath

(R) Waterworks Rd.
Get on trail after
crossing tracks

State Capitol
Building

Midtown Express

24 / 27 Miles

Depart from the Lock & Dam parking lot underneath the west end of the Stone Arch bridge. From Washington Avenue, go east on Portland, past West River Road, and down the short steep hill to the parking lot. This is a figure eight loop, traveling the Kenilworth Trail twice. Many variations are possible to shorten or lengthen the route. To shorten, forego the loop to Hopkins. To lengthen, take West River Road from downtown to the Midtown Greenway. The flat route is conducive to single speed and fixed gear bikes, except for the short steep hill out of the Lock and Dam parking lot (and West River Road if you lengthen the route)!

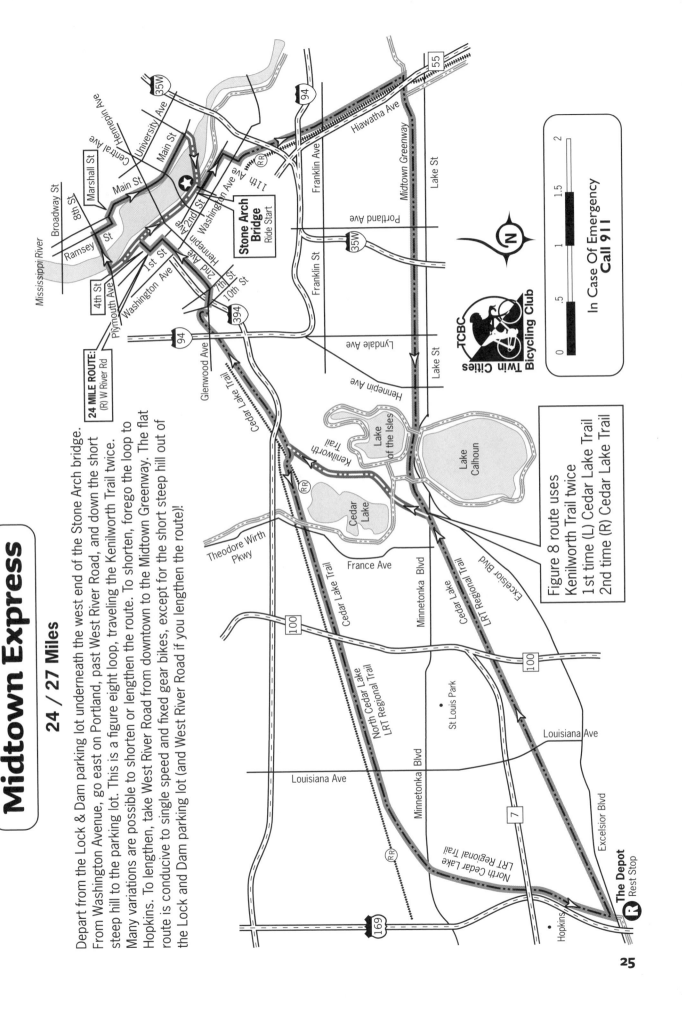

Stone Arch Bridge Ride Start

24 MILE ROUTE: (R) W River Rd

Figure 8 route uses
Kenilworth Trail twice
1st time (L) Cedar Lake Trail
2nd time (R) Cedar Lake Trail

TCBC
Twin Cities Bicycling Club

In Case Of Emergency
Call 911

0 .5 1 1.5 2

N

The Depot
Rest Stop

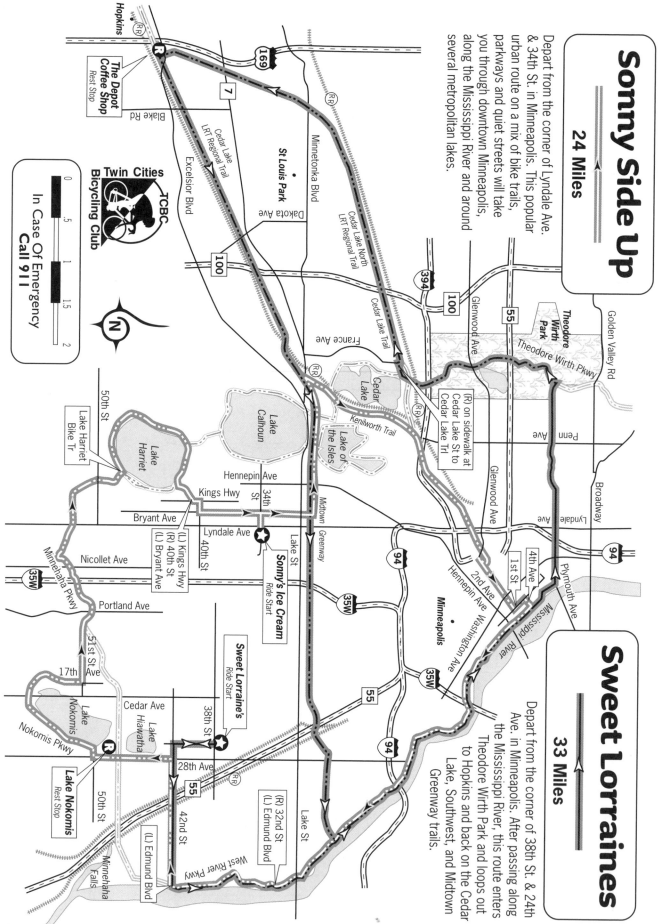

Sonny Side Up

24 Miles

Depart from the corner of Lyndale Ave. & 34th St. in Minneapolis. This popular urban route on a mix of bike trails, parkways and quiet streets will take you through downtown Minneapolis, along the Mississippi River and around several metropolitan lakes.

Sweet Lorraines

33 Miles

Depart from the corner of 38th St. & 24th Ave. in Minneapolis. After passing along the Mississippi River, this route enters Theodore Wirth Park and loops out to Hopkins and back on the Cedar Lake, Southwest, and Midtown Greenway trails.

Twin Cities Bicycling Club
TCBC

In Case Of Emergency
Call 9 1 1

0   .5   1   1.5   2

The Depot Coffee Shop
Rest Stop

Lake Nokomis
Rest Stop

Sonny's Ice Cream
Ride Start

Sweet Lorraine's
Ride Start

(L) Kings Hwy
(R) 40th St
(L) Bryant Ave

Lake Harriet Bike Tr

(R) on sidewalk at Cedar Lake St to Cedar Lake Trl

(R) 32nd St
(L) Edmund Blvd

(L) Edmund Blvd

Hopkins

St Louis Park

Theodore Wirth Park

Minneapolis

Lake Calhoun

Lake Harriet

Lake of the Isles

Cedar Lake

Lake Hiawatha

Lake Nokomis

Minnehaha Falls

Mississippi River

Kenilworth Trail

Cedar Lake Trail

Cedar Lake North LRT Regional Trail

Cedar Lake LRT Regional Trail

Blake Rd

Excelsior Blvd

Minnetonka Blvd

Dakota Ave

France Ave

Glenwood Ave

Glenwood Ave

Penn Ave

Broadway

Lyndale Ave

Golden Valley Rd

Theodore Wirth Pkwy

Hennepin Ave

Washington Ave

2nd Ave

1st St

4th Ave

Plymouth Ave

50th St

Kings Hwy

Bryant Ave

Hennepin Ave

34th St

Lyndale Ave

40th St

Nicollet Ave

Portland Ave

Minnehaha Pkwy

51st St

17th Ave

Nokomis Pkwy

50th St

Cedar Ave

38th St

28th Ave

42nd St

West River Pkwy

Lake St

Lake St

Midtown Greenway

169
7
100
100
394
55
94
94
55
35W
35W
35W
55

N

26

Pleasant on Pleasant

25 Miles

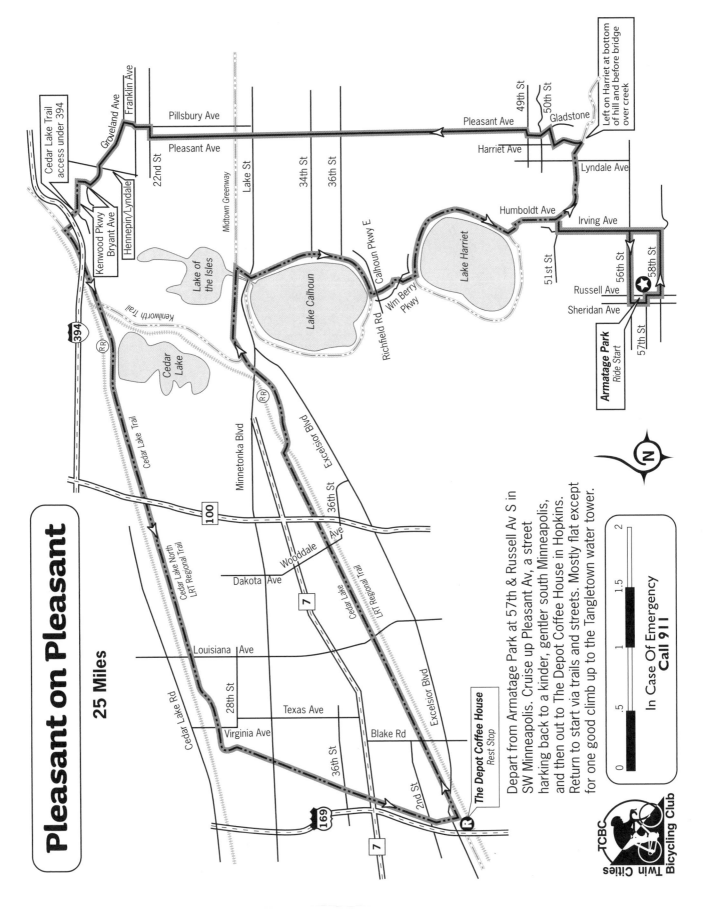

Left on Harriet at bottom of hill and before bridge over creek

Armatage Park
Ride Start

The Depot Coffee House
Rest Stop

Depart from Armatage Park at 57th & Russell Av S in SW Minneapolis. Cruise up Pleasant Av, a street harking back to a kinder, gentler south Minneapolis, and then out to The Depot Coffee House in Hopkins. Return to start via trails and streets. Mostly flat except for one good climb up to the Tangletown water tower.

In Case Of Emergency
Call 9 1 1

0   .5   1   1.5   2

Twin Cities Bicycling Club
TCBC

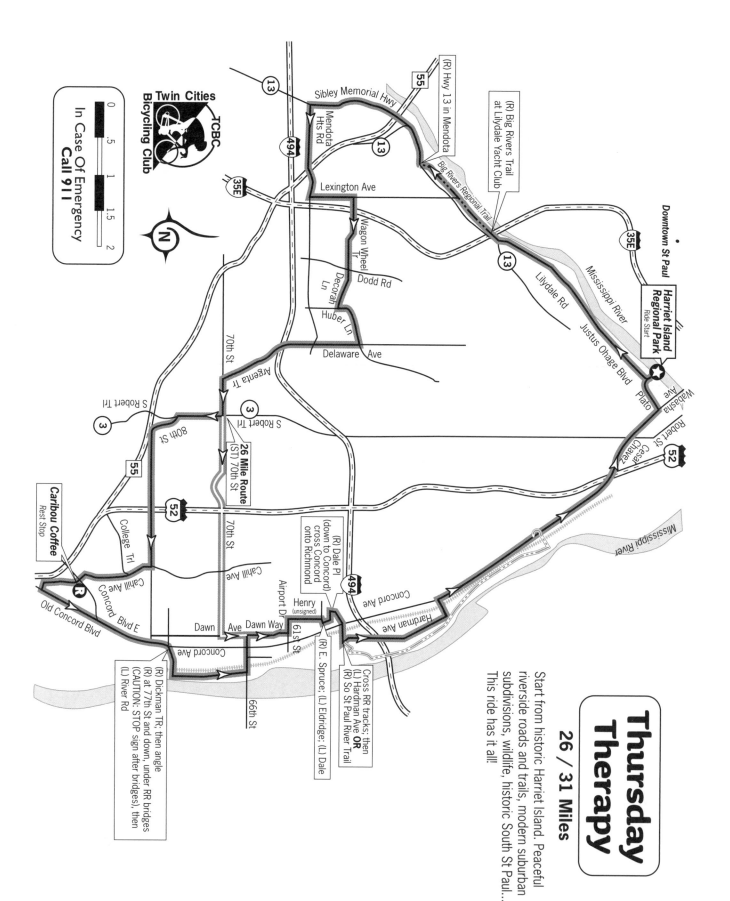

Thursday Therapy

26 / 31 Miles

Start from historic Harriet Island. Peaceful riverside roads and trails, modern suburban subdivisions, wildlife, historic South St Paul. This ride has it all!

In Case Of Emergency
Call 911

Twin Cities
Bicycling Club
TCBC

Downtown St Paul

Harriet Island
Regional Park
Ride Start

(R) Hwy 13 in Mendota

(R) Big Rivers Trail
at Lilydale Yacht Club

(R) Big Rivers Trail
at Lilydale Yacht Club

Sibley Memorial Hwy

Mendota Hts Rd

Lexington Ave

Wagon Wheel Tr

Dodd Rd

Decorah Ln

Huber Ln

Delaware Ave

Big Rivers Regional Trail

Mississippi River

Lilydale Rd

Justus Ohage Blvd

Plato

Wabasha Ave

Robert St

Cesar Chavez

Mississippi River

70th St

Argenta Tr

S Robert Trl

3

80th St

S Robert Trl

26 Mile Route
(ST) 70th St

55

52

70th St

Cahill Ave

(R) Dale Pl
(down to Concord)
cross Concord
onto Richmond

494

Concord Ave

Hardman Ave

Caribou Coffee
Rest Stop

College Trl

Concord Blvd E

Old Concord Blvd

Cahill Ave

Airport Dr

Henry
(unsigned)

Dawn Ave Dawn Way

61st St

Cross RR tracks; then
(L) Hardman Ave **OR**
(R) So St Paul River Trail
(R) E. Spruce; (L) Eldridge; (L) Dale

Concord Ave

66th St

(R) Dickman TR; then angle
(R) at 77th St and down, under RR bridges
(CAUTION: STOP sign after bridges), then
(L) River Rd

28

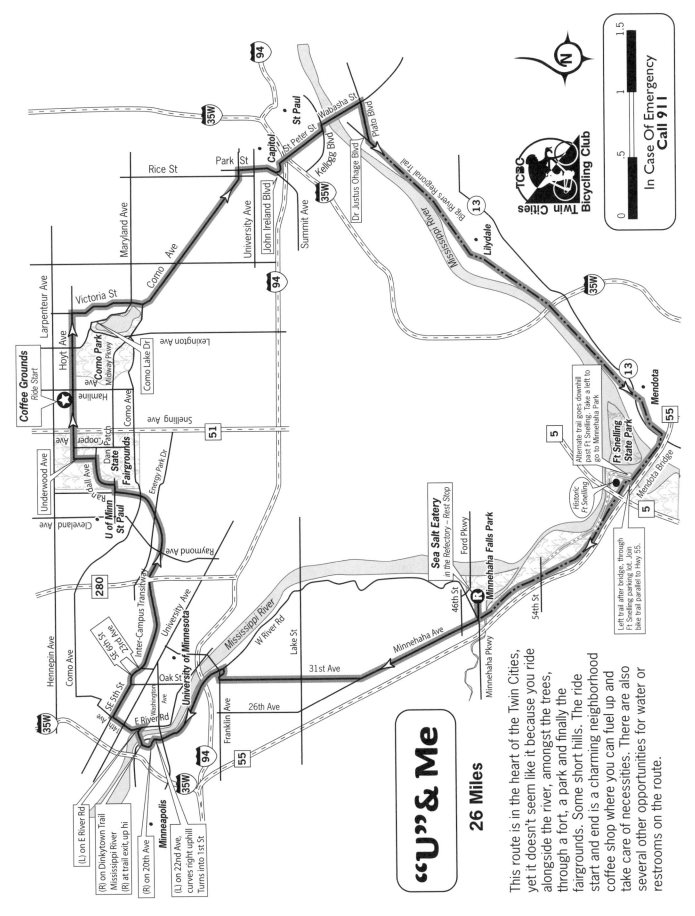

"U" & Me

26 Miles

This route is in the heart of the Twin Cities, yet it doesn't seem like it because you ride alongside the river, amongst the trees, through a fort, a park and finally the fairgrounds. Some short hills. The ride start and end is a charming neighborhood coffee shop where you can fuel up and take care of necessities. There are also several other opportunities for water or restrooms on the route.

In Case Of Emergency Call 911

Twin Cities Bicycling Club

N

0   .5   1   1.5

Coffee Grounds
Ride Start

Como Park

State Fairgrounds

U of Minn St Paul

Dan Patch

Minneapolis

University of Minnesota

Sea Salt Eatery
in the Refectory – Rest Stop

Minnehaha Falls Park

Ft Snelling State Park

Historic Ft Snelling

Alternate trail goes downhill past Ft Snelling. Take a left to go to Minnehaha Park

Left trail after bridge, through Ft Snelling parking lot. Join bike trail parallel to Hwy 55.

St Paul

Capitol

Mendota

Lilydale

Mississippi River

Big Rivers Regional Trail

Mendota Bridge

(L) on E River Rd

(R) on Dinkytown Trail Mississippi River

(R) at trail exit, up hi

(R) on 20th Ave

(L) on 22nd Ave, curves right uphill Turns into 1st St

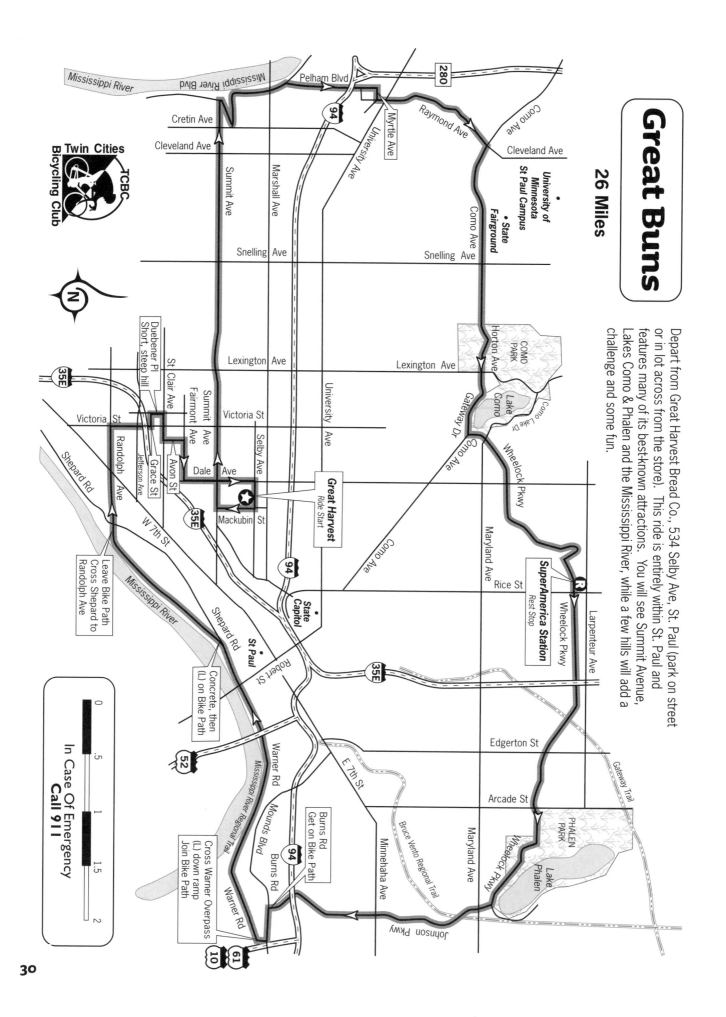

Great Buns

26 Miles

Depart from Great Harvest Bread Co., 534 Selby Ave, St. Paul (park on street or in lot across from the store). This ride is entirely within St. Paul and features many of its best-known attractions. You will see Summit Avenue, Lakes Como & Phalen and the Mississippi River, while a few hills will add a challenge and some fun.

Twin Cities Bicycling Club TCBC

Great Harvest Ride Start

SuperAmerica Station Rest Stop

Duebener Pl Short, steep hill

Leave Bike Path Cross Shepard to Randolph Ave

Concrete, then (L) on Bike Path

Burns Rd Get on Bike Path

Cross Warner Overpass (L) down ramp Join Bike Path

In Case Of Emergency Call 911

0   .5   1   1.5   2

30

The Whole Enchilada

26 / 33 Miles

There are two different rides that depart from the Roseville Professional Center (SW corner of Hwy 36 and Hamline Ave in Roseville). The 26 mile route goes through the Roseville Reservoir trails and the St. Paul Water Works, with a moderate climb up Snail Lake Blvd. The 33 mile route goes northeast to White Bear Lake and back with a couple moderate climbs on County Rd B. Both routes utilize flat-to-gently rolling roads and pass by many area lakes. After the ride, join your compadres at La Casita, just west of Rosedale, for fun and refueling. Andele! Andele! Epa! Epa! Yeehah!!

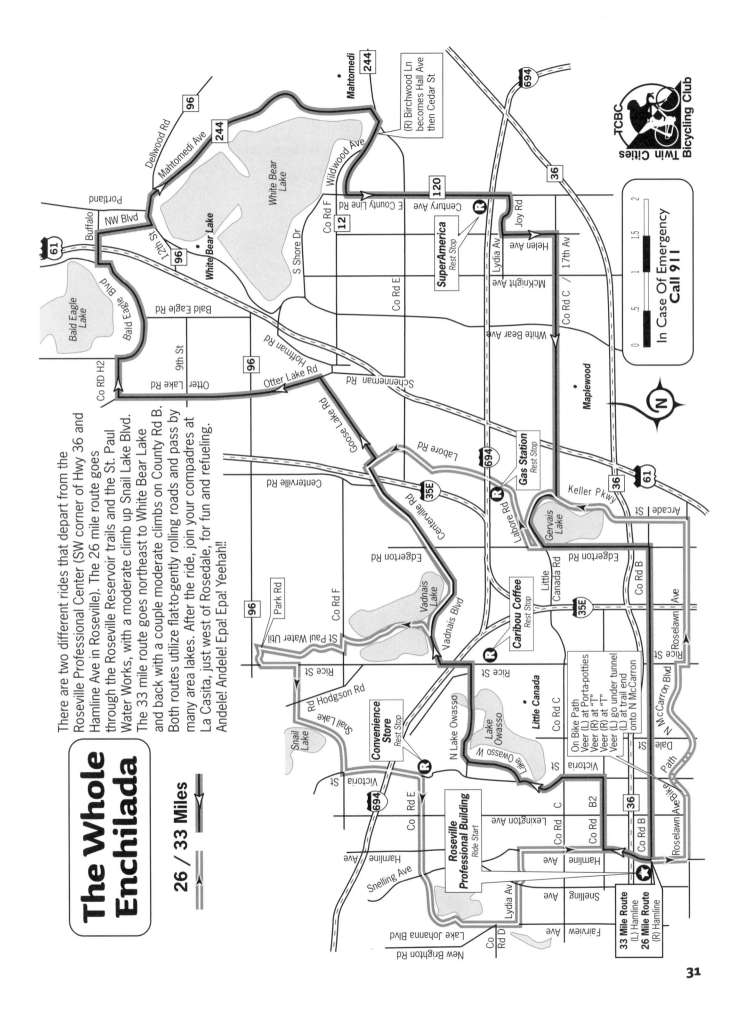

TCBC Twin Cities Bicycling Club

Mahtomedi 244

(R) Birchwood Ln becomes Hall Ave then Cedar St

SuperAmerica Rest Stop

Gas Station Rest Stop

Caribou Coffee Rest Stop

Convenience Store Rest Stop

Roseville Professional Building Ride Start

On Bike Path
Veer (L) at Porta-potties
Veer (R) at "T"
Veer (R) at "T"
Veer (L) go under tunnel
Veer (L) at trail end onto N McCarron

33 Mile Route (L) Hamline
26 Mile Route (R) Hamline

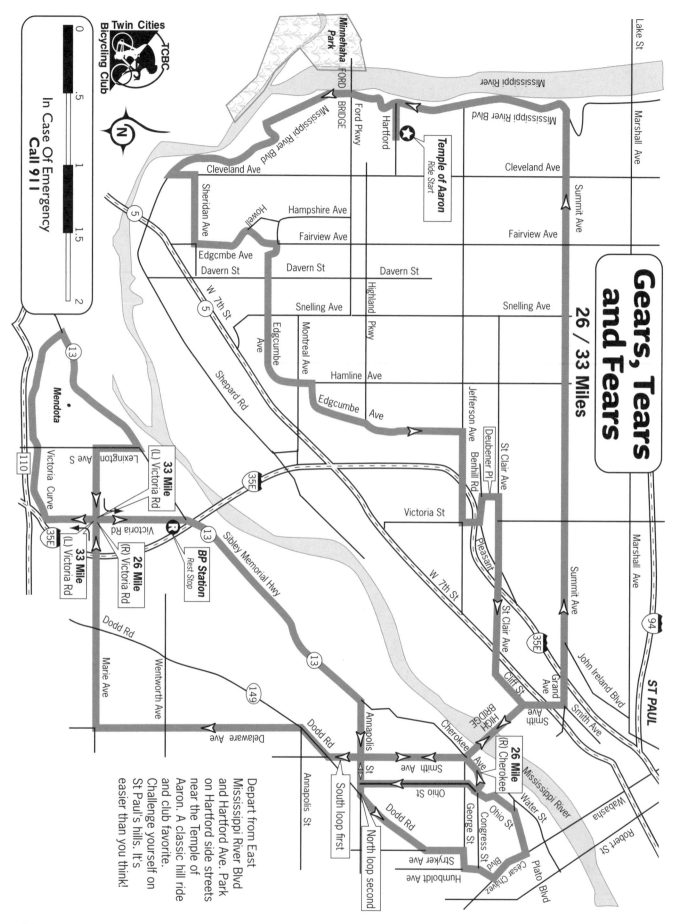

Gears, Tears and Fears

26 / 33 Miles

Temple of Aaron
Ride Start

33 Mile
(L) Victoria Rd

26 Mile
(R) Victoria Rd

33 Mile
(L) Victoria Rd

BP Station
Rest Stop

26 Mile
(R) Cherokee

South loop first

North loop second

Depart from East Mississippi River Blvd and Hartford Ave. Park on Hartford side streets near the Temple of Aaron. A classic hill ride and club favorite. Challenge yourself on St Paul's hills. It's easier than you think!

Minnehaha Park

Mendota

ST PAUL

Twin Cities Bicycling Club
TCBC

In Case Of Emergency
Call 9 1 1

0   .5   1   1.5   2

N

Stone Arch Express

27 Miles

Depart from Lock & Dam parking lot underneath the west end of the Stone Arch Bridge in downtown Minneapolis. Go north on Portland from Washington Av, then just past West River Rd down a short steep hill to the Lock & Dam parking lot. No water at start. The route uses East and West River Roads, Summit Av, and the High Bridge.

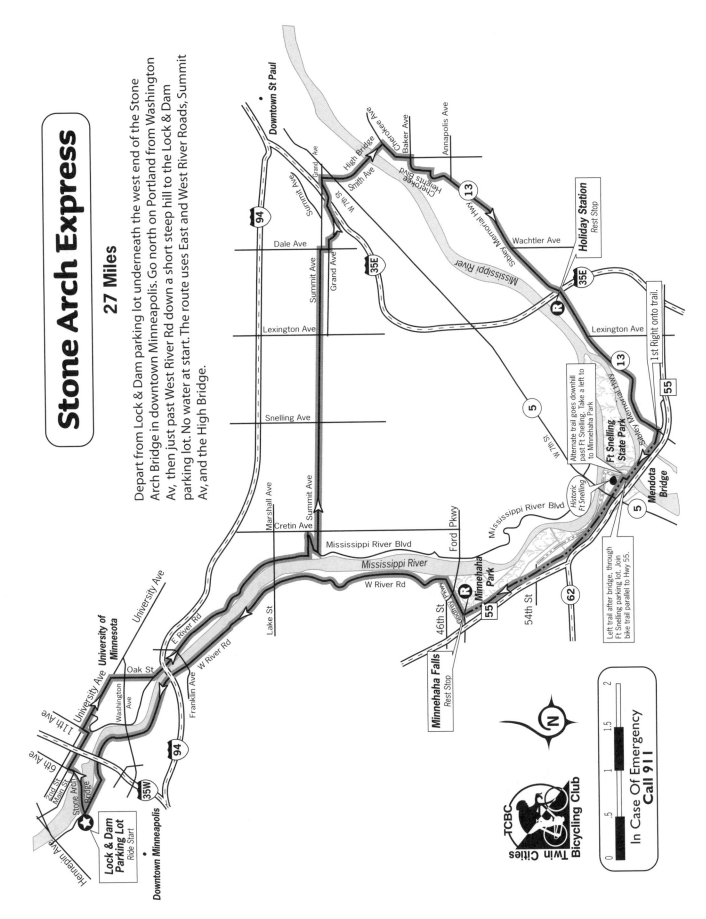

Lock & Dam Parking Lot
Ride Start

Downtown Minneapolis

Hennepin Ave

11th Ave

6th Ave

2nd St

Main St

35W

Stone Arch Bridge

94

University Ave

University Ave

University of Minnesota

Washington Ave

Oak St

Franklin Ave

E River Rd

W River Rd

Lake St

Marshall Ave

Cretin Ave

Summit Ave

Mississippi River

W River Rd

Mississippi River Blvd

Ford Pkwy

Godfrey Pkwy

46th St

Minnehaha Falls
Rest Stop

Minnehaha Park

54th St

55

62

Downtown St Paul

94

Summit Ave

Grand Ave

Dale Ave

Summit Ave

Grand Ave

Lexington Ave

Snelling Ave

W 7th St

Grand Ave

High Bridge

Smith Ave

Cherokee Ave

Baker Ave

Cherokee Heights Blvd

Annapolis Ave

13

Sibley Memorial Hwy

Wachtler Ave

Holiday Station
Rest Stop

35E

35E

Lexington Ave

13

5

Mississippi River

Mississippi River Blvd

Alternate trail goes downhill past Ft Snelling. Take a left to to Minnehaha Park

Historic Ft Snelling

Ft Snelling State Park

W 7th St

Sibley Memorial Hwy

5

Mendota Bridge

55

1st Right onto trail.

Left trail after bridge, through Ft Snelling parking lot. Join bike trail parallel to Hwy 55.

N

In Case Of Emergency
Call 911

0   .5   1   1.5   2

TCBC
Twin Cities Bicycling Club

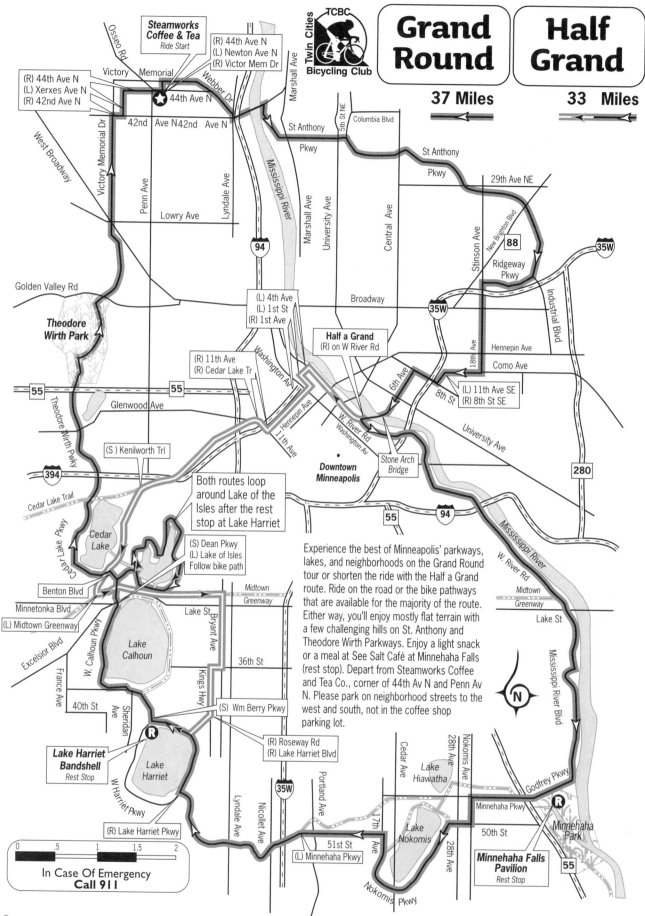

Grand Round
37 Miles

Half Grand
33 Miles

TCBC
Twin Cities
Bicycling Club

Steamworks Coffee & Tea
Ride Start

(R) 44th Ave N
(L) Newton Ave N
(R) Victor Mem Dr

(R) 44th Ave N
(L) Xerxes Ave N
(R) 42nd Ave N

Osseo Rd
Victory Memorial
44th Ave N
42nd Ave N 42nd Ave N

Webber Dr
Marshall Ave
5th St NE
Columbia Blvd

St Anthony Pkwy

St Anthony Pkwy

29th Ave NE

New Brighton Blvd
88
Ridgeway Pkwy

35W

West Broadway

Victory Memorial Dr
Penn Ave
Lowry Ave
Lyndale Ave

Mississippi River

94

Stinson Ave

Industrial Blvd

Golden Valley Rd

Marshall Ave
University Ave
Central Ave
Broadway

35W

18th Ave
Hennepin Ave
Como Ave

Theodore Wirth Park

(L) 4th Ave
(L) 1st St
(R) 1st Ave

Half a Grand
(R) on W River Rd

6th Ave
8th St

(L) 11th Ave SE
(R) 8th St SE

(R) 11th Ave
(R) Cedar Lake Tr

55
55
Glenwood Ave

Washington Av

Hennepin Ave

11th Ave

W. River Rd
Washington Av

University Ave

280

Downtown Minneapolis

Stone Arch Bridge

Theodore Wirth Pkwy

(S) Kenilworth Trl

394

Cedar Lake Trail

Both routes loop around Lake of the Isles after the rest stop at Lake Harriet

Cedar Lake Pkwy

Cedar Lake

(S) Dean Pkwy
(L) Lake of Isles
Follow bike path

Benton Blvd

Minnetonka Blvd

(L) Midtown Greenway

Excelsior Blvd

France Ave

W. Calhoun Pkwy

Sheridan Ave

Lake Calhoun

Midtown Greenway

Lake St

Bryant Ave

Kings Hwy

36th St

40th St

(S) Wm Berry Pkwy

55

94

55

Mississippi River

W. River Rd

Midtown Greenway

Lake St

Mississippi River Blvd

Experience the best of Minneapolis' parkways, lakes, and neighborhoods on the Grand Round tour or shorten the ride with the Half a Grand route. Ride on the road or the bike pathways that are available for the majority of the route. Either way, you'll enjoy mostly flat terrain with a few challenging hills on St. Anthony and Theodore Wirth Parkways. Enjoy a light snack or a meal at See Salt Café at Minnehaha Falls (rest stop). Depart from Steamworks Coffee and Tea Co., corner of 44th Av N and Penn Av N. Please park on neighborhood streets to the west and south, not in the coffee shop parking lot.

N

R

Lake Harriet Bandshell
Rest Stop

Lake Harriet

(R) Roseway Rd
(R) Lake Harriet Blvd

W Harriet Pkwy

Lyndale Ave

Nicollet Ave

35W

Portland Ave

17th Ave

Cedar Ave

28th Ave

Nokomis Ave

Lake Hiawatha

Minnehaha Pkwy

Godfrey Pkwy

R

Minnehaha Park

(R) Lake Harriet Pkwy

Lake Nokomis

28th Ave

50th St

Minnehaha Falls Pavilion
Rest Stop

55

0 .5 1 1.5 2

51st St
(L) Minnehaha Pkwy

Nokomis Pkwy

In Case Of Emergency Call 911

Winter Warmer West

33 / 39 Miles

This is an urban route which takes you along scenic parkways with lower traffic areas for the majority of the route. The course is moderately hilly with rollers and one large challenging hill. There are numerous rest stop opportunities along the way.

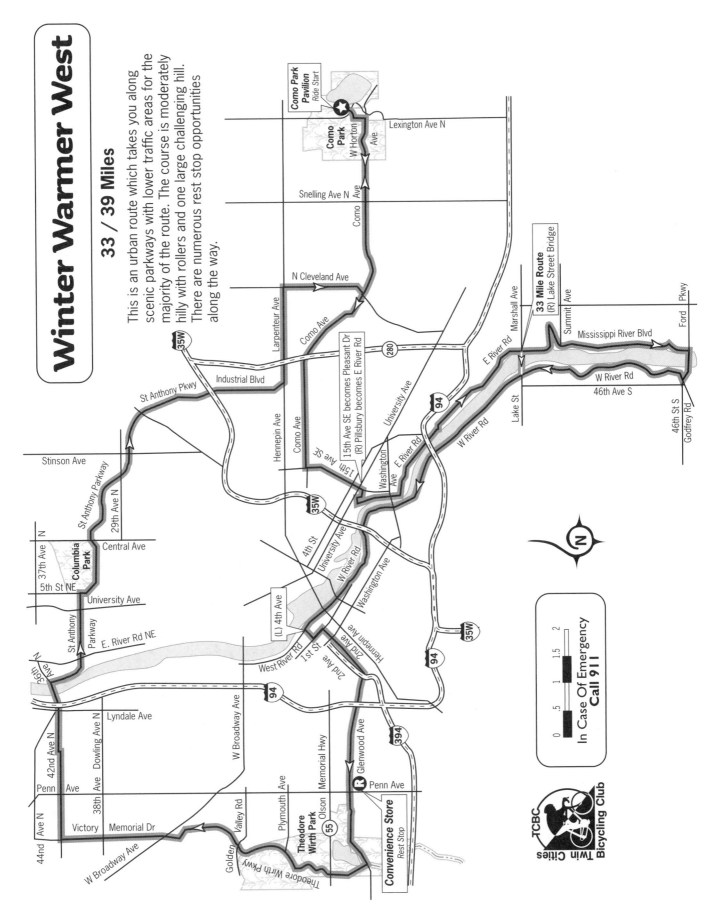

Como Park Pavilion
Ride Start

Como Park

Lexington Ave N

W Horton Ave

Snelling Ave N

Como Ave

N Cleveland Ave

Larpenteur Ave

Como Ave

35W

Industrial Blvd

St Anthony Pkwy

Stinson Ave

St Anthony Parkway

29th Ave N

Central Ave

Columbia Park

37th Ave

5th St NE

University Ave

N

St Anthony Parkway

E. River Rd NE

36th Ave N

Hennepin Ave

Como Ave

15th Ave SE

15th Ave SE becomes Pleasant Dr
(R) Pillsbury becomes E River Rd

280

University Ave

94

Washington Ave

E River Rd

W River Rd

E River Rd

Marshall Ave

33 Mile Route
(R) Lake Street Bridge

Summit Ave

Mississippi River Blvd

Lake St

W River Rd

46th Ave S

Ford Pkwy

46th St S

Godfrey Rd

35W

4th St

University Ave

W River Rd

Washington Ave

(L) 4th Ave

4th Ave

1st St

2nd Ave

Hennepin Ave

West River Rd

35W

94

94

394

Lyndale Ave

Dowling Ave N

W Broadway Ave

Glenwood Ave

Memorial Hwy

R Penn Ave

42nd Ave N

Penn Ave

38th Ave

Valley Rd

Plymouth Ave

Olson

Theodore Wirth Park

55

Convenience Store
Rest Stop

44th

Ave N

Victory Memorial Dr

W Broadway Ave

Golden Valley Rd

Theodore Wirth Pkwy

N

In Case Of Emergency
Call 911

0   .5   1   1.5   2

TCBC
Twin Cities Bicycling Club

35

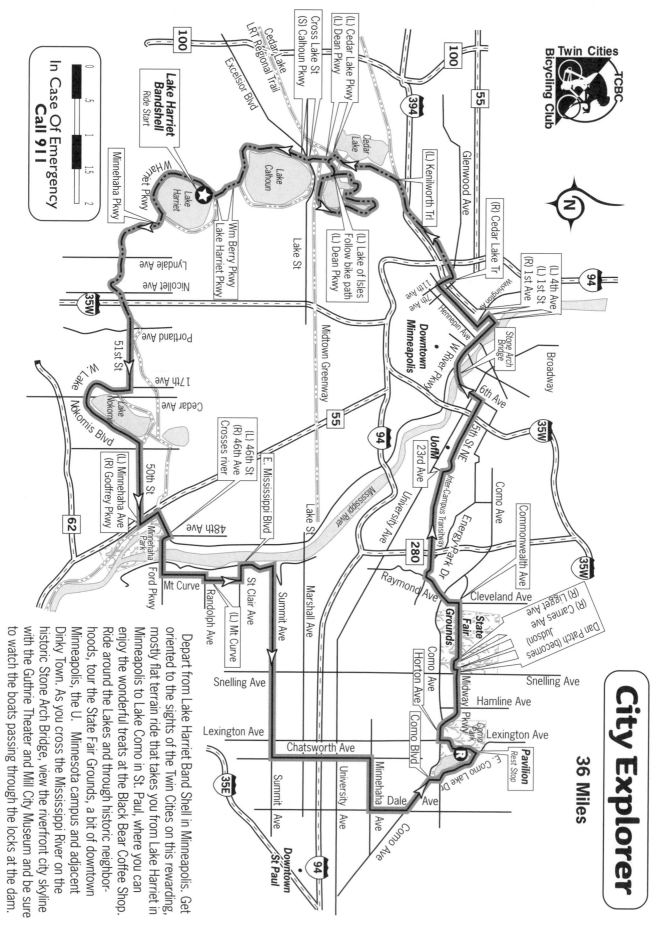

City Explorer

36 Miles

Depart from Lake Harriet Band Shell in Minneapolis. Get oriented to the sights of the Twin Cities on this rewarding, mostly flat terrain ride that takes you from Lake Harriet in Minneapolis to Lake Como in St. Paul, where you can enjoy the wonderful treats at the Black Bear Coffee Shop. Ride around the Lakes and through historic neighborhoods, tour the State Fair Grounds, a bit of downtown Minneapolis, the U. Minnesota campus and adjacent Dinky Town. As you cross the Mississippi River on the historic Stone Arch Bridge, view the riverfront city skyline with the Guthrie Theater and Mill City Museum and be sure to watch the boats passing through the locks at the dam.

Twin Cities Bicycling Club

In Case Of Emergency
Call 911

0   .5   1   1.5   2

Metro Ride Journal

Date _____ Mileage _____

Route _____

Notes _____

_____

Date _____ Mileage _____

Route _____

Notes _____

_____

Date _____ Mileage _____

Route _____

Notes _____

_____

Date _____ Mileage _____

Route _____

Notes _____

_____

Date _____ Mileage _____

Route _____

Notes _____

_____

Date _____ Mileage _____

Route _____

Notes _____

_____

Date _____ Mileage _____

Route _____

Notes _____

_____

Date _____ Mileage _____

Route _____

Notes _____

_____

Date _____ Mileage _____

Route _____

Notes _____

_____

Date _____ Mileage _____

Route _____

Notes _____

_____

Date _____ Mileage _____

Route _____

Notes _____

_____

Date _____ Mileage _____

Route _____

Notes _____

_____

Northeast

NW NE WI
MET
SW SE

A WELCOME REST STOP IN SCANDIA
NEW SCANDIA TOWNSHIP TOUR - PAGE 45

REST STOP MARINE ON ST. CROIX
SUNRISE SOLITUDE - PAGE 56

CRUSING INTO THE SUNSET
STRAW MAN - PAGE 51

THE GATEWAY TRAIL
AN APPLE A DAY - PAGE 54

Legend													
FOOD	WATER	TOILET	FLAT	ROLLING	HILLY	CLIMBS	ROADS	TRAILS	LT TRAFFIC	TRAFFIC	SCENIC	TREATS	

Page	Ride	Miles	At Ride Start	Terrain	Highlights
40	Watermelon-Family Ride	15	water, toilet	flat, climbs, roads, trails, lt traffic	scenic
41	Here We Come 'Owasso'ling	21		rolling, roads, trails, lt traffic	treats
42	Watermelon Traditional	22/33	water, toilet	rolling, climbs, roads, trails, lt traffic	
43	Acapulco	24 29/36	food, water, toilet	rolling, roads, lt traffic	scenic
44	Miles from Maplewood	25/35		rolling, roads, trails, traffic	treats
45	Scandia Township Tour	27	water, toilet	flat, climbs, roads, trails, lt traffic	scenic, treats
46	White Bear Lake Loop	28/36	water, toilet	flat, climbs, roads, trails, traffic	
47	Pink Express	29	food, water, toilet	flat, roads, lt traffic	
48	Winter Warmer	29/43		rolling, roads, lt traffic	
49	Paper Man	30/62	water, toilet	rolling, roads, lt traffic	scenic
50	Wolfgang's Bistro	31	food, water, toilet	flat, climbs, roads, trails, lt traffic	
51	Straw Man	26/33	water, toilet	flat, climbs, roads, trails, lt traffic	scenic
52	Chain of Fools	44/46 55/62		rolling, roads, lt traffic	
53	Tin Man	47/76		rolling, roads, trails, lt traffic	scenic
54	An Apple a Day	53		rolling, roads, trails, lt traffic	scenic, treats
55	Snooze Button Metric	62		roads, trails, traffic	
56	Sunrise Solitude	62 79/101	food, water, toilet	flat, climbs, roads, trails, lt traffic	scenic

Family Friendly Trail Route

15 Miles

Watermelon BIKE RIDE & PICNIC

July 4

TCBC Twin Cities Bicycling Club

Annual **Watermelon Ride**, on July 4th. This route connects several trail segments and parks. The trails wind through wooded areas with occasional wildlife sightings. A few sections are on crushed limestone or gravel. A few short portions of the route use streets with shoulders. Restrooms and water available at Island Lake Park.

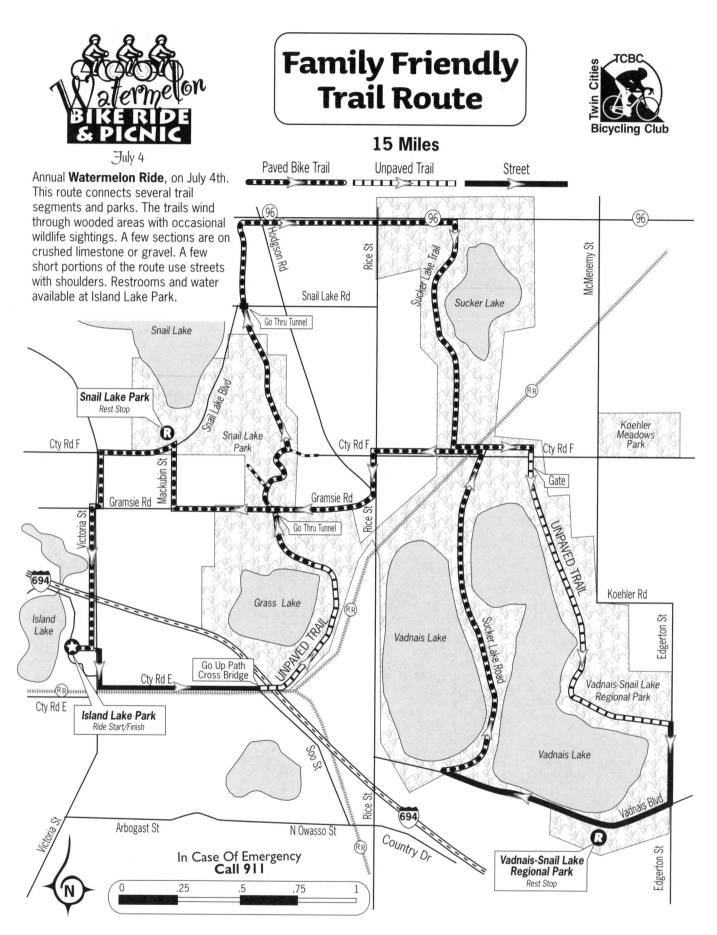

Paved Bike Trail   Unpaved Trail   Street

96
Hodgson Rd
Snail Lake Rd
Snail Lake
Snail Lake Park
Rest Stop
Cty Rd F
Mackubin St
Snail Lake Blvd
Snail Lake Park
Go Thru Tunnel
Gramsie Rd
Victoria St
694
Island Lake
Gramsie Rd
Go Thru Tunnel
Grass Lake
UNPAVED TRAIL
Go Up Path Cross Bridge
Cty Rd E
Island Lake Park
Ride Start/Finish
Cty Rd E
Soo St
Rice St
Victoria St
Arbogast St
N Owasso St
694
Country Dr

Rice St
96
Sucker Lake Trail
Sucker Lake
McMenemy St
96
Cty Rd F
Koehler Meadows Park
Gate
Cty Rd F
Vadnais Lake
Sucker Lake Road
Vadnais Lake
UNPAVED TRAIL
Koehler Rd
Edgerton St
Vadnais-Snail Lake Regional Park
Vadnais Lake
Vadnais Blvd
Vadnais-Snail Lake Regional Park
Rest Stop
Edgerton St

In Case Of Emergency
Call 911

0   .25   .5   .75   1

N

Here We Come 'Owasso'ling

21 Miles

Depart from the Roseville Professional Center (SW corner of Hwy 36 and Hamline Ave in Roseville). " Here We Come 'Owasso'ling among the Owasso streets!" Here's your chance to ride many of the "Owassos" of the area: North Owasso, South Owasso, West Owasso... even East Owasso! This route primarily utilizes trails and low-traffic roads as it passes by Lake Owasso (go figure), Sucker Lake and Vadnais Lake. To avoid a long stretch of gravel, take McMenemy/Koehler/Edgerton instead of the gravel trail off of Cty Rd F.

(R) stay on trail

Shoreview

(S) Under Snail Lake Rd

Hodgson Rd

96

96

Rice St

Sucker Lake Rd

(R) on trail into Sucker Lake Park

Sucker Lake

Snail Lake Rd

Snail Lake

(R) at trail Fork

Snail Lake Rd

CR F

Gravel

CR F

(R) at trail "T"

Gramsie Rd

Sucker Lake Rd

Gravel Trl

Mc Menemy St

Vadnais Heights

(R) Under Gramsie

Grass Lake

Gravel

Koehler Rd

694

49

Rice St

Vadnais Lake

Edgerton St

CR E

(L) Bike Path Double back over bridge

Soo St

N Owasso

R

Country Dr

Vadnais Blvd

Caribou Coffee
Rest Stop

Lake Owasso

(R) E Owasso Ln
(R) Woodbridge
(R) Jerrold
(R) Soo
(R) Edgewater
(L) Woodbridge
(L) E Owasso Ln
(R) Rice St

35E 694

Victoria St

W Owasso

Little Bay

Sandy Hook

S Owasso

R

S Owasso Blvd

35E

Owasso Hills

Western St

Rice St

A & W Restaurant
Rest Stop

Dale St

CR C

CR C

CR C

Lexington Ave

Victoria St

Dale St

Cohansey

Transit

CR B2

CR B2

Professional Bldg
Ride Start

36

Hamline Ave

CR B

36

36

N

0 .25 .5 .75 1

In Case Of Emergency
Call 911

Roseville

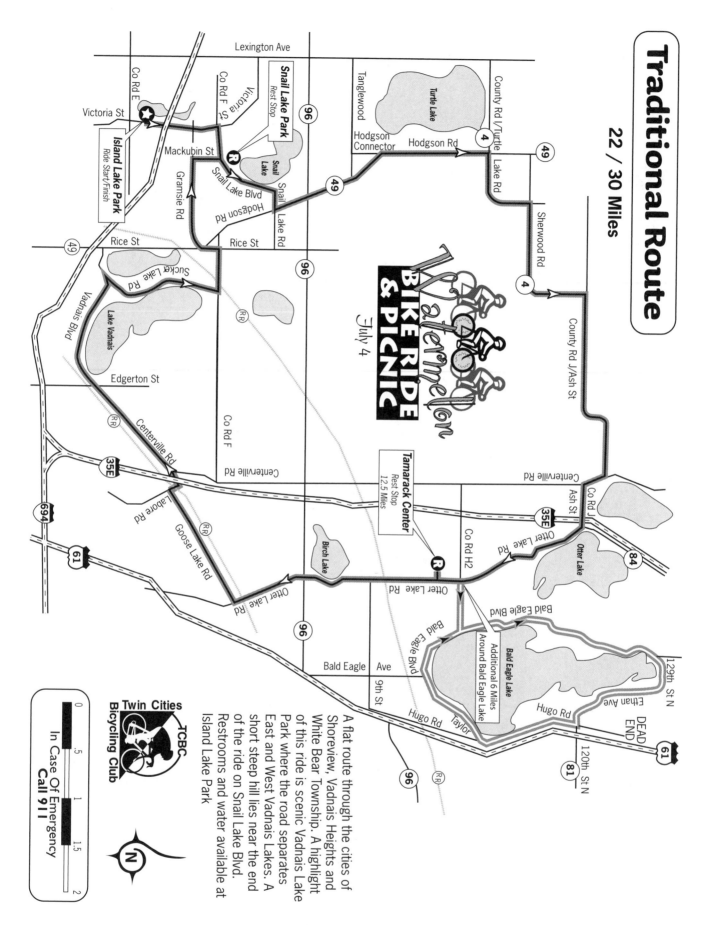

Traditional Route

22 / 30 Miles

Watermelon
BIKE RIDE & PICNIC
July 4

Island Lake Park
Ride Start/Finish

Snail Lake Park
Rest Stop

Tamarack Center
Rest Stop
12.5 Miles

Around Bald Eagle Lake
Additional 6 Miles

A flat route through the cities of Shoreview, Vadnais Heights and White Bear Township. A highlight of this ride is scenic Vadnais Lake Park where the road separates East and West Vadnais Lakes. A short steep hill lies near the end of the ride on Snail Lake Blvd. Restrooms and water available at Island Lake Park

Twin Cities Bicycling Club
TCBC

In Case Of Emergency
Call 911

N

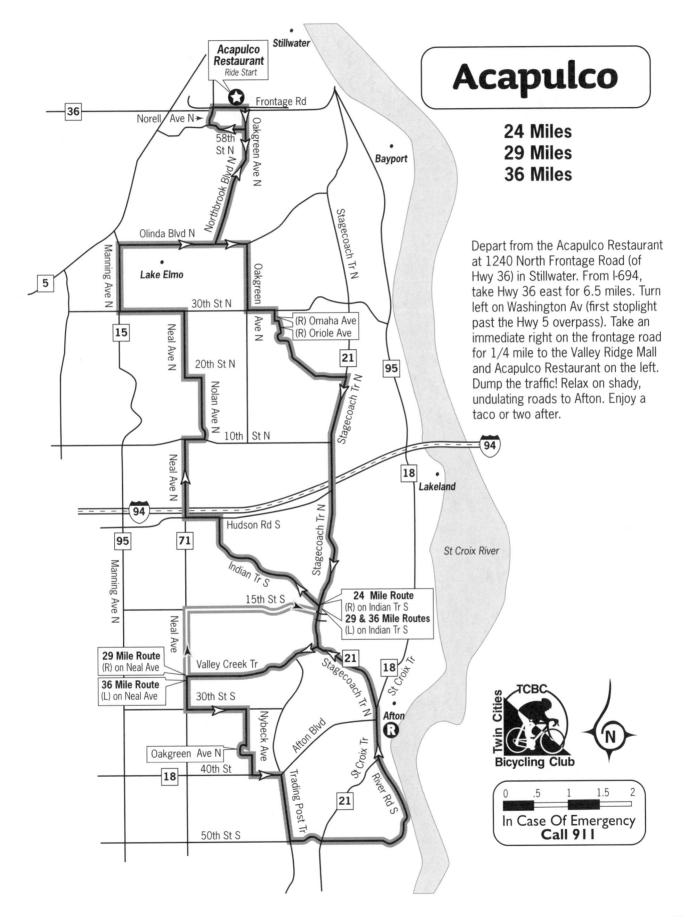

Acapulco

24 Miles
29 Miles
36 Miles

Depart from the Acapulco Restaurant at 1240 North Frontage Road (of Hwy 36) in Stillwater. From I-694, take Hwy 36 east for 6.5 miles. Turn left on Washington Av (first stoplight past the Hwy 5 overpass). Take an immediate right on the frontage road for 1/4 mile to the Valley Ridge Mall and Acapulco Restaurant on the left. Dump the traffic! Relax on shady, undulating roads to Afton. Enjoy a taco or two after.

Acapulco Restaurant
Ride Start

Stillwater

Frontage Rd

Norell Ave N

58th St N

Oakgreen Ave N

Northbrook Blvd N

Bayport

Olinda Blvd N

Stagecoach Tr N

Manning Ave N

Lake Elmo

Oakgreen Ave N

30th St N

(R) Omaha Ave
(R) Oriole Ave

15

Neal Ave N

20th St N

Nolan Ave N

21

95

10th St N

Neal Ave N

94

18

Lakeland

94

95

71

Hudson Rd S

Stagecoach Tr N

St Croix River

Indian Tr S

15th St S

24 Mile Route
(R) on Indian Tr S
29 & 36 Mile Routes
(L) on Indian Tr S

29 Mile Route
(R) on Neal Ave

Neal Ave

Valley Creek Tr

21

18

St Croix Tr

36 Mile Route
(L) on Neal Ave

30th St S

Nybeck Ave

Afton Blvd

Afton

R

Oakgreen Ave N

18

40th St

Trading Post Tr

St Croix Tr

River Rd S

21

50th St S

Manning Ave N

Twin Cities Bicycling Club TCBC

N

0 .5 1 1.5 2

In Case Of Emergency
Call 911

Miles From Maplewood

25 / 35 Miles

Hop on the Gateway trail for a shady ride to Highway 12. Choose either the wide shoulder or bike path over the rollers on 12 to Stillwater. After an ice cream break head South and then West on lightly traveled road with wide shoulders. Just enough hills to work off your ice cream treat.

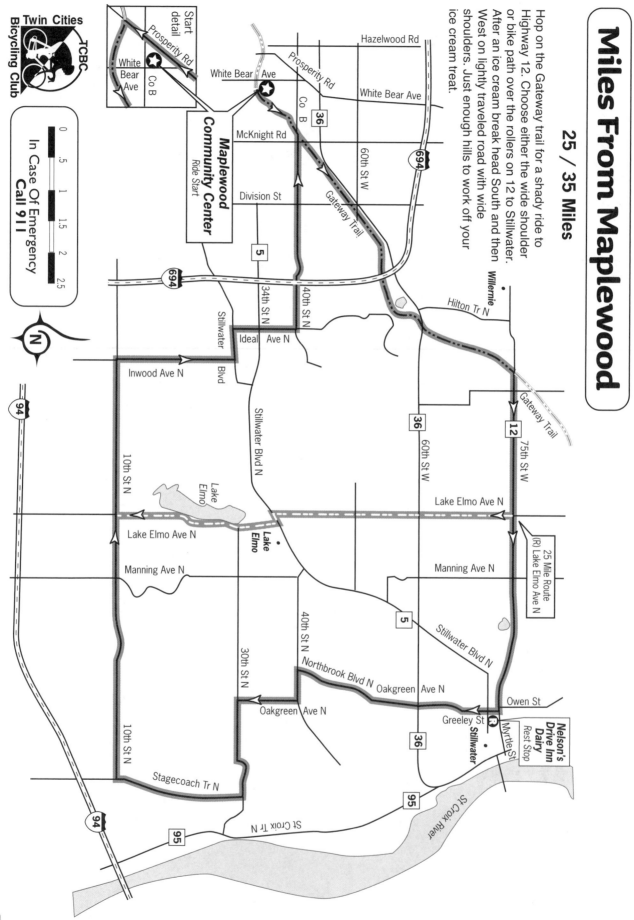

Start detail

Prosperity Rd

White Bear Ave

Co B

Hazelwood Rd

White Bear Ave

Prosperity Rd

White Bear Ave

Co B

36

694

McKnight Rd

60th St W

Maplewood Community Center
Ride Start

Division St

Gateway Trail

5

694

34th St N

40th St N

Ideal Ave N

Stillwater Blvd

Willernie

Hilton Tr N

Gateway Trail

36

60th St W

12

75th St W

Inwood Ave N

94

Stillwater Blvd N

10th St N

Lake Elmo

Lake Elmo Ave N

Lake Elmo Ave N

Lake Elmo

Lake Elmo Ave N

Manning Ave N

Manning Ave N

5

Stillwater Blvd N

25 Mile Route
(R) Lake Elmo Ave N

40th St N

30th St N

Northbrook Blvd N

Oakgreen Ave N

Oakgreen Ave N

36

Owen St

Greeley St

Myrtle St

Stillwater

Nelson's Drive Inn Dairy
Rest Stop

10th St N

Stagecoach Tr N

St Croix Tr N

95

95

St Croix River

94

N

In Case Of Emergency
Call 911

0   .5   1   1.5   2   2.5

Twin Cities
Bicycling Club
TCBC

New Scandia Township Tour

27 Miles

Depart from New Scandia Community Center, 209th St N in Scandia, MN. From Twin Cities take I-35 to Hwy 97 (exit 129) and continue to Scandia. Take a right on Cty 3, cross Cty 52 and a left on 209 N to Community Center lot on right. Tour the paved back roads and trails through New Scandia Township and St Croix. There are some hills.

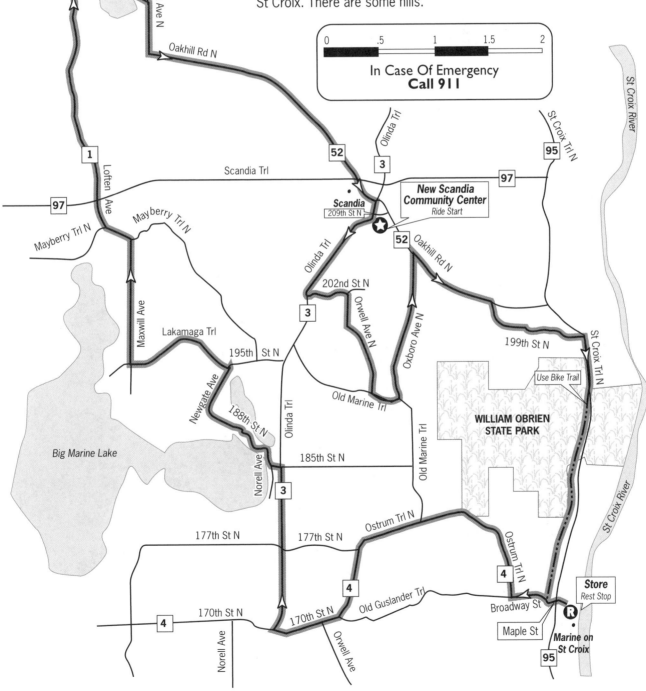

In Case Of Emergency
Call 911

White Bear Lake Loop

28 / 36 Miles

Depart from Island Lake Park in Shoreview on the SW corner of 694 & Victoria St. This route is primarily on gently rolling roads and passes by a few lakes en route to, and around, White Bear Lake.

Twin Cities Bicycling Club
TCBC

In Case Of Emergency
Call 911

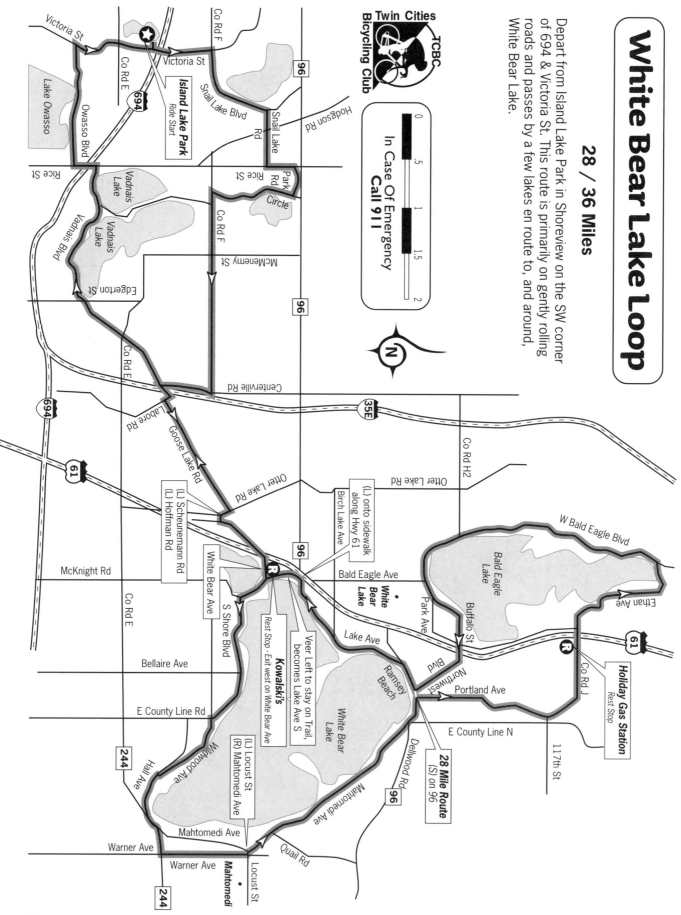

Pink Express

29 Miles

Start at: County Cycles Bike Shop
2700 Lexington Av N, Roseville.
Park on Woodhill Drive.

A relatively flat route. Passes 3 lakes,
scenic, low traffic route. Restroom
and water at start and end when
bike store is open. Rest stop has
food, snacks and restroom.

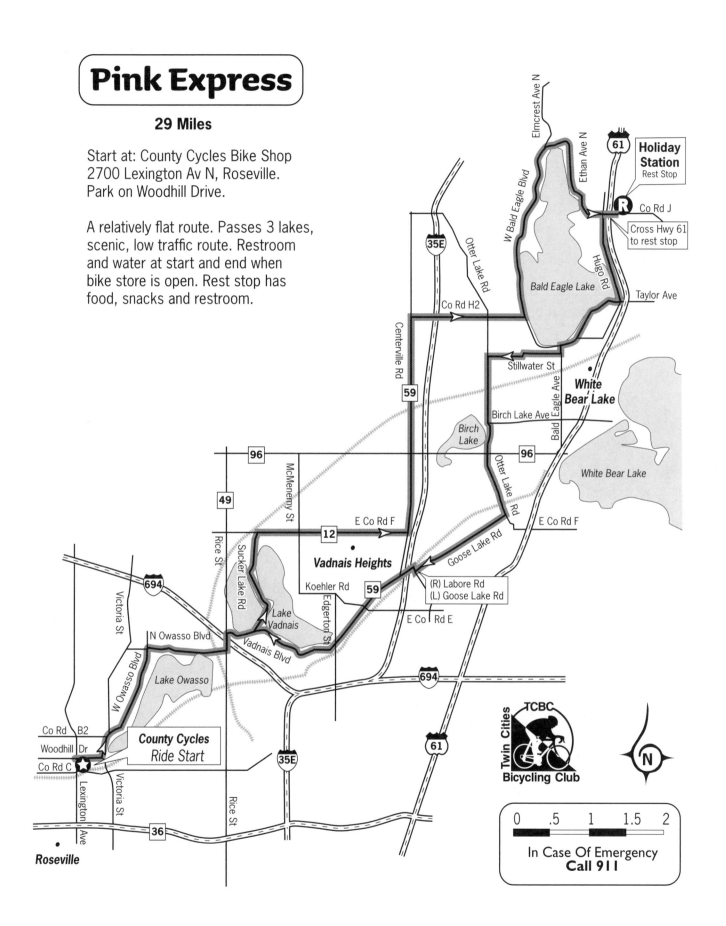

Holiday
Station
Rest Stop

Cross Hwy 61
to rest stop

(R) Labore Rd
(L) Goose Lake Rd

County Cycles
Ride Start

Twin Cities
TCBC
Bicycling Club

In Case Of Emergency
Call 911

Winter Warmer

29 / 43

Hilly, with three challenging hills along route. Shorter route still contains all of the challenging hills, longer route has mainly rollers on extension portion of route. Route is mainly urban, but does go by several scenic areas and area lakes. There are restrooms and food at the start.

29 mile Route
(L) Goose Lake Rd
(L) Centerville Rd

Return Route
(R) Little Canada Rd
County Rd E

Route Outbound
(R) Keller Pkwy

Convenience Store
Rest Stop

Como Park Pavilion
Ride Start

Twin Cities Bicycling Club TCBC

In Case Of Emergency
Call 911

Downtown St Paul (detail)

48

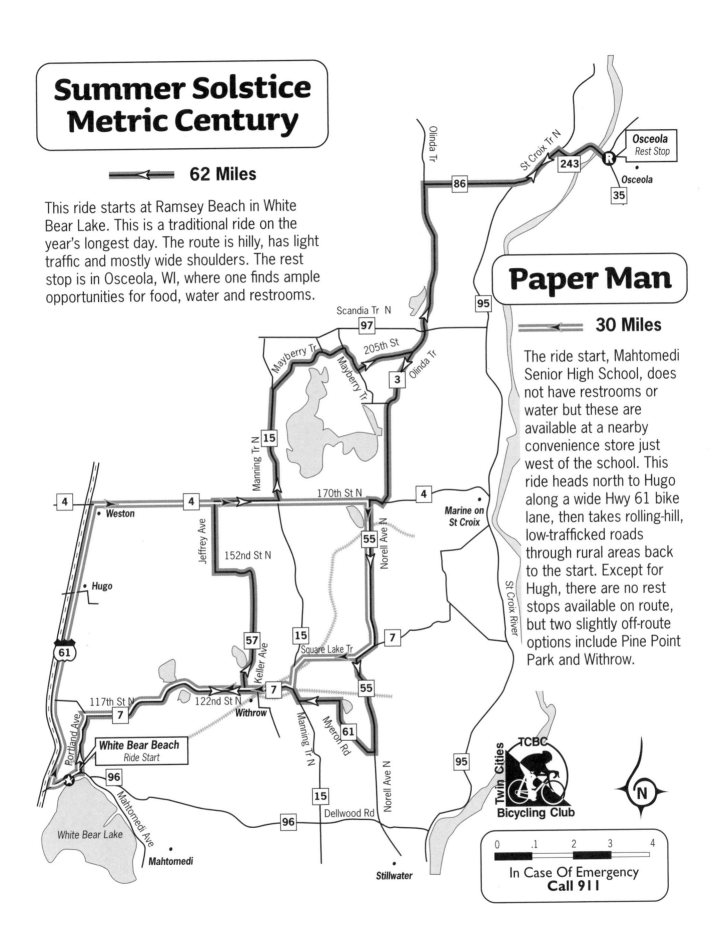

Summer Solstice Metric Century

⟵ **62 Miles**

This ride starts at Ramsey Beach in White Bear Lake. This is a traditional ride on the year's longest day. The route is hilly, has light traffic and mostly wide shoulders. The rest stop is in Osceola, WI, where one finds ample opportunities for food, water and restrooms.

Paper Man

⟵ **30 Miles**

The ride start, Mahtomedi Senior High School, does not have restrooms or water but these are available at a nearby convenience store just west of the school. This ride heads north to Hugo along a wide Hwy 61 bike lane, then takes rolling-hill, low-trafficked roads through rural areas back to the start. Except for Hugh, there are no rest stops available on route, but two slightly off-route options include Pine Point Park and Withrow.

Osceola
Rest Stop

Osceola

St Croix River

Marine on St Croix

White Bear Lake

Mahtomedi

Stillwater

TCBC
Twin Cities
Bicycling Club

0 .1 2 3 4

In Case Of Emergency
Call 911

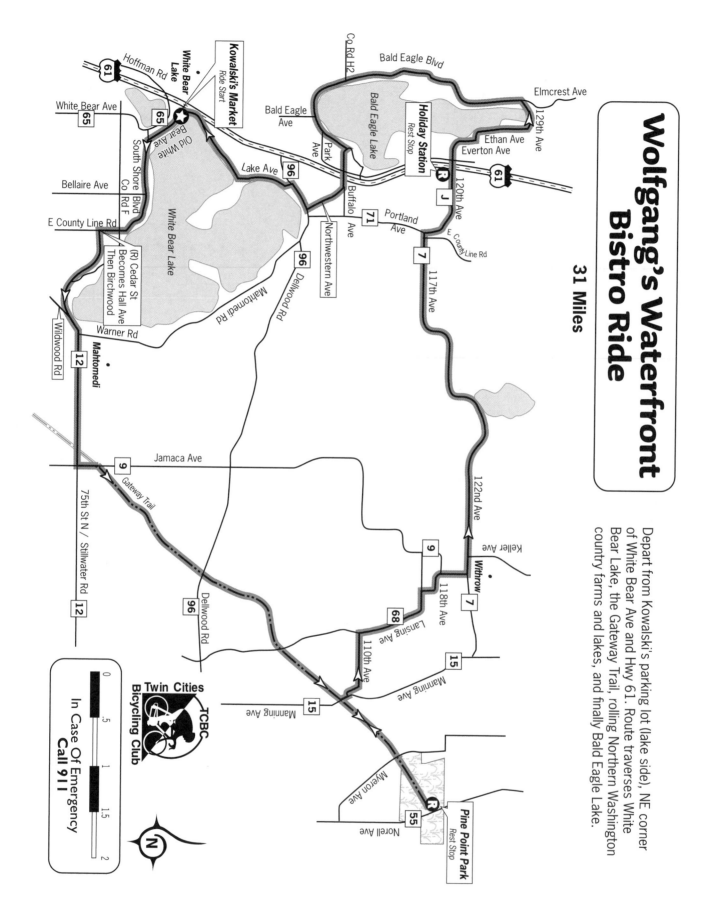

Wolfgang's Waterfront Bistro Ride

31 Miles

Depart from Kowalski's parking lot (lake side), NE corner of White Bear Ave and Hwy 61. Route traverses White Bear Lake, the Gateway Trail, rolling Northern Washington country farms and lakes, and finally Bald Eagle Lake.

Kowalski's Market
Ride Start

Holiday Station
Rest Stop

Pine Point Park
Rest Stop

Twin Cities
Bicycling Club
TCBC

In Case Of Emergency
Call 911

50

Straw Man

39 Miles

The ride start, Ramsey Beach, has restrooms and water during the summer; restrooms may be closed early or late season. The closest gas station is on highway 61 about 1/2 mile before the turn onto highway 96. The terrain of this ride is generally rolling. The most significant climb will be on highway 7 out of Marine on St. Croix (Nason Hill). The General Store in Marine is a great rest stop; or if you want to mingle with the motorcyclists, stop by the Brookside Bar and Grill.

Aluminum Man

52 Miles

The ride start, Ramsey Beach, has restrooms and water during the summer; restrooms may be closed early or late season. The closest gas station is on highway 61 about 1/2 mile before the turn on to highway 96. Like Straw Man, this ride features rolling terrain and a climb out of Marine on St. Croix on Nason Hill. The roads on the way to Scandia are a particular treat - lightly trafficked and scenic, with lakes and woods.

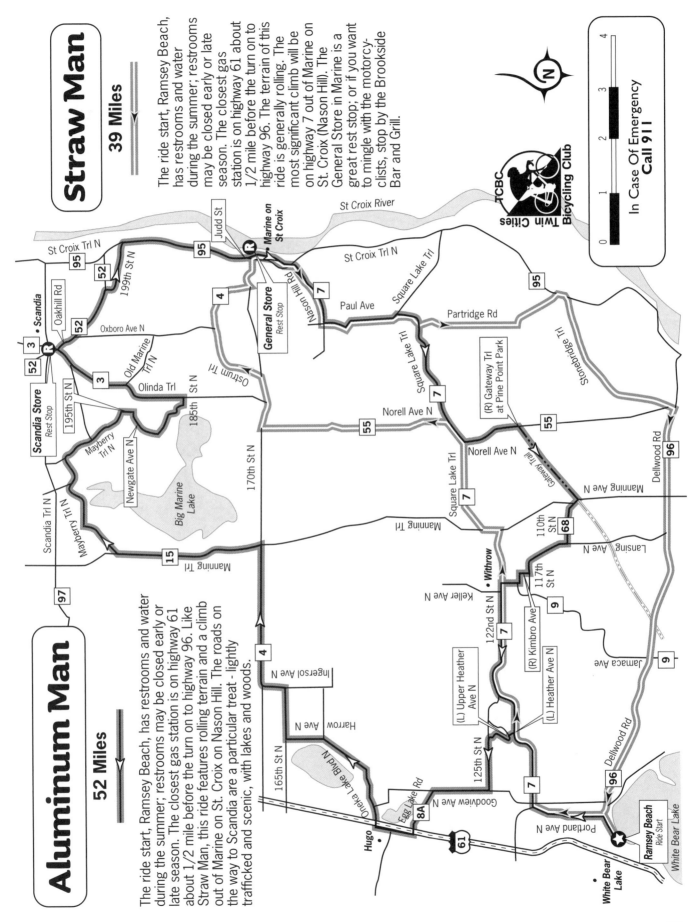

TCBC
Twin Cities
Bicycling Club

In Case Of Emergency
Call 911

0 1 2 3 4

N

51

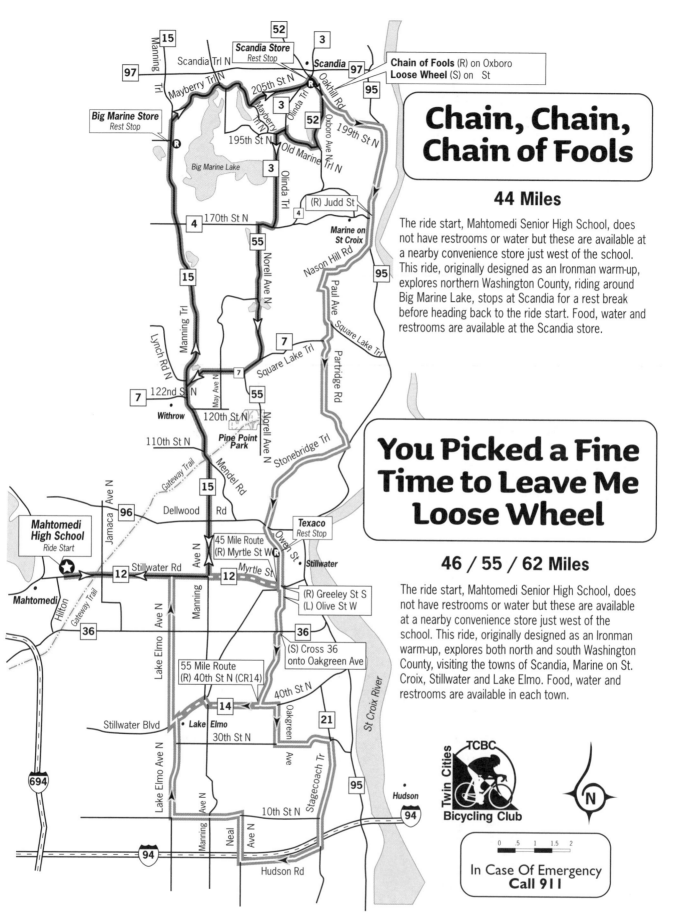

Chain, Chain, Chain of Fools

44 Miles

The ride start, Mahtomedi Senior High School, does not have restrooms or water but these are available at a nearby convenience store just west of the school. This ride, originally designed as an Ironman warm-up, explores northern Washington County, riding around Big Marine Lake, stops at Scandia for a rest break before heading back to the ride start. Food, water and restrooms are available at the Scandia store.

You Picked a Fine Time to Leave Me Loose Wheel

46 / 55 / 62 Miles

The ride start, Mahtomedi Senior High School, does not have restrooms or water but these are available at a nearby convenience store just west of the school. This ride, originally designed as an Ironman warm-up, explores both north and south Washington County, visiting the towns of Scandia, Marine on St. Croix, Stillwater and Lake Elmo. Food, water and restrooms are available in each town.

Map labels

Manning Trl N
15
97
52
Scandia Store *Rest Stop*
3
Scandia
97
3
95
Chain of Fools (R) on Oxboro
Loose Wheel (S) on   St
Scandia Trl N
Mayberry Trl N
205th St N
Oakhill Rd
Big Marine Store *Rest Stop*
R
Mayberry Trl N
Olinda Trl
52
Oxboro Ave Trl N
199th St N
195th St N
Old Marine Trl N
3
Big Marine Lake
Olinda Trl
4
(R) Judd St
Marine on St Croix
170th St N
4
55
Nason Hill Rd
95
15
Norell Ave N
Paul Ave
95
Manning Trl
7
Square Lake Trl
Lynch Rd N
7
Square Lake Trl
Partridge Rd
7
122nd St N
55
May Ave N
Withrow
120th St N
Norell Ave N
110th St N
Pine Point Park
Stonebridge Trl
Gateway Trail
Mendel Rd
15
Jamaca Ave N
96
Dellwood Rd
Mahtomedi High School *Ride Start*
Texaco *Rest Stop*
Owen St
45 Mile Route (R) Myrtle St W
Stillwater
Stillwater Rd
12
Ave N
12
Myrtle St
Mahtomedi
Hilton
Gateway Trail
Manning
(R) Greeley St S
(L) Olive St W
36
Lake Elmo Ave N
Manning
36
(S) Cross 36 onto Oakgreen Ave
55 Mile Route (R) 40th St N (CR14)
40th St N
14
Oakgreen Ave
21
Stillwater Blvd
Lake Elmo
30th St N
St Croix River
Lake Elmo Ave N
Ave N
Stagecoach Tr
95
Hudson
694
Manning
Neal Ave N
10th St N
94
94
Hudson Rd

TCBC
Twin Cities Bicycling Club

0   .5   1   1.5   2

In Case Of Emergency
Call 911

N

Tin Man

47 / 76 Miles

The ride start, Mahtomedi Senior High School, does not have restrooms or water. The closest gas station is just west of the high school on county road 12. This route has rolling terrain with a few steep climbs. Afton and Marine on St. Croix are both very cute little towns that are great for a rest stop.

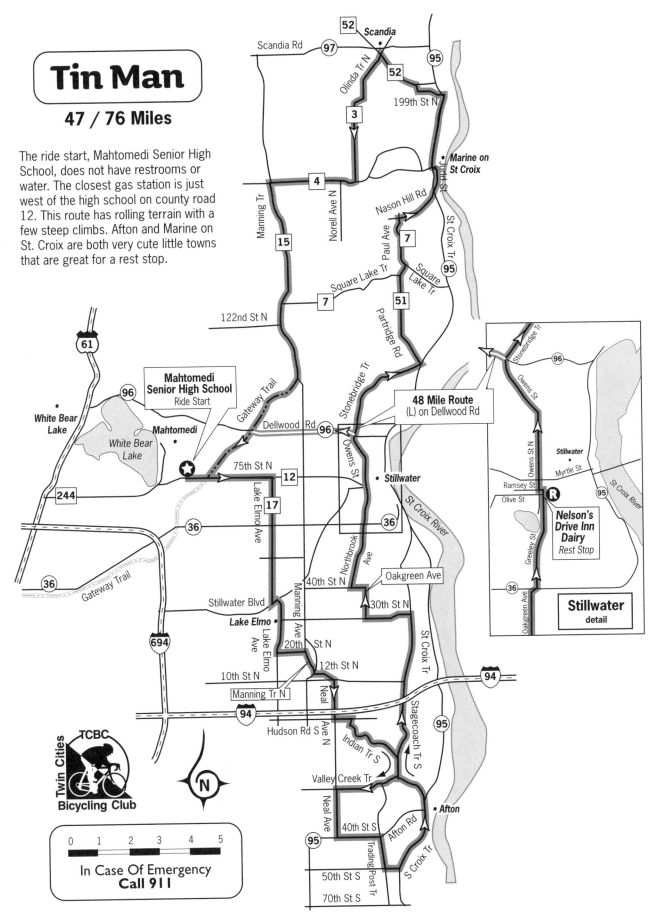

Twin Cities Bicycling Club
TCBC

In Case Of Emergency
Call 911

0 1 2 3 4 5

An Apple a Day

24 / 36 / 53 Miles

Depart from Mahtomedi High School on Hwy 12 (take Hwy 36 just east of I-694, north on Hilton Trail, east on Hwy 12, then left into the school.) Keep the doctor away by eating an apple or two on this ride that meanders along the quiet rolling roads of the area en route to Scandia and back with a rest stop at the Pine Tree Apple Orchard. Never mind that those apples may be covered with caramel sauce and ice cream or tucked inside of pies and turnovers! The route can be shortened to 24 or 36 miles while still including a stop at the orchard. In early summer, enjoy strawberry treats at the orchard!

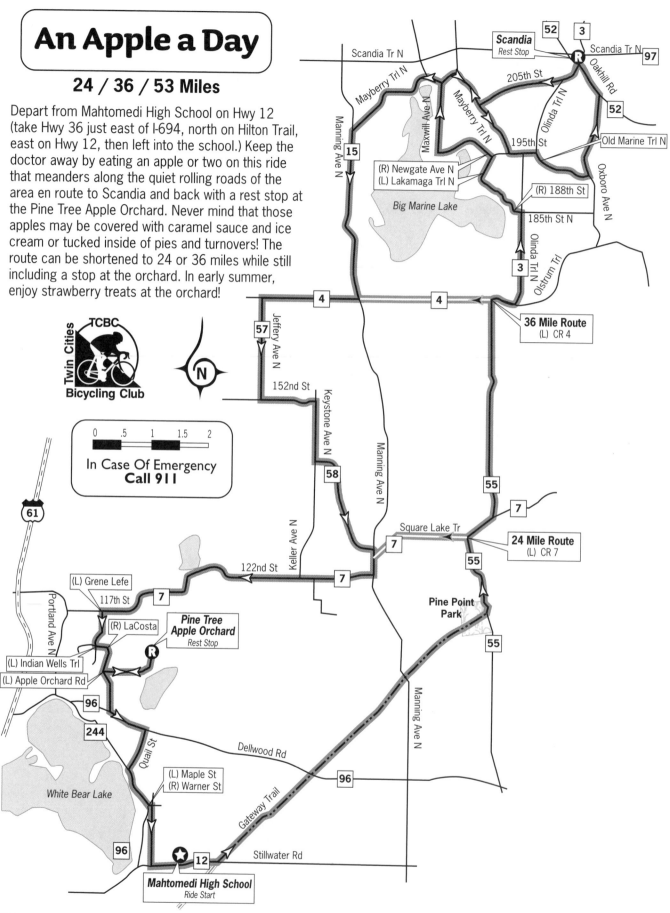

TCBC
Twin Cities
Bicycling Club

0 .5 1 1.5 2

In Case Of Emergency
Call 911

Scandia Tr N

Scandia
Rest Stop

52 3 Scandia Tr N 97

205th St

Mayberry Trl N

Maxwill Ave N

Olinda Trl N

Oakhill Rd

52

195th St

Old Marine Trl N

Manning Ave N

15

(R) Newgate Ave N
(L) Lakamaga Trl N

(R) 188th St

Oxboro Ave N

Big Marine Lake

185th St N

3

Olinda Trl N

Olstrum Trl

4   4

36 Mile Route
(L) CR 4

57

Jeffery Ave N

152nd St

Keystone Ave N

Manning Ave N

58

55

7

61

Keller Ave N

Square Lake Tr

24 Mile Route
(L) CR 7

7

55

122nd St

7

(L) Grene Lefe
117th St

7

Pine Point Park

55

(R) LaCosta

Pine Tree Apple Orchard
Rest Stop

R

Portland Ave N

(L) Indian Wells Trl

(L) Apple Orchard Rd

96

244

Quail St

Dellwood Rd

Manning Ave N

96

(L) Maple St
(R) Warner St

White Bear Lake

Gateway Trail

96

12 Stillwater Rd

Mahtomedi High School
Ride Start

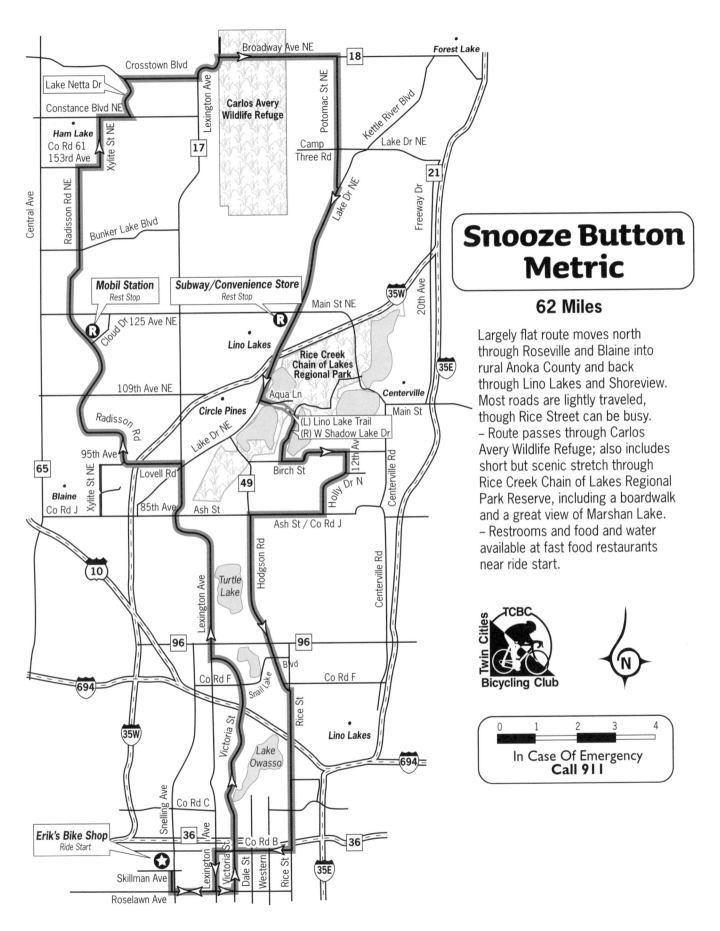

Snooze Button Metric

62 Miles

Largely flat route moves north through Roseville and Blaine into rural Anoka County and back through Lino Lakes and Shoreview. Most roads are lightly traveled, though Rice Street can be busy.
- Route passes through Carlos Avery Wildlife Refuge; also includes short but scenic stretch through Rice Creek Chain of Lakes Regional Park Reserve, including a boardwalk and a great view of Marshan Lake.
- Restrooms and food and water available at fast food restaurants near ride start.

Twin Cities **TCBC** Bicycling Club

In Case Of Emergency
Call 911

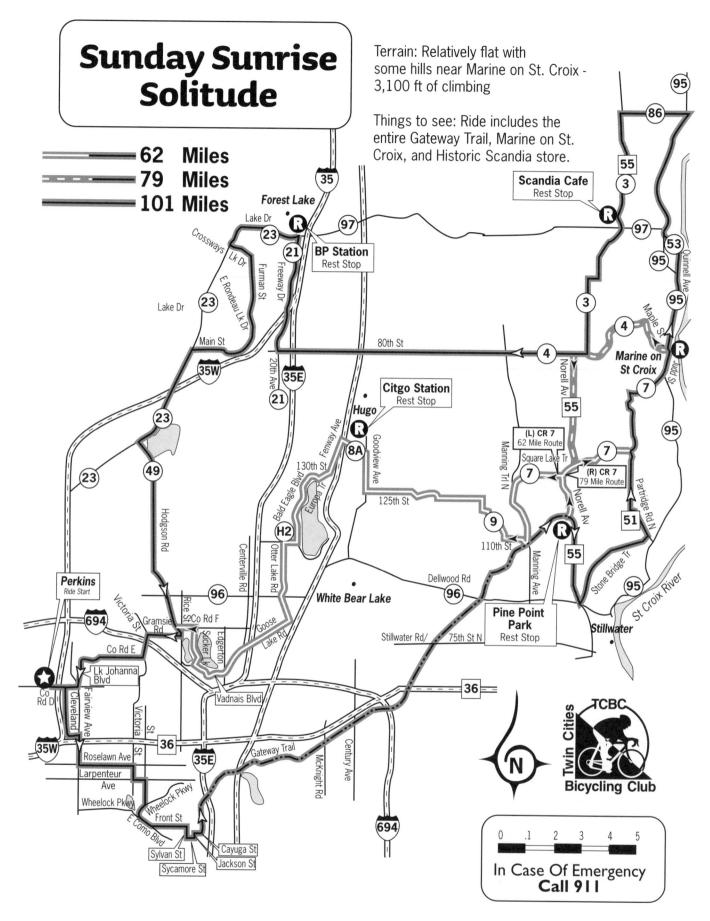

Sunday Sunrise Solitude

Terrain: Relatively flat with some hills near Marine on St. Croix - 3,100 ft of climbing

Things to see: Ride includes the entire Gateway Trail, Marine on St. Croix, and Historic Scandia store.

62 Miles
79 Miles
101 Miles

Forest Lake

Scandia Cafe
Rest Stop

BP Station
Rest Stop

Citgo Station
Rest Stop

Hugo

(L) CR 7
62 Mile Route

Square Lake Tr

(R) CR 7
79 Mile Route

Marine on St Croix

Perkins
Ride Start

White Bear Lake

Dellwood Rd

Pine Point Park
Rest Stop

Stillwater

St Croix River

Gateway Trail

Lk Johanna Blvd

Vadnais Blvd

Stillwater Rd/ 75th St N

TCBC
Twin Cities
Bicycling Club

N

0 .1 2 3 4 5

In Case Of Emergency
Call 911

Northeast Ride Journal

Date _____ Mileage _____

Route _____

Notes _____

_____

_____

Date _____ Mileage _____

Route _____

Notes _____

_____

_____

Date _____ Mileage _____

Route _____

Notes _____

_____

_____

Date _____ Mileage _____

Route _____

Notes _____

_____

_____

Date _____ Mileage _____

Route _____

Notes _____

_____

_____

Date _____ Mileage _____

Route _____

Notes _____

_____

_____

Date _____ Mileage _____

Route _____

Notes _____

_____

_____

Date _____ Mileage _____

Route _____

Notes _____

_____

_____

Date _____ Mileage _____

Route _____

Notes _____

_____

_____

Date _____ Mileage _____

Route _____

Notes _____

_____

_____

Southeast

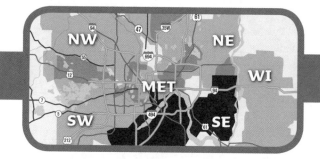

GREY CLOUD ISLAND
RIDE IN THE CLOUDS - PAGE 72

HISTORIC COVERED BRIDGE - GREAT
RIDE OF THE PUDDING BOY - PAGE 71

GREAT RIVER TRAIL
URBAN WILDLIFE - PAGE 67

THE EAGLE'S NEST IS A
WELCOME REST STOP ON
THE PEDAL PEPIN RIDE
- PAGE 76

Legend: FOOD · WATER · TOILET · FLAT · ROLLING · HILLY · CLIMBS · ROADS · TRAILS · LT TRAFFIC · TRAFFIC · SCENIC · TREATS

Page	Ride	Miles	At Ride Start	Terrain	Highlights
60	Explore Dakota County	22	Water, Toilet	Flat, Roads, LT Traffic	Scenic, Treats
61	It's Not S'more - 'UMore	23	Water, Toilet	Flat, Rolling, Roads, Traffic	Scenic
62	Spring Brake	25/30	Food, Water, Toilet	Rolling, Roads, Trails, LT Traffic	Scenic, Treats
63	Johnny's Traveling Crystal	29	Toilet	Rolling, Roads, LT Traffic	
64	Ironman 30	30		Rolling, Roads, LT Traffic	
65	Farquar Park Loop	30/36	Toilet	Rolling, Climbs, Roads, Traffic	
66	Morning Glory	30/40	Toilet	Rolling, Climbs, Roads, Traffic	Treats
67	Urban Wildlife	32/46	Water	Rolling, Roads, Trails, LT Traffic	
68	Afton to Elmo	33/37	Toilet	Rolling, Climbs, Roads, Traffic	Scenic, Treats
69	Washington County Whirl	34/45	Toilet	Rolling, Roads, LT Traffic	Scenic, Treats
70	Dakota Badlands	45	Food, Water, Toilet	Rolling, Roads, LT Traffic	Scenic
71	Great Ride of Pudding Boy	50/78		Climbs, Roads, LT Traffic	Scenic, Treats
72	Ride in the Clouds	53/67	Water, Toilet	Rolling, Climbs, Roads, Traffic	Scenic, Treats
73	Ironman 62 & 100	62/100		Flat, Climbs, Roads, Traffic	
74	Bloomington Ferry Bridge	64	Toilet	Rolling, Roads, LT Traffic	Scenic
75	Goodhue County Canter	71	Water, Toilet	Rolling, Roads, Trails, LT Traffic	Scenic, Treats
76	Pedal Pepin	76	Food, Water, Toilet	Rolling, Climbs, Roads, Traffic	Scenic, Treats

Disclaimer: The Twin Cities Bicycling Club, Hostelling International USA – Minnesota Council, and their respective officers, employees, trip leaders and members, and those whose work appears in this Atlas, and those people and establishments who distribute this Atlas, cannot be held responsible for the future condition of any of these routes, or for any injuries or damages sustained or occuring while using these routes.

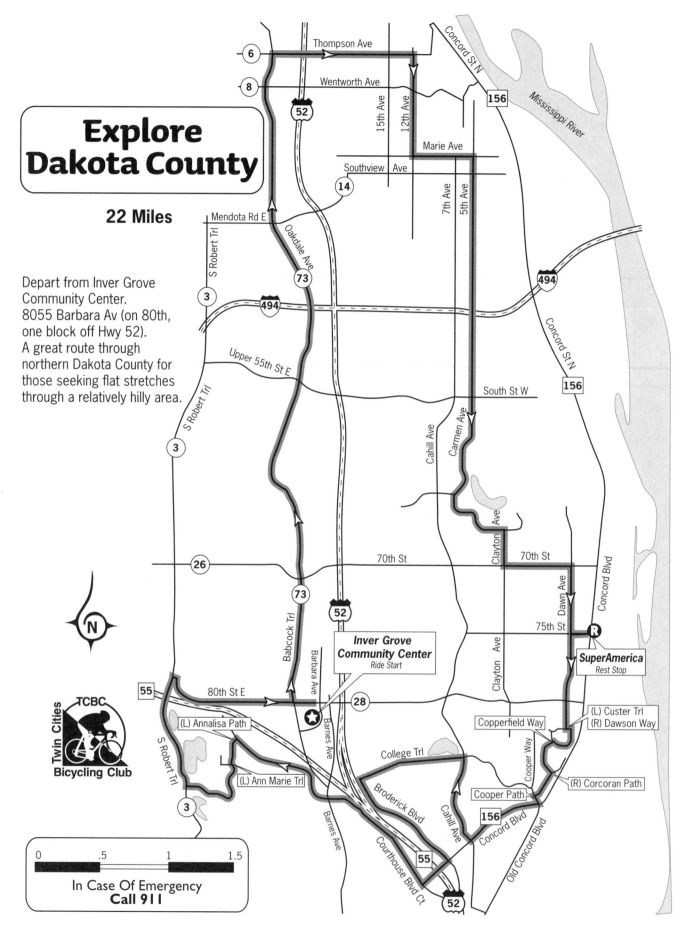

Explore Dakota County

22 Miles

Depart from Inver Grove Community Center. 8055 Barbara Av (on 80th, one block off Hwy 52). A great route through northern Dakota County for those seeking flat stretches through a relatively hilly area.

Thompson Ave

Wentworth Ave

Marie Ave

Southview Ave

Mendota Rd E

Oakdale Ave

Upper 55th St E

South St W

Mississippi River

15th Ave

12th Ave

7th Ave

5th Ave

Concord St N

S Robert Trl

Cahill Ave

Carmen Ave

Concord St N

70th St

70th St

Clayton Ave

Concord Blvd

Babcock Trl

Barbara Ave

Dawn Ave

75th St

Inver Grove Community Center
Ride Start

SuperAmerica
Rest Stop

80th St E

Clayton Ave

Copperfield Way

(L) Custer Trl
(R) Dawson Way

(L) Annalisa Path

Barnes Ave

College Trl

Cooper Way

Cooper Path

(R) Corcoran Path

(L) Ann Marie Trl

S Robert Trl

Broderick Blvd

Cahill Ave

Concord Blvd

Old Concord Blvd

Courthouse Blvd Ct

Barnes Ave

TCBC
Twin Cities Bicycling Club

0   .5   1   1.5

In Case Of Emergency
Call 911

It's Not S'more It's UMORE

23 Miles

Depart from Inver Grove Community Center, 8055 Barbara Ave, on 80th Street, one block off Hwy 52.

No, you won't be able to roast marshmallows in the fires you see coming from the refinery in the distance, but you will get a nice ride through the rolling hills of the southeastern metro, including a trip through UMore Park (University of Minnesota Outreach, Research and Education Park)

TCBC
Twin Cities
Bicycling Club

0 .5 1 1.5 2

In Case Of Emergency
Call 911

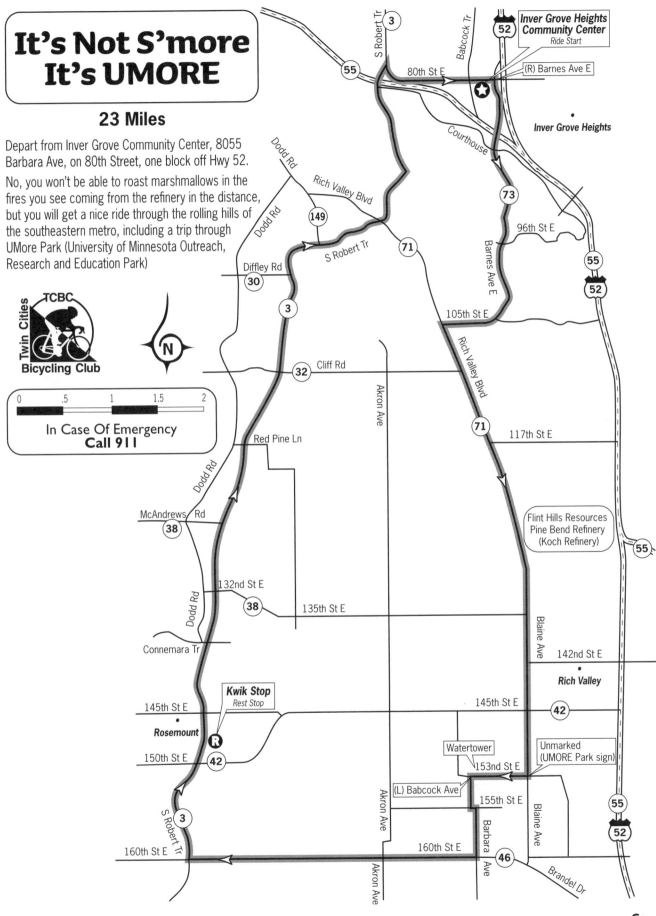

Inver Grove Heights
Community Center
Ride Start

(R) Barnes Ave E

Inver Grove Heights

Dodd Rd
Rich Valley Blvd
149
S Robert Tr
Diffley Rd
30
3
32 Cliff Rd
Red Pine Ln
McAndrews Rd
38
Dodd Rd
132nd St E
38
135th St E
Connemara Tr
145th St E
Rosemount
150th St E
42
S Robert Tr
3
160th St E

80th St E
Babcock Tr
52
S Robert Tr
3
55
Courthouse
73
96th St E
Barnes Ave E
105th St E
55
52
Rich Valley Blvd
71
71
117th St E
Flint Hills Resources
Pine Bend Refinery
(Koch Refinery)
55
Blaine Ave
142nd St E
Rich Valley
145th St E
42
Watertower
153nd St E
Unmarked
(UMORE Park sign)
(L) Babcock Ave
155th St E
Barbara Ave
Blaine Ave
160th St E
46
Brandel Dr
55
52

Akron Ave

Kwik Stop
Rest Stop
R

N

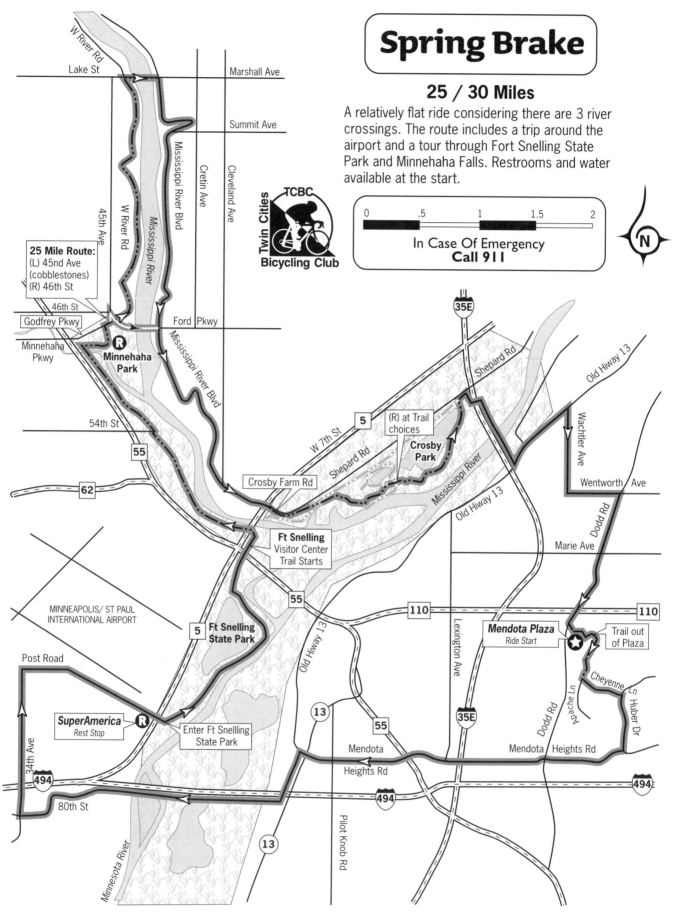

Spring Brake

25 / 30 Miles

A relatively flat ride considering there are 3 river crossings. The route includes a trip around the airport and a tour through Fort Snelling State Park and Minnehaha Falls. Restrooms and water available at the start.

TCBC
Twin Cities Bicycling Club

0   .5   1   1.5   2

In Case Of Emergency
Call 911

N

25 Mile Route:
(L) 45nd Ave (cobblestones)
(R) 46th St

Godfrey Pkwy

Minnehaha Pkwy

R Minnehaha Park

Lake St
Marshall Ave
Summit Ave
W River Rd
Mississippi River Blvd
Cretin Ave
Cleveland Ave
45th Ave
W River Rd
Mississippi River
46th St
Ford Pkwy

Mississippi River Blvd

54th St
55
62

Crosby Farm Rd

W 7th St
Shepard Rd
5
(R) at Trail choices
Crosby Park
Shepard Rd
Mississippi River
Old Hiway 13
Wachtler Ave
Wentworth Ave
Dodd Rd

35E

Ft Snelling
Visitor Center
Trail Starts

MINNEAPOLIS/ ST PAUL
INTERNATIONAL AIRPORT

55

5 **Ft Snelling State Park**

Post Road

SuperAmerica
Rest Stop R

Enter Ft Snelling State Park

34th Ave

494

80th St

Minnesota River

13

Old Hiway 13

Pilot Knob Rd

Mendota Heights Rd

55

110
Marie Ave

Mendota Plaza
Ride Start

Trail out of Plaza

Cheyenne Ln
Huber Dr
Apache Ln
Dodd Rd

Lexington Ave

35E

110

494

Mendota Heights Rd

Old Hiway 13

Johnny's Traveling Diamond Crystal

29 Miles

Depart from Thomas Lake Park in Eagan (approximately 2 miles South of 35E on Pilot Knob Rd). Wander through suburban neighborhoods via the rolling hills of the area. Johnny Cake's quest begins on the Highline Trail which leads him to a familiar place, his own Ridge Road. He then follows the Diamond Path on his search for the Crystal Lake. Return home along the Travelers Trail with any treasures found on this journey through the rolling hills and neighborhoods of the south metro.

In Case Of Emergency
Call 911

Twin Cities
Bicycling Club
TCBC

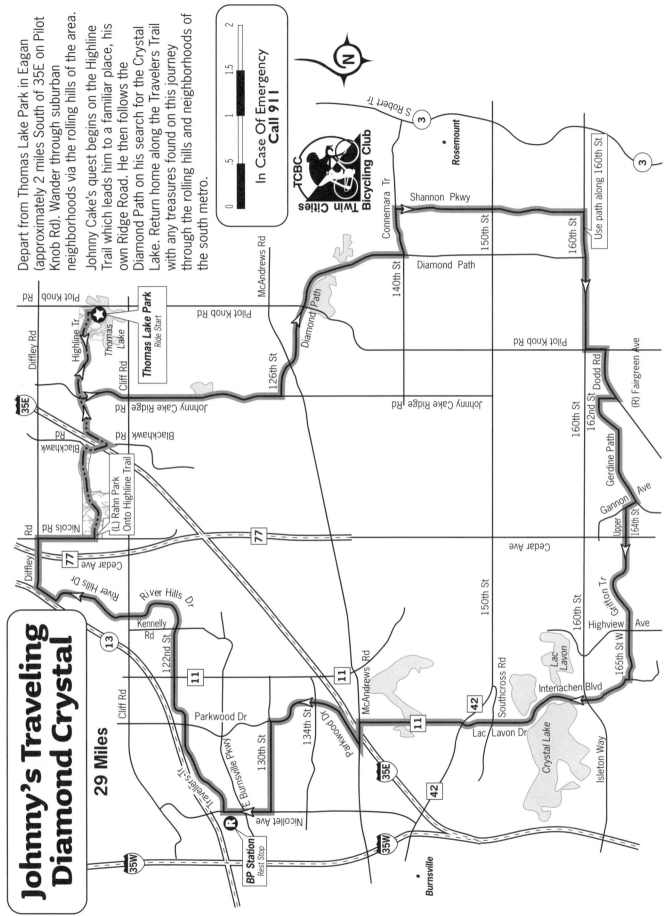

Thomas Lake Park
Ride Start

(L) Rahn Park Onto Highline Trail

BP Station
Rest Stop

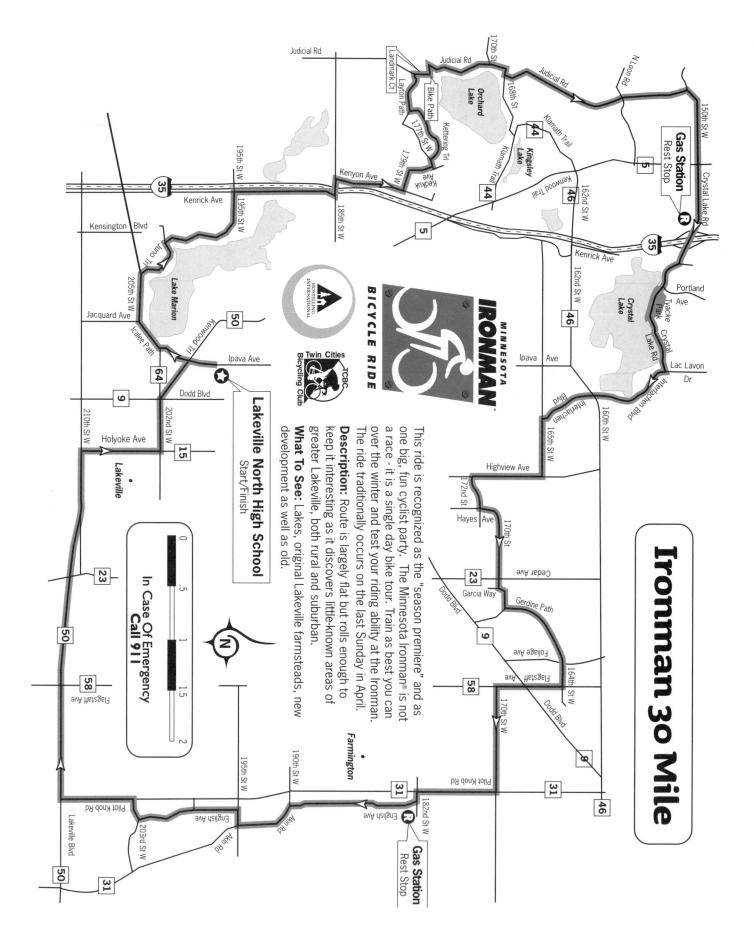

Ironman 30 Mile

Lakeville North High School
Start/Finish

MINNESOTA IRONMAN
BICYCLE RIDE

Twin Cities Bicycling Club
TCBC

HOSTELLING INTERNATIONAL

This ride is recognized as the "season premiere" and as one big, fun cyclist party. The Minnesota Ironman® is not a race - it is a single day bike tour. Train as best you can over the winter and test your riding ability at the Ironman. The ride traditionally occurs on the last Sunday in April.

Description: Route is largely flat but rolls enough to keep it interesting as it discovers little-known areas of greater Lakeville, both rural and suburban.

What To See: Lakes, original Lakeville farmsteads, new development as well as old.

In Case Of Emergency Call 911

0   .5   1   1.5   2

N

Gas Station
Rest Stop

Gas Station
Rest Stop

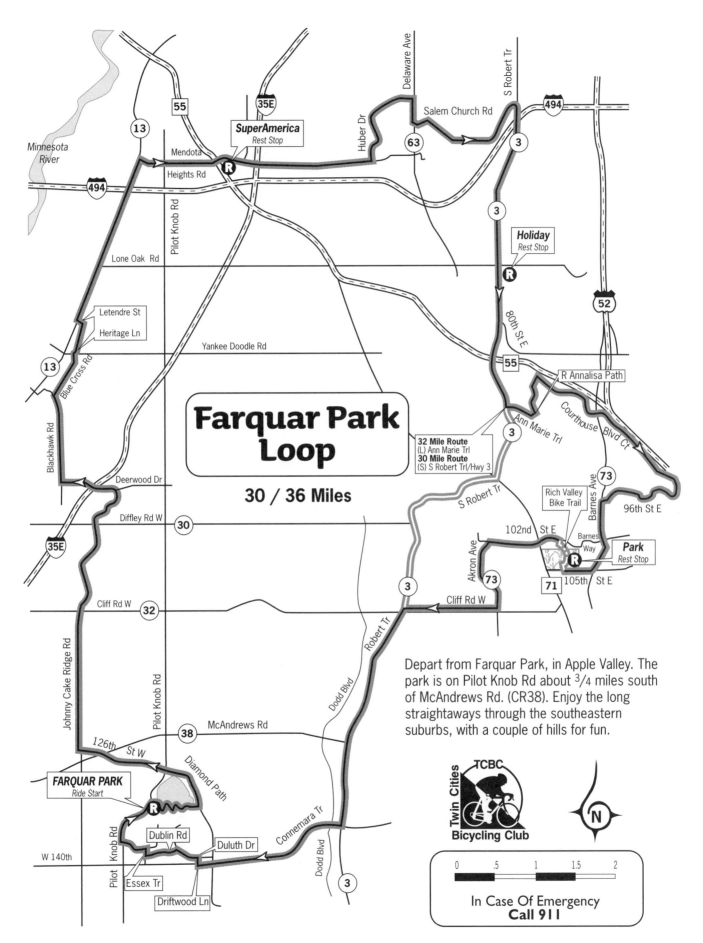

Farquar Park Loop

30 / 36 Miles

32 Mile Route
(L) Ann Marie Trl
30 Mile Route
(S) S Robert Trl/Hwy 3

Depart from Farquar Park, in Apple Valley. The park is on Pilot Knob Rd about 3/4 miles south of McAndrews Rd. (CR38). Enjoy the long straightaways through the southeastern suburbs, with a couple of hills for fun.

SuperAmerica *Rest Stop*

Holiday *Rest Stop*

Park *Rest Stop*

FARQUAR PARK *Ride Start*

Minnesota River

TCBC
Twin Cities
Bicycling Club

In Case Of Emergency
Call 911

0   .5   1   1.5   2

65

Morning Glory

30 / 40 Miles

Depart from the parking lot of Harriet Island regional Park, across the Wabasha St. Bridge from downtown St. Paul. Ride to Rosemount and back, via the rolling hills of the area, with the opportunity for a rest stop at the Morning Glory Cafe.

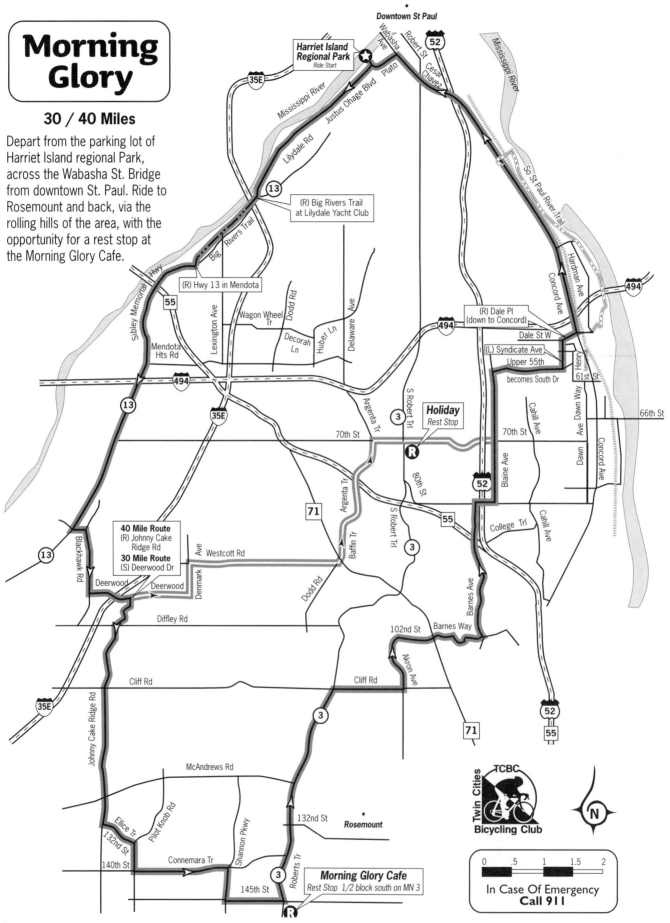

Downtown St Paul

Harriet Island Regional Park
Ride Start

(R) Big Rivers Trail at Lilydale Yacht Club

(R) Hwy 13 in Mendota

(R) Dale Pl (down to Concord)

(L) Syndicate Ave

Holiday Rest Stop

40 Mile Route
(R) Johnny Cake Ridge Rd
30 Mile Route
(S) Deerwood Dr

Rosemount

Morning Glory Cafe
Rest Stop 1/2 block south on MN 3

TCBC
Twin Cities Bicycling Club

0   .5   1   1.5   2

In Case Of Emergency
Call 911

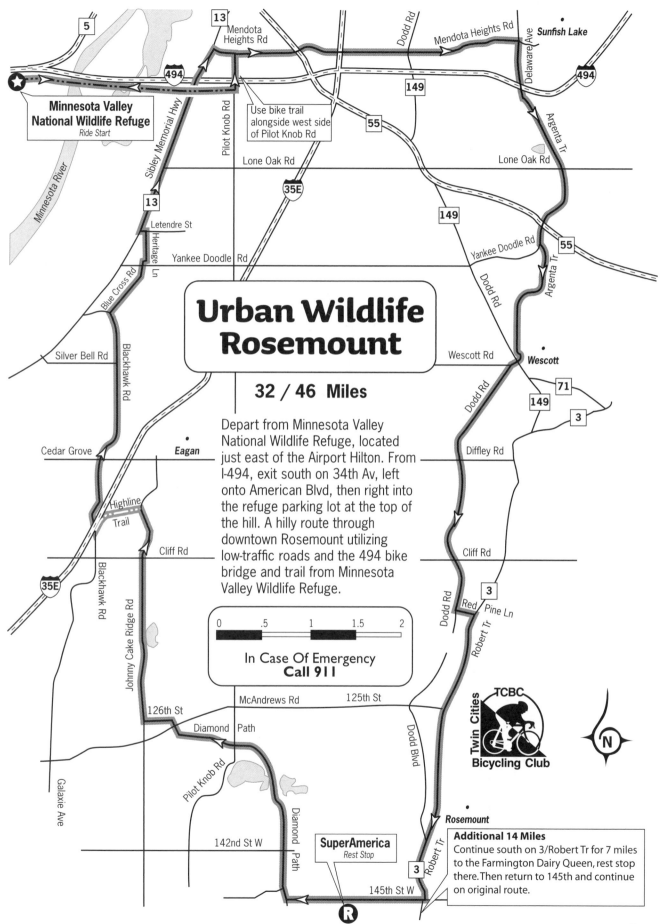

Urban Wildlife Rosemount

32 / 46 Miles

Depart from Minnesota Valley National Wildlife Refuge, located just east of the Airport Hilton. From I-494, exit south on 34th Av, left onto American Blvd, then right into the refuge parking lot at the top of the hill. A hilly route through downtown Rosemount utilizing low-traffic roads and the 494 bike bridge and trail from Minnesota Valley Wildlife Refuge.

0   .5   1   1.5   2

In Case Of Emergency
Call 911

Minnesota Valley
National Wildlife Refuge
Ride Start

Use bike trail
alongside west side
of Pilot Knob Rd

Additional 14 Miles
Continue south on 3/Robert Tr for 7 miles to the Farmington Dairy Queen, rest stop there. Then return to 145th and continue on original route.

SuperAmerica
Rest Stop

TCBC
Twin Cities
Bicycling Club

5
13
Mendota Heights Rd
Dodd Rd
Mendota Heights Rd
Sunfish Lake
494
494
Delaware Ave
Pilot Knob Rd
Sibley Memorial Hwy
13
149
55
Argenta Tr
Lone Oak Rd
Lone Oak Rd
35E
149
55
Letendre St
Heritage Ln
Yankee Doodle Rd
Yankee Doodle Rd
Argenta Tr
Blue Cross Rd
Dodd Rd
Silver Bell Rd
Blackhawk Rd
Wescott Rd
Wescott
71
149
3
Cedar Grove
Eagan
Diffley Rd
Highline
Trail
35E
Blackhawk Rd
Cliff Rd
Cliff Rd
3
Dodd Rd
Johnny Cake Ridge Rd
Red Pine Ln
Robert Tr
McAndrews Rd   125th St
126th St
Diamond Path
Dodd Blvd
Galaxie Ave
Pilot Knob Rd
142nd St W
Diamond Path
Rosemount
3
Robert Tr
R
145th St W

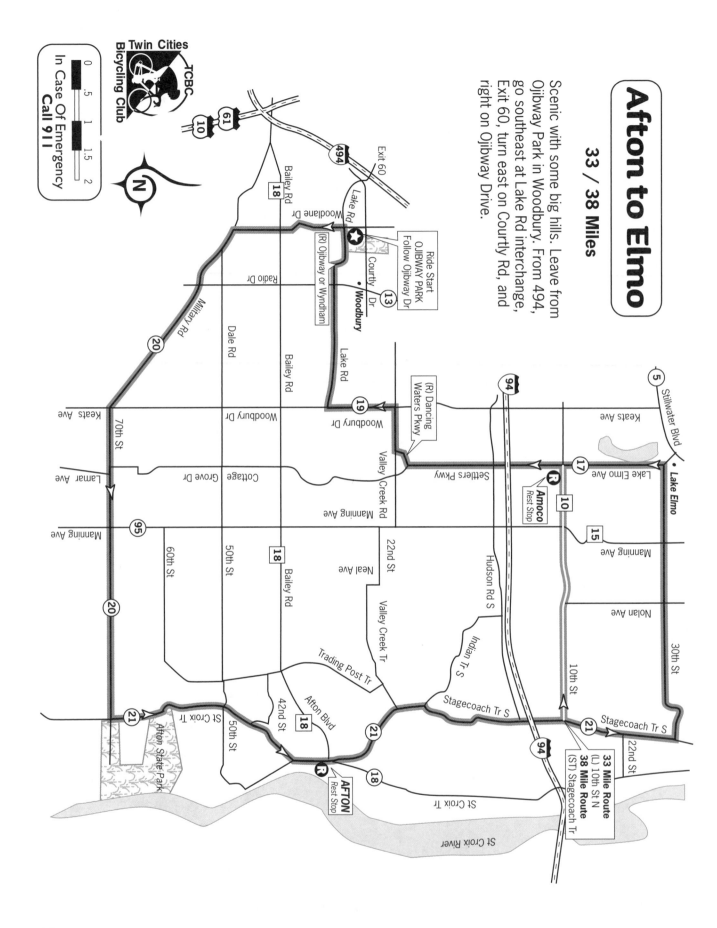

Afton to Elmo
33 / 38 Miles

Scenic with some big hills. Leave from Ojibway Park in Woodbury. From 494, go southeast at Lake Rd interchange, Exit 60, turn east on Courtly Rd, and right on Ojibway Drive.

Twin Cities Bicycling Club
TCBC

In Case Of Emergency Call 911

0 .5 1 1.5 2

N

Ride Start OJIBWAY PARK Follow Ojibway Dr

(R) Ojibway or Wyndham

Woodbury

Courtly Dr

Woodlane Dr

Exit 60

Lake Rd

Bailey Rd

Radio Dr

Dale Rd

Bailey Rd

Military Rd

Lake Rd

(R) Dancing Waters Pkwy

Settlers Pkwy

Stilwater Blvd

Keats Ave

Lake Elmo Ave

Lake Elmo

Woodbury Dr

Woodbury Dr

Keats Ave

70th St

Lamar Ave

Grove Dr

Cottage

Valley Creek Rd

Manning Ave

Amoco Rest Stop

Manning Ave

Manning Ave

Nolan Ave

30th St

60th St

50th St

Bailey Rd

Neal Ave

22nd St

Valley Creek Tr

Hudson Rd S

10th St

Indian Tr S

Stagecoach Tr S

Stagecoach Tr S

Stagecoach Tr S

22nd St

Trading Post Tr

Afton Blvd

42nd St

50th St

St Croix Tr

Afton State Park

AFTON Rest Stop

St Croix Tr

St Croix Tr

St Croix River

33 Mile Route
(L) 10th St N
38 Mile Route
(ST) Stagecoach Tr

68

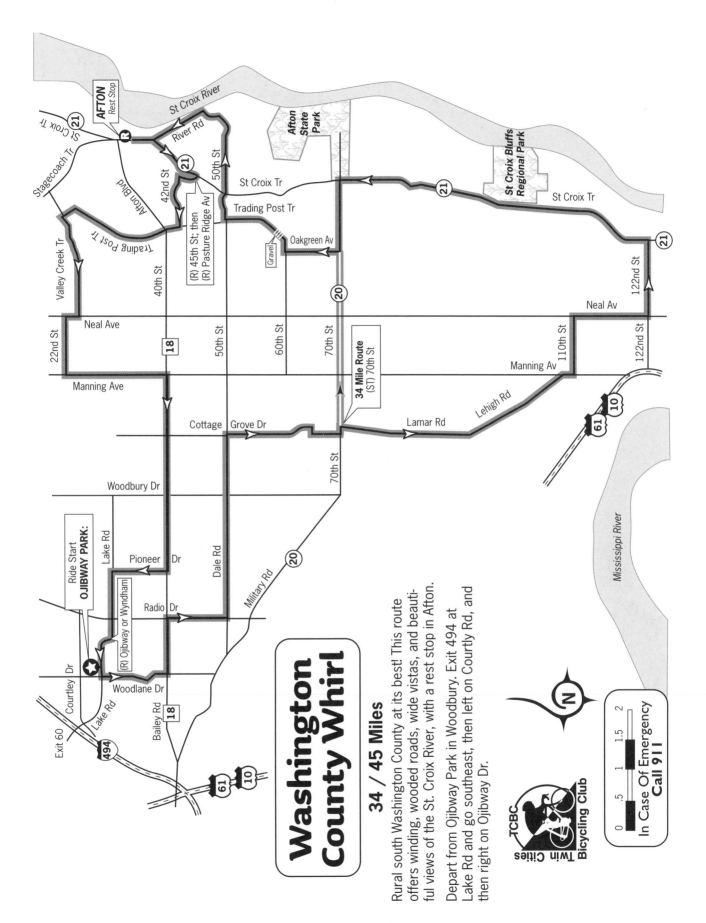

Washington County Whirl

34 / 45 Miles

Rural south Washington County at its best! This route offers winding, wooded roads, wide vistas, and beautiful views of the St. Croix River, with a rest stop in Afton.

Depart from Ojibway Park in Woodbury. Exit 494 at Lake Rd and go southeast, then left on Courtly Rd, and then right on Ojibway Dr.

In Case Of Emergency
Call 911

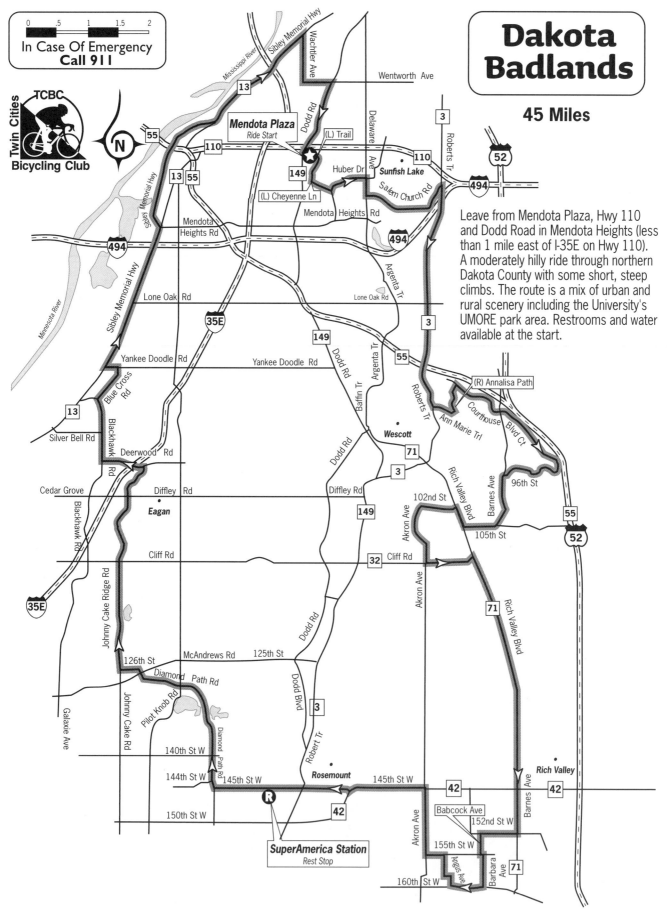

Dakota Badlands

45 Miles

Leave from Mendota Plaza, Hwy 110 and Dodd Road in Mendota Heights (less than 1 mile east of I-35E on Hwy 110). A moderately hilly ride through northern Dakota County with some short, steep climbs. The route is a mix of urban and rural scenery including the University's UMORE park area. Restrooms and water available at the start.

In Case Of Emergency
Call 911

TCBC
Twin Cities
Bicycling Club

N

Mendota Plaza
Ride Start

(L) Trail

(L) Cheyenne Ln

Huber Dr

Sunfish Lake

Mendota Heights Rd

Mendota Heights Rd

Wentworth Ave

Delaware Ave

Salem Church Rd

Argenta Tr

Sibley Memorial Hwy

Wachtler Ave

Mississippi River

Minnesota River

Sibley Memorial Hwy

Mendota Heights Rd

Lone Oak Rd

Lone Oak Rd

Yankee Doodle Rd

Yankee Doodle Rd

Blue Cross Rd

Blackhawk Rd

Silver Bell Rd

Deerwood Rd

Cedar Grove

Diffley Rd

Diffley Rd

Eagan

Blackhawk Rd

Cliff Rd

Cliff Rd

Johnny Cake Ridge Rd

Dodd Rd

Dodd Rd

Dodd Rd

Baffin Tr

Wescott

Roberts Tr

Ann Marie Trl

(R) Annalisa Path

Courthouse Blvd Ct

96th St

Barnes Ave

102nd St

105th St

Akron Ave

Rich Valley Blvd

Rich Valley Blvd

Johnny Cake Rd

126th St

McAndrews Rd

125th St

Diamond Path Rd

Pilot Knob Rd

Galaxie Ave

140th St W

144th St W

145th St W

150th St W

Diamond Path Rd

Dodd Blvd

Robert Tr

Rosemount

145th St W

Akron Ave

Babcock Ave

152nd St W

155th St W

160th St W

Angus Ave

Barbara Ave

Barnes Ave

Rich Valley

SuperAmerica Station
Rest Stop

70

Great Ride of the Pudding Boy

50 / 78 Miles

Depart from Northfield High School, 1400 Division St. South, just south of town. From I-35 or US 52, take MN 19 to Division St. in Northfield and turn south. High School is on your right. At the age of 10, on his single speed, balloon-tired red Schwinn Wasp, THE PUDDING BOY made his great lonely ride. This time, you come too. See Valley Grove Church, most of Nerstrand, Kenyon's Blvd of Roses, Zumbrota's covered bridge, downtown Wanamingo, the Sogn Valley, the Al Quie post office, and Malto Meal Dam. Climb PUDDING BOY HILL, a fairly steep 1.1 mile climb. Beautiful rolling farm country route that goes right through the heart of all that is good.

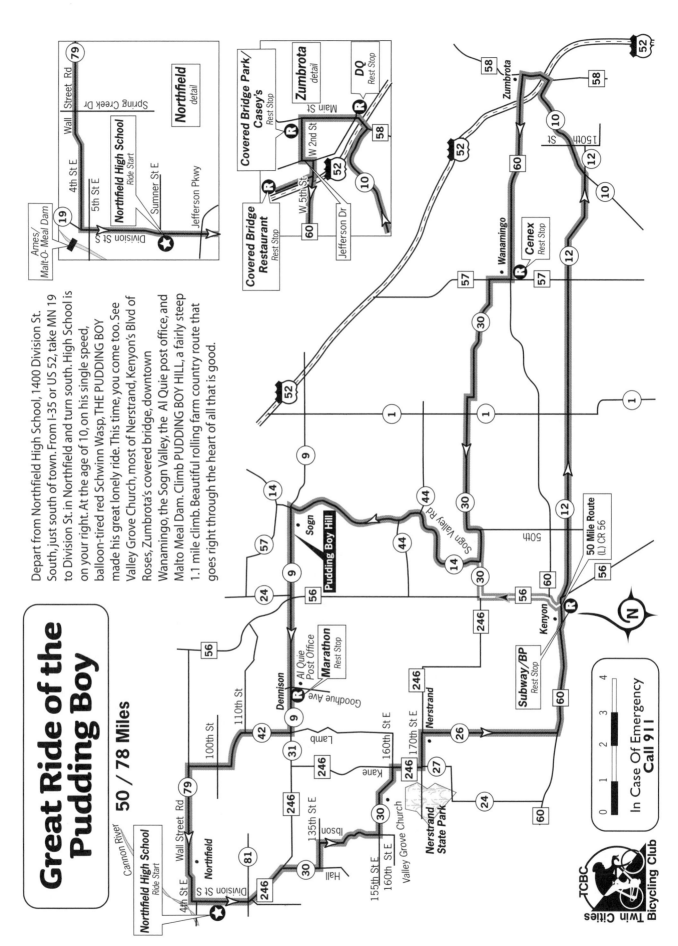

Northfield High School
Ride Start

Cannon River

Northfield *detail*

Ames/
Malt-O-Meal Dam

Northfield High School
Ride Start

Covered Bridge Park/ Casey's
Rest Stop

Zumbrota *detail*

DQ
Rest Stop

Covered Bridge Restaurant
Rest Stop

Wanamingo

Cenex
Rest Stop

Marathon
Rest Stop

Al Quie
Post Office

Dennison

Pudding Boy Hill

Sogn

Sogn Valley Rd

50 Mile Route
(L) CR 56

Kenyon

Subway/BP
Rest Stop

Nerstrand

Nerstrand State Park

Valley Grove Church

In Case Of Emergency
Call 911

TCBC
Twin Cities Bicycling Club

71

Ride in the Clouds

53 / 67 Miles

Ride Start
OJIBWAY PARK:
Follow Ojibway Dr

53 Mile Route
(L) Valley Creek
67 Mile Route
(S) Stagecoach

AFTON
Rest Stop

Gravel

53 Mile Route
(L) Lamar Rd
67 Mile Route
(R) Lamar Rd

Cottage Grove Ravine Park

Trail By Lake

Picnic Bldg
Rest Stop

St Croix Bluffs Regional Park

Afton State Park

Depart from Ojibway Park in Woodbury. Exit 494 at Lake Rd and head east. At the light on Courtly, go SE (left) to Ojibway Drive, then right into the park. Scenic route through southern Washington County including Grey Cloud Island, Cottage Grove Ravine Park and a rest stop in Afton. Some hilly sections that appear to lead up into the clouds.

Twin Cities Bicycling Club

In Case Of Emergency Call 911

Ironman 100 & 62 Mile Routes

Description: Route showcases a little bit of everything from winding, wooded hills to wide-open agricultural fields. Roadways are largely quiet and traffic is light. Shoulders are rare however.

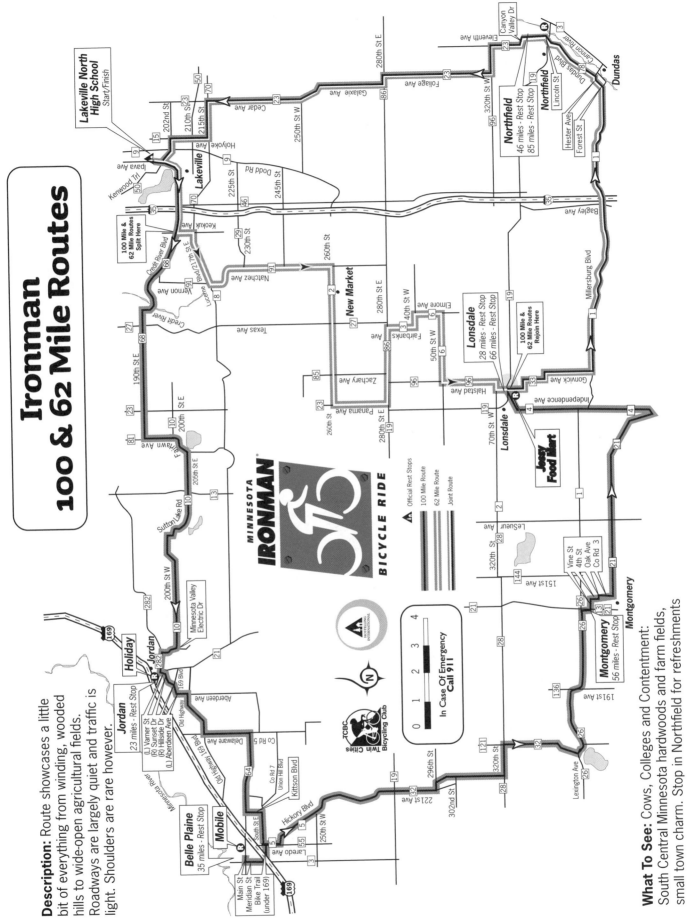

Lakeville North High School
Start/Finish

Northfield
46 miles - Rest Stop
85 miles - Rest Stop

100 Mile & 62 Mile Routes Split Here

Lonsdale
28 miles - Rest Stop
66 miles - Rest Stop

100 Mile & 62 Mile Routes Rejoin Here

New Market

Jordan
23 miles - Rest Stop
(L) Varner St
(R) Sunset Dr
(R) Hillside Dr
(L) Aberdeen Ave

Belle Plaine
35 miles - Rest Stop

Mobile

Montgomery
56 miles - Rest Stop

Joey Food Mart

MINNESOTA IRONMAN BICYCLE RIDE

In Case Of Emergency Call 911

TCBC Twin Cities Bicycling Club

HOSTELLING INTERNATIONAL

▲ Official Rest Stops
— 100 Mile Route
— 62 Mile Route
— Joint Route

What To See: Cows, Colleges and Contentment: South Central Minnesota hardwoods and farm fields, small town charm. Stop in Northfield for refreshments

73

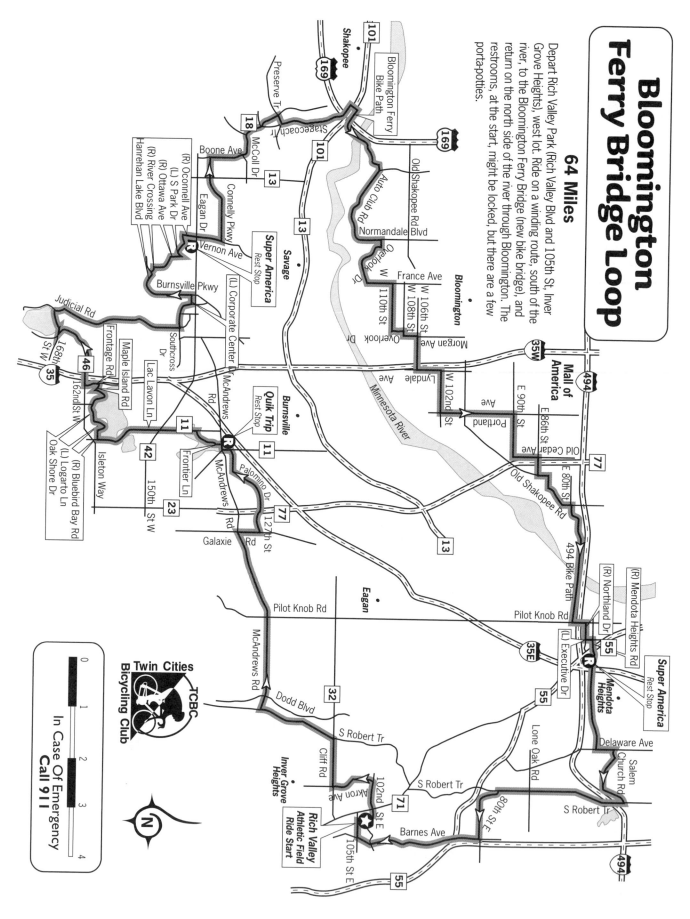

Bloomington Ferry Bridge Loop

64 Miles

Depart Rich Valley Park (Rich Valley Blvd and 105th St, Inver Grove Heights), west lot. Ride on a winding route, south of the river, to the Bloomington Ferry Bridge (new bike bridge), and return on the north side of the river through Bloomington. The restrooms, at the start, might be locked, but there are a few portapotties.

Twin Cities Bicycling Club
TCBC

In Case Of Emergency
Call 911

0 1 2 3 4

N

Shakopee

101

169

Bloomington Ferry Bike Path

169

Preserve Tr

Stagecoach Tr

18

101

McColl Dr

Boone Ave

13

Connelly Pkwy

Eagan Dr

(R) Oconnell Ave
(L) S Park Dr
(R) Ottawa Ave
(R) River Crossing
Hanrehan Lake Blvd

Vernon Ave

Super America
Rest Stop

Savage

13

Burnsville Pkwy

Southcross Dr

(L) Corporate Center Dr

McAndrews Rd

Lac Lavon Ln

Maple Island Rd

Frontage Rd

Judicial Rd

168th St W

162nd St W

35

46

Isleton Way

(R) Bluebird Bay Rd
(L) Logarto Ln
Oak Shore Dr

11

42

150th St W

23

Frontier Ln

Burnsville

Quik Trip
Rest Stop

11

McAndrews Rd

Palomino Dr

127th St

77

Galaxie Rd

13

Minnesota River

Auto Club Rd

Old Shakopee Rd

Normandale Blvd

Overlook Dr

W France Ave

W 106th St

W 108th St

110th St

Overlook Dr

Morgan Ave

Bloomington

Lyndale Ave

W 102nd St

35W

Mall of America

494

E 90th St

E 86th St

Portland Ave

Old Cedar Ave

77

E 80th St

Old Shakopee Rd

494 Bike Path

Pilot Knob Rd

(R) Northland Dr

(R) Mendota Heights Rd

55

Super America
Rest Stop

Mendota Heights

(L) Executive Dr

35E

Pilot Knob Rd

Eagan

McAndrews Rd

Pilot Knob Rd

Dodd Blvd

32

S Robert Tr

Cliff Rd

Inver Grove Heights

Akron Ave

102nd St E

71

105th St E

Rich Valley Athletic Field
Ride Start

Barnes Ave

S Robert Tr

80th St E

Lone Oak Rd

55

Delaware Ave

Salem Church Rd

S Robert Tr

494

55

74

Goodhue County Canter

71 Miles

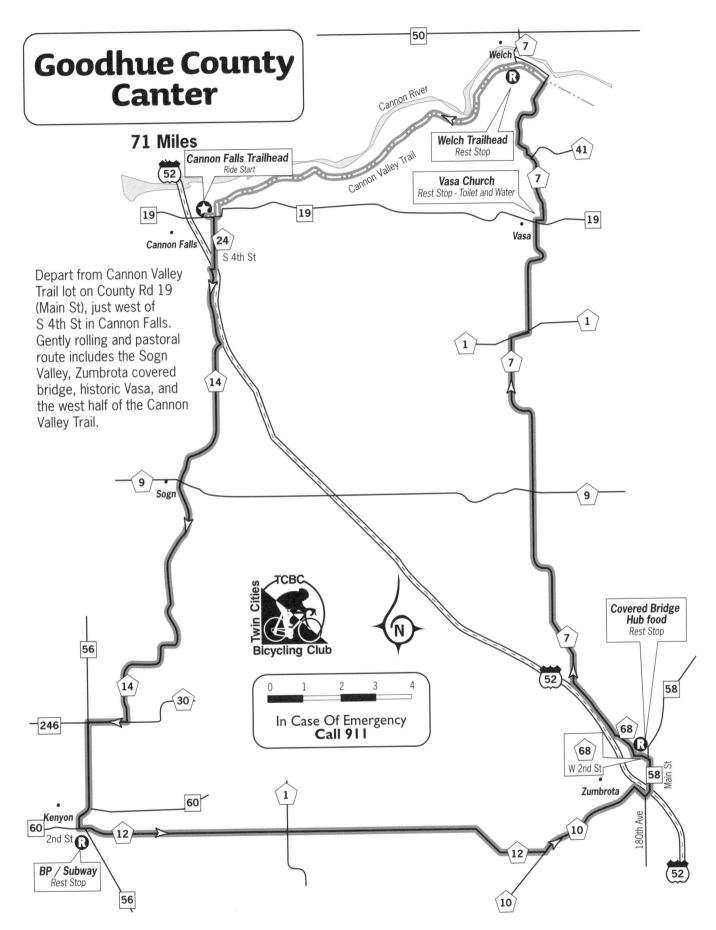

Cannon Falls Trailhead
Ride Start

Welch Trailhead
Rest Stop

Vasa Church
Rest Stop - Toilet and Water

Depart from Cannon Valley Trail lot on County Rd 19 (Main St), just west of S 4th St in Cannon Falls. Gently rolling and pastoral route includes the Sogn Valley, Zumbrota covered bridge, historic Vasa, and the west half of the Cannon Valley Trail.

Cannon River

Cannon Valley Trail

Welch

Cannon Falls

S 4th St

Sogn

Vasa

TCBC
Twin Cities
Bicycling Club

N

0 1 2 3 4

In Case Of Emergency
Call 911

Covered Bridge Hub food
Rest Stop

W 2nd St

Zumbrota

Main St

180th Ave

Kenyon

2nd St

BP / Subway
Rest Stop

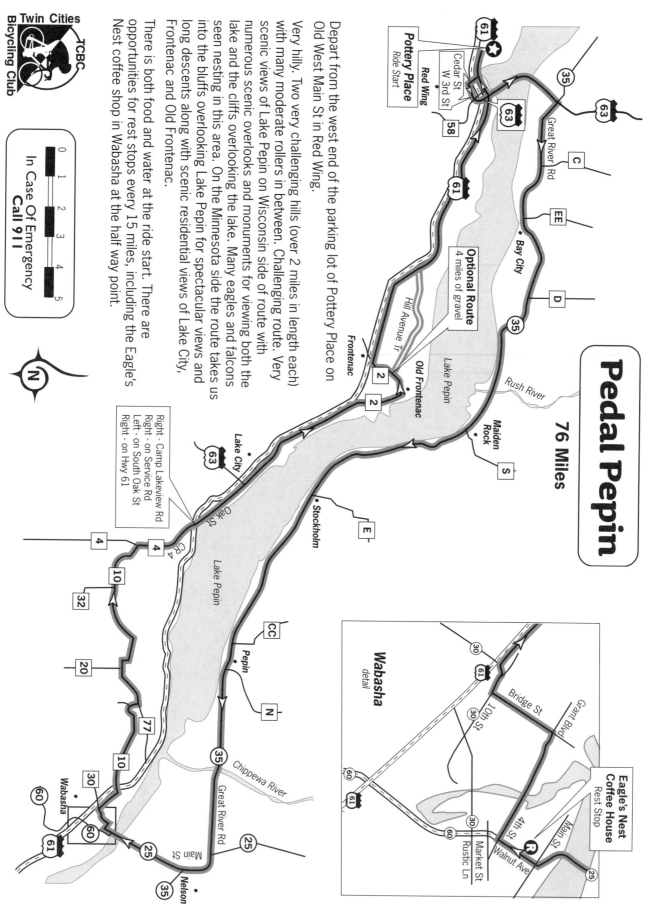

Pedal Pepin

76 Miles

Depart from the west end of the parking lot of Pottery Place on Old West Main St in Red Wing.

Very hilly. Two very challenging hills (over 2 miles in length each) with many moderate rollers in between. Challenging route. Very scenic views of Lake Pepin on Wisconsin side of route with numerous scenic overlooks and monuments for viewing both the lake and the cliffs overlooking the lake. Many eagles and falcons seen nesting in this area. On the Minnesota side the route takes us into the bluffs overlooking Lake Pepin for spectacular views and long descents along with scenic residential views of Lake City, Frontenac and Old Frontenac.

There is both food and water at the ride start. There are opportunities for rest stops every 15 miles, including the Eagle's Nest coffee shop in Wabasha at the half way point.

Right - Camp Lakeview Rd
Right - on Service Rd
Left - on South Oak St
Right - on Hwy 61

Optional Route
4 miles of gravel

Pottery Place
Ride Start

Eagle's Nest Coffee House
Rest Stop

Wabasha
detail

In Case Of Emergency
Call **911**

Twin Cities
Bicycling Club
TCBC

76

Southeast Ride Journal

Date _____ Mileage _____

Route _____

Notes _____

_____

_____

Date _____ Mileage _____

Route _____

Notes _____

_____

_____

Date _____ Mileage _____

Route _____

Notes _____

_____

_____

Date _____ Mileage _____

Route _____

Notes _____

_____

_____

Date _____ Mileage _____

Route _____

Notes _____

_____

_____

Date _____ Mileage _____

Route _____

Notes _____

_____

_____

Date _____ Mileage _____

Route _____

Notes _____

_____

_____

Date _____ Mileage _____

Route _____

Notes _____

_____

_____

Date _____ Mileage _____

Route _____

Notes _____

_____

_____

Date _____ Mileage _____

Route _____

Notes _____

_____

_____

Southwest

JORDAN VALLEY / MONTY MARATHON - PAGE 93

SMITH DOUGLAS MORE HOUSE 1877
DUNN BROS OUT & BACK - PAGE 91

AN EASY RIDE BACK ON THE LRT
CANTERBURY TRAILS - PAGE 86

NATURAL SPRING WATER
REST STOP NEAR THE BOTTOM
OF SPRING ROAD
THIGHS SIGHS & CRIES - PAGE 84

BEAUTIFUL CLIMB UP
BLUFF CREEK DRIVE
EATIN' PRAIRIE - PAGE 85

Legend: FOOD · WATER · TOILET · FLAT · ROLLING · HILLY · CLIMBS · ROADS · TRAILS · LT TRAFFIC · TRAFFIC · SCENIC · TREATS

Page	Ride	Miles	At Ride Start	Terrain	Highlights
80	Twisted Bloomington	19	Water, Toilet	Flat, Roads, LT Traffic	
81	Indian Hills & River Bluff	20 27/39	Water, Toilet	Rolling, Roads, LT Traffic	Treats
82	Mini Tonka Trekking	22	Water, Toilet	Hilly, Roads, LT Traffic	Scenic, Treats
83	Tupelo Honey	22/29	Food, Water, Toilet	Hilly, Roads, LT Traffic	
84	Thighs Sighs & Cries	22/30	Food, Water, Toilet	Hilly, Climbs, Roads, Traffic	
85	Eatin' Prairie	30	Food, Water, Toilet	Hilly, Climbs, Roads, Trails, LT Traffic	Scenic, Treats
86	Canterbury Trails	30	Food, Water, Toilet	Flat, Rolling, Roads, Trails, LT Traffic	Scenic
87	Minnetonka Miles	31	Water, Toilet	Rolling, Roads, Traffic	Treats
88	Belle Plaine Pedal	31 46/65	Food, Water, Toilet	Climbs, Roads, LT Traffic	Scenic, Treats
89	Adele's Frozen Custard	32	Food, Water, Toilet	Flat, Hilly, Roads, Traffic	Scenic, Treats
90	Fridays to the Lake	32/43	Food, Water, Toilet	Hilly, Roads, Trails, Traffic	Scenic, Treats
91	Dunn Bros and Back	33	Food, Water, Toilet	Rolling, Roads, Trails, LT Traffic	Scenic, Treats
92	Excelsior Sampler	35	Water, Toilet	Rolling, Roads, LT Traffic	
93	Jordan Valley / Monty	35/60	Water, Toilet	Flat, Roads, LT Traffic	Scenic
94	Trail Out Trail Back	36	Food, Water, Toilet	Flat, Roads, Trails, LT Traffic	Treats
95	Rolling on the West Side	44	Food, Water, Toilet	Climbs, Roads, LT Traffic	Treats
96	Scott Carver Trails	45	Water, Toilet	Rolling, Roads, LT Traffic	Scenic

Disclaimer: The Twin Cities Bicycling Club, Hostelling International USA – Minnesota Council, and their respective officers, employees, trip leaders and members, and those whose work appears in this Atlas, and those people and establishments who distribute this Atlas, cannot be held responsible for the future condition of any of these routes, or for any injuries or damages sustained or occuring while using these routes.

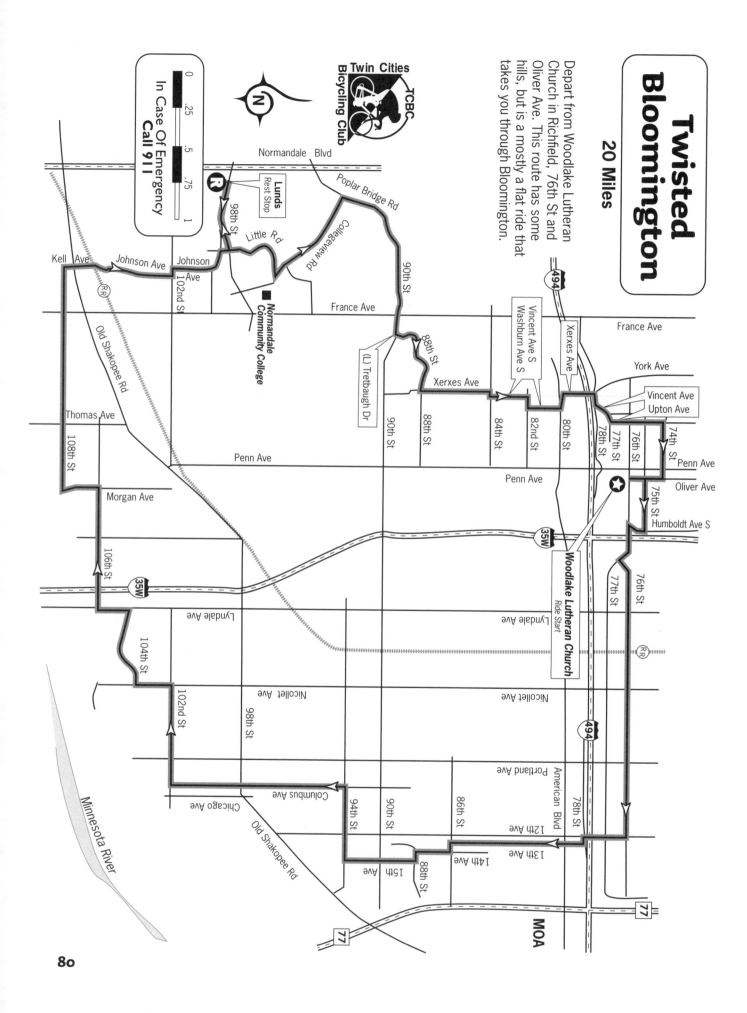

Twisted Bloomington

20 Miles

Depart from Woodlake Lutheran Church in Richfield, 76th St and Oliver Ave. This route has some hills, but is a mostly a flat ride that takes you through Bloomington.

Twin Cities Bicycling Club
TCBC

In Case Of Emergency
Call 911

0 .25 .5 .75 1

Normandale Blvd

Lunds
Rest Stop

98th St

Little Rd

Poplar Bridge Rd

Collegeview Rd

Johnson Ave

Johnson Ave

Kell Ave

102nd St

Normandale Community College

France Ave

90th St

88th St

(L) Tretbaugh Dr

Xerxes Ave

Vincent Ave S
Washburn Ave S

Xerxes Ave

France Ave

York Ave

Vincent Ave
Upton Ave

90th St

88th St

84th St

82nd St

80th St

78th St

77th St

76th St

74th St

Penn Ave

Old Shakopee Rd

Thomas Ave

108th St

Penn Ave

Penn Ave

Oliver Ave

75th St
Humboldt Ave S

Morgan Ave

35W

Woodlake Lutheran Church
Ride Start

77th St

76th St

106th St

35W

Lyndale Ave

Lyndale Ave

Nicollet Ave

Nicollet Ave

78th St

104th St

102nd St

98th St

Portland Ave

American Blvd

Minnesota River

Old Shakopee Rd

Chicago Ave

Columbus Ave

94th St

90th St

88th St

86th St

15th Ave

14th Ave

13th Ave

12th Ave

MOA

77

77

80

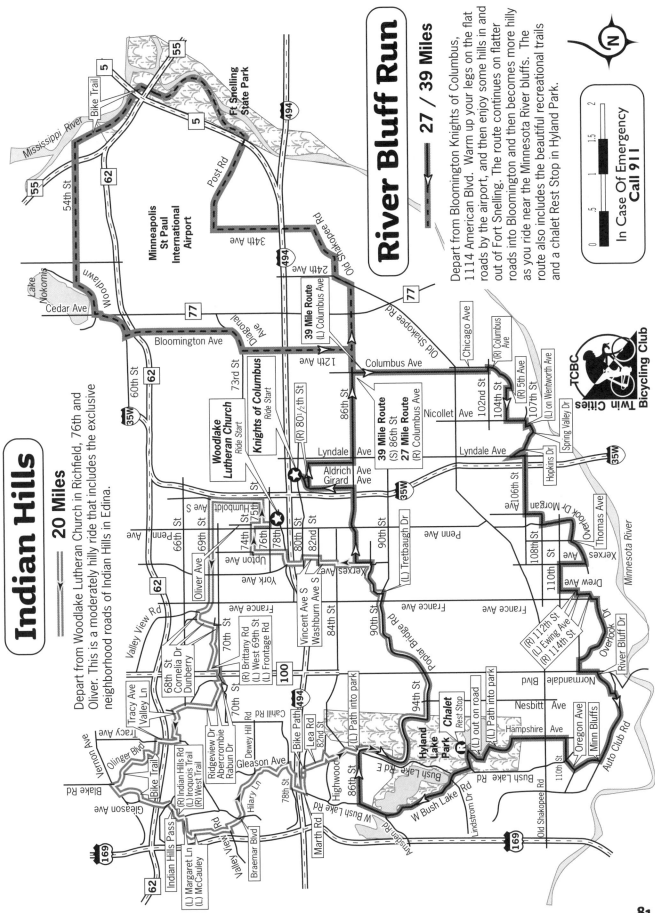

River Bluff Run
27 / 39 Miles

Depart from Bloomington Knights of Columbus, 1114 American Blvd. Warm up your legs on the flat roads by the airport, and then enjoy some hills in and out of Fort Snelling. The route continues on flatter roads into Bloomington and then becomes more hilly as you ride near the Minnesota River bluffs. The route also includes the beautiful recreational trails and a chalet Rest Stop in Hyland Park.

In Case Of Emergency
Call 911

Indian Hills
20 Miles

Depart from Woodlake Lutheran Church in Richfield, 76th and Oliver. This is a moderately hilly ride that includes the exclusive neighborhood roads of Indian Hills in Edina.

TCBC
Twin Cities
Bicycling Club

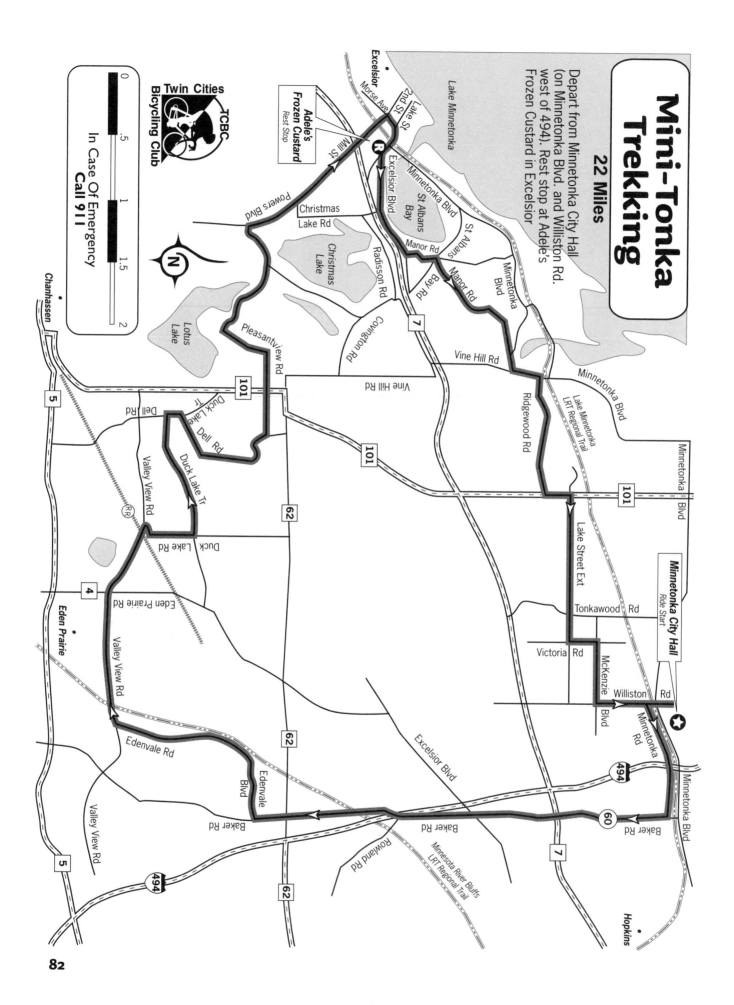

Mini-Tonka Trekking

22 Miles

Depart from Minnetonka City Hall (on Minnetonka Blvd. and Williston Rd. west of 494). Rest stop at Adele's Frozen Custard in Excelsior

Adele's Frozen Custard
Rest Stop

Minnetonka City Hall
Ride Start

Twin Cities Bicycling Club
TCBC

In Case Of Emergency
Call 911

0 .5 1 1.5 2

Tupelo Honey

22 / 29 Miles

Depart from Edina Bike and Sport Shop, 4504 Valley View, Edina. A nice ride in the Edina and Eden Prairie metro area. After the ride stay for a burger and share a malt at Snuffy's Malt Shop

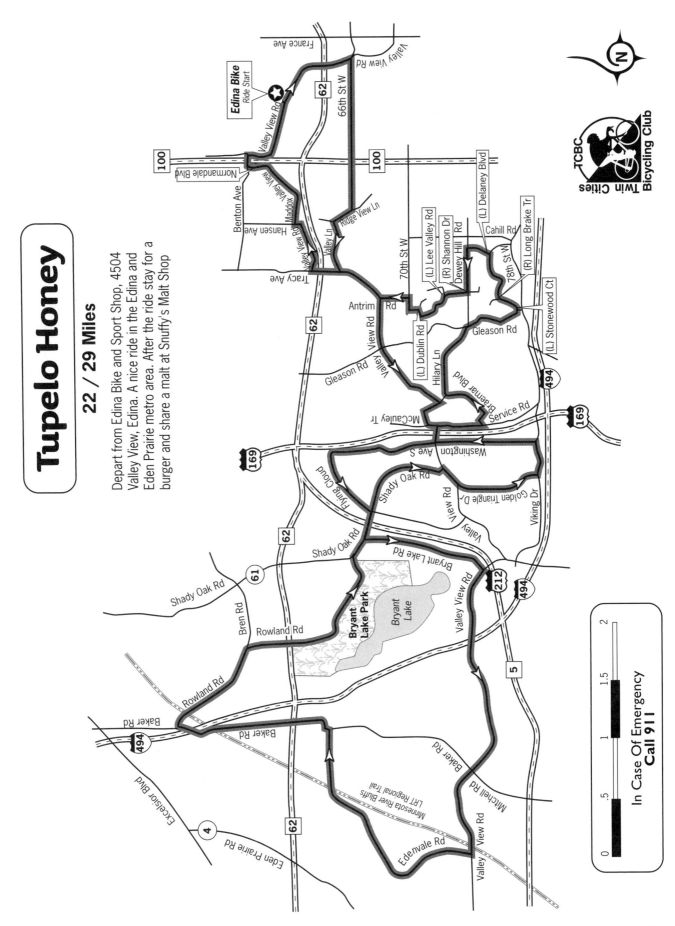

In Case Of Emergency
Call 911

Twin Cities
Bicycling Club

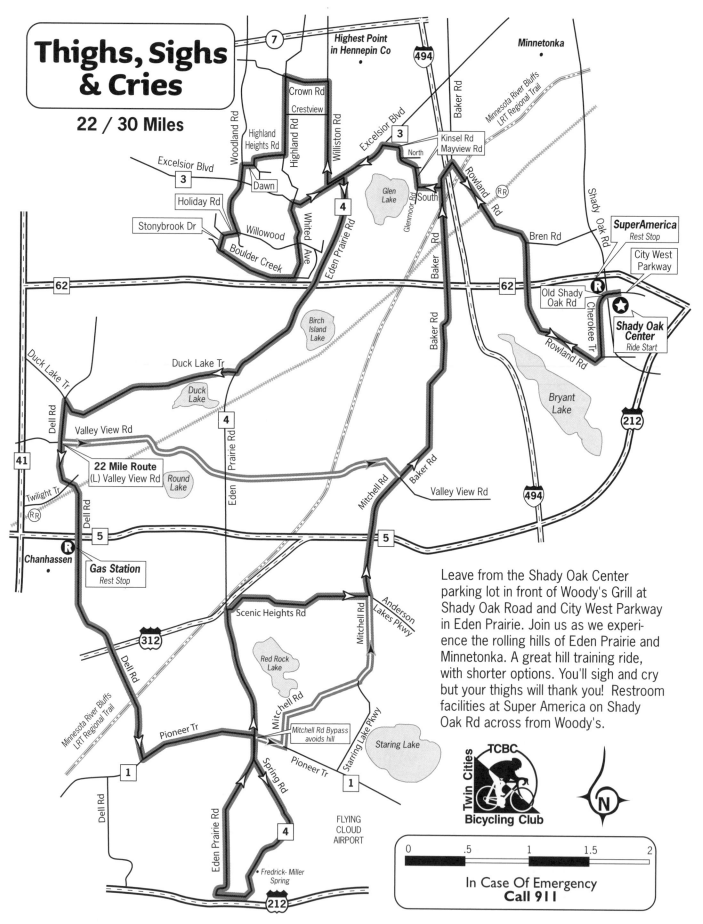

Thighs, Sighs & Cries

22 / 30 Miles

7

Highest Point in Hennepin Co

Minnetonka

494

Crown Rd
Crestview

Minnesota River Bluffs LRT Regional Trail

Woodland Rd

Highland Heights Rd

Highland Rd

Williston Rd

Excelsior Blvd

3

Baker Rd

Kinsel Rd
Mayview Rd

Rowland Rd

Shady Oak Rd

Excelsior Blvd

3

Dawn

Holiday Rd

Stonybrook Dr

Willowood

Boulder Creek

Whited Ave

Eden Prairie Rd

Glen Lake

Glenmoor Rd

North

South

RR

Bren Rd

SuperAmerica
Rest Stop

City West Parkway

62

Birch Island Lake

Baker Rd

62

Old Shady Oak Rd

Cherokee Tr

R

Shady Oak Center
Ride Start

Duck Lake Tr

Duck Lake Tr

Duck Lake

4

Baker Rd

Rowland Rd

Bryant Lake

212

Dell Rd

Valley View Rd

41

22 Mile Route
(L) Valley View Rd

Round Lake

Eden Prairie Rd

Baker Rd

Valley View Rd

494

Twilight Tr

RR

Dell Rd

5

Mitchell Rd

Valley View Rd

R

Chanhassen

Gas Station
Rest Stop

5

US 312

Dell Rd

Scenic Heights Rd

Mitchell Rd

Anderson Lakes Pkwy

Mitchell Rd

Red Rock Lake

Mitchell Rd

Starring Lake Pkwy

Minnesota River Bluffs LRT Regional Trail

Pioneer Tr

Mitchell Rd Bypass avoids hill

Staring Lake

1

Spring Rd

Pioneer Tr

1

Dell Rd

Eden Prairie Rd

4

FLYING CLOUD AIRPORT

Fredrick- Miller Spring

212

Leave from the Shady Oak Center parking lot in front of Woody's Grill at Shady Oak Road and City West Parkway in Eden Prairie. Join us as we experience the rolling hills of Eden Prairie and Minnetonka. A great hill training ride, with shorter options. You'll sigh and cry but your thighs will thank you! Restroom facilities at Super America on Shady Oak Rd across from Woody's.

TCBC
Twin Cities Bicycling Club

N

0   .5   1   1.5   2

In Case Of Emergency
Call 911

Eatin' Prairie

29 Miles

Depart from Round Lake Park, located at Valley View Rd & Eden Prairie Rd. Start this ride on the flat LRT gravel trail, then a climb up Bluff Creek Dr to Pioneer Trail. Out past the classic planned community of Jonathan, then into Excelsior for a refreshing rest stop of Ice Cream, at Lick's Unlimited on Water St.

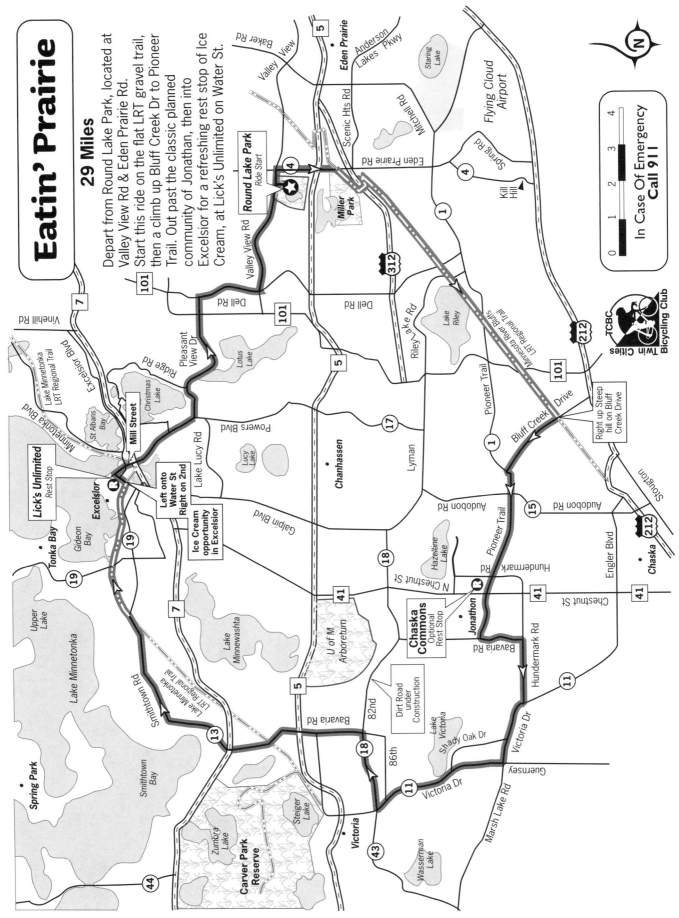

In Case Of Emergency
Call 911

Round Lake Park
Ride Start

Eden Prairie

Flying Cloud Airport

Staring Lake

Kill Hill

Miller Park

Lake Riley

Minnesota River Bluffs LRT Regional Trail

Right up Steep hill on Bluff Creek Drive

Bluff Creek Drive

Chaska

Lake Minnetonka LRT Regional Trail

Lick's Unlimited
Rest Stop

Mill Street

Christmas Lake

Lotus Lake

Pleasant View Dr

Left onto Water St
Right on 2nd

Ice Cream opportunity in Excelsior

Excelsior

Tonka Bay

Gideon Bay

St Albans Bay

Lucy Lake

Chanhassen

Lyman

Upper Lake

Lake Minnewashta

U of M Arboretum

Lake Minnetonka

Spring Park

Smithtown Bay

Carver Park Reserve

Zumbra Lake

Steiger Lake

Victoria

Chaska Commons
Optional Rest Stop

Jonathon

Dirt Road under Construction

Lake Victoria

Shady Oak Dr

Victoria Dr

Wasserman Lake

Marsh Lake Rd

Guernsey

Hundermark Rd

Bavaria Rd

Engler Blvd

Chestnut St

N Chestnut St

Hazeltine Lake

Audubon Rd

Pioneer Trail

Stoughton

TCBC
Twin Cities Bicycling Club

85

Canterbury Trails
30 Miles

Depart from Miller Park, located just west of Eden Prairie Rd on the LRT trail. This route is mostly flat with a few hills thrown in to make it interesting. It goes into the Minnesota River Valley along the Bloomington Ferry Trail. A long slightly downhill stretch on Eagle Creek Blvd will get speed up. A steep climb on Bluff Creek Dr with an optional bail out on the LRT.

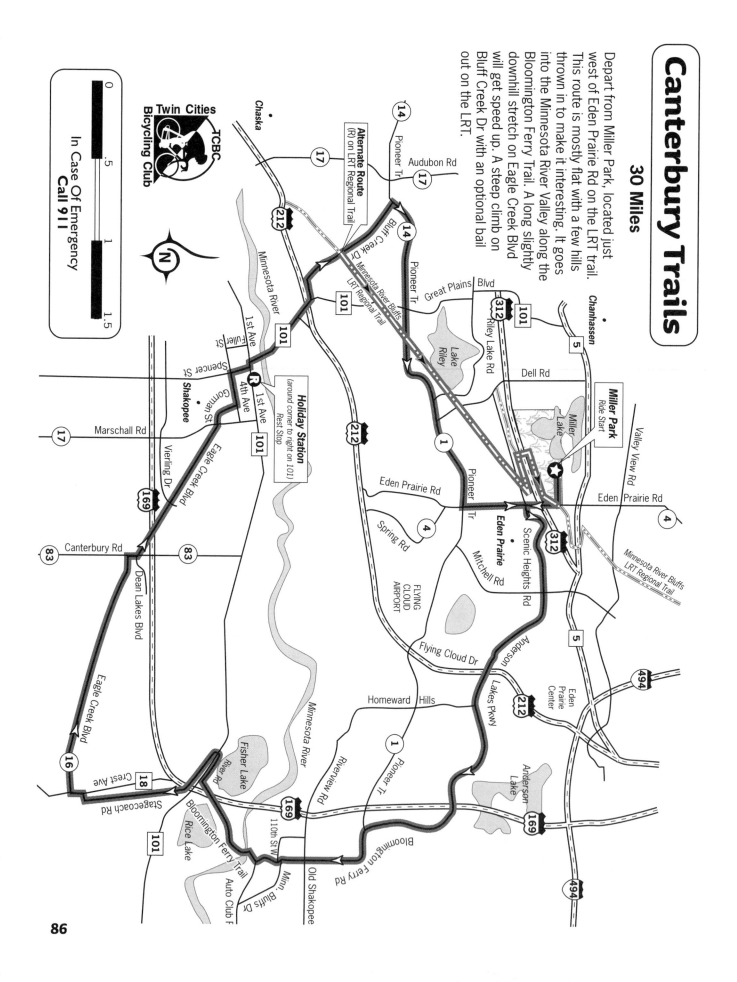

Twin Cities Bicycling Club — TCBC

In Case Of Emergency
Call 911

0   .5   1   1.5

Alternate Route
(R) on LRT Regional Trail

Holiday Station
(around corner to right on 101)
Rest Stop

Miller Park
Ride Start

Eden Prairie

Shakopee

Chaska

Chanhassen

Minnesota River Bluffs LRT Regional Trail
Minnesota River Bluffs LRT Regional Trail

Minnesota River

Eagle Creek Blvd
Dean Lakes Blvd
Canterbury Rd
Marschall Rd
Vierling Dr
Gorman St
Spencer St
Fuller St
1st Ave
4th Ave
Crest Ave
Stagecoach Rd
River Rd
Fisher Lake
Rice Lake
Bloomington Ferry Trail
Auto Club F
Minn. Bluffs Dr
110th St W
Old Shakopee
Bloomington Ferry Rd
Riverview Rd
Pioneer Tr
Homeward Hills
Flying Cloud Dr
FLYING CLOUD AIRPORT
Anderson Lakes Pkwy
Anderson Lake
Eden Prairie Center
Mitchell Rd
Scenic Heights Rd
Spring Rd
Eden Prairie Rd
Pioneer Tr
Valley View Rd
Eden Prairie Rd
Dell Rd
Riley Lake Rd
Lake Riley
Great Plains Blvd
Pioneer Tr
Bluff Creek Dr
Audubon Rd
Pioneer Tr
Miller Lake

83   83   17   16   18   169   101   101   212   1   4   312   312   5   5   494   494   169   169   17   17   14   14   101   101   212

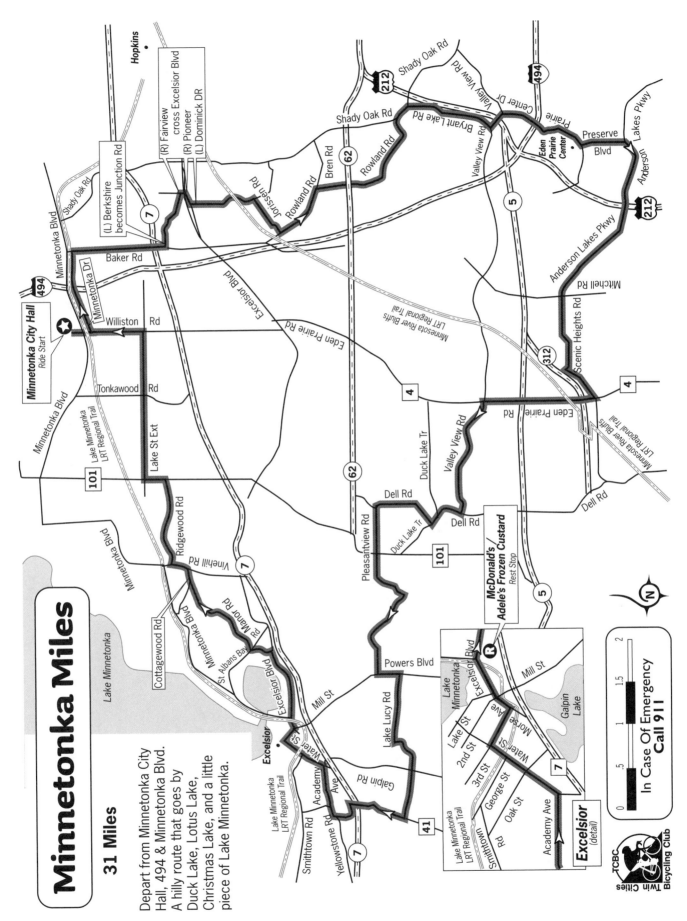

Minnetonka Miles

31 Miles

Depart from Minnetonka City Hall, 494 & Minnetonka Blvd. A hilly route that goes by Duck Lake, Lotus Lake, Christmas Lake, and a little piece of Lake Minnetonka.

Hopkins

Minnetonka City Hall
Ride Start

(R) Fairview
cross Excelsior Blvd
(R) Pioneer
(L) Dominick DR

(L) Berkshire
becomes Junction Rd

McDonald's/
Adele's Frozen Custard
Rest Stop

Excelsior
(detail)

In Case Of Emergency
Call 911

TCBC
Twin Cities Bicycling Club

87

Belle Plaine Pedal

31 / 46 / 65 Miles

Depart from Holiday Gas Station in Eden Prairie, Dell Road and 62, 3.5 miles west of 494 on 62. Park at far end of lot, next to Dell Rd. An excellent training ride in the western suburbs to Belle Plaine and back through Victoria.

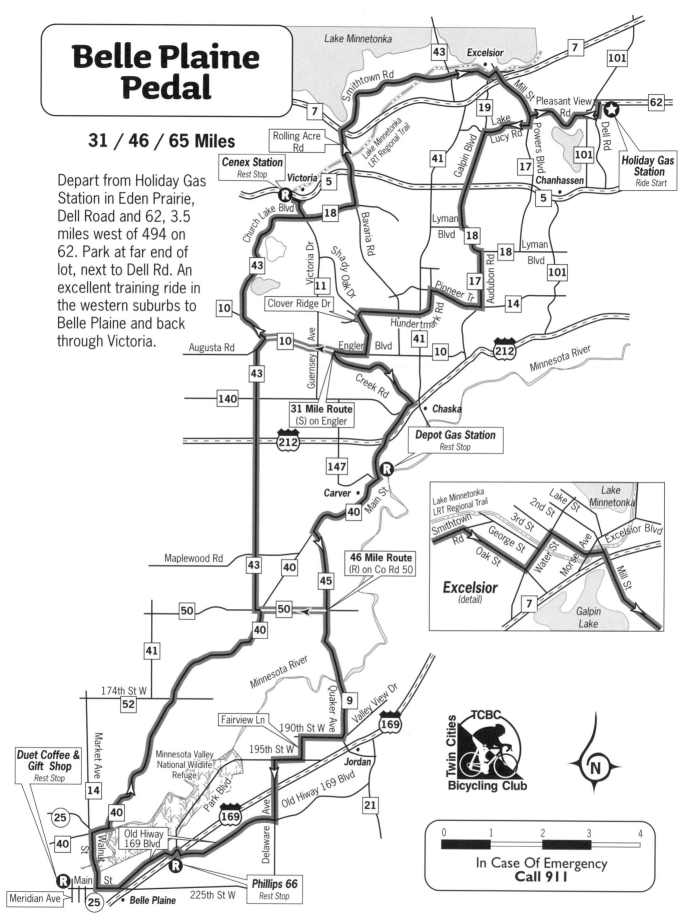

Lake Minnetonka

Excelsior

Smithtown Rd

Lake Minnetonka LRT Regional Trail

Rolling Acre Rd

Cenex Station Rest Stop

Victoria

Church Lake Blvd

Victoria Dr

Shady Oak Dr

Bavaria Rd

Clover Ridge Dr

Augusta Rd

Guernsey Ave

Engler Blvd

Creek Rd

31 Mile Route (S) on Engler

Chaska

Depot Gas Station Rest Stop

Carver

Main St

Maplewood Rd

46 Mile Route (R) on Co Rd 50

Mill St

Pleasant View Rd

Lake

Lucy Rd

Powers Blvd

Galpin Blvd

Chanhassen

Holiday Gas Station Ride Start

Lyman Blvd

Lyman Blvd

Audubon Rd

Pioneer Tr

Hundertmark Rd

Minnesota River

174th St W

Market Ave

Duet Coffee & Gift Shop Rest Stop

Minnesota Valley National Wildlife Refuge

Park Blvd

Quaker Ave

Fairview Ln

190th St W

195th St W

Jordan

Valley View Dr

Old Hiway 169 Blvd

Old Hiway 169 Blvd

Delaware Ave

Walnut St

Main St

Meridian Ave

Belle Plaine

225th St W

Phillips 66 Rest Stop

Excelsior (detail)

Lake Minnetonka LRT Regional Trail

Smithtown Rd

Oak St

George St

3rd St

2nd St

Water St

Morse Ave

Lake St

Excelsior Blvd

Mill St

Lake Minnetonka

Galpin Lake

TCBC
Twin Cities
Bicycling Club

N

0 1 2 3 4

In Case Of Emergency Call 911

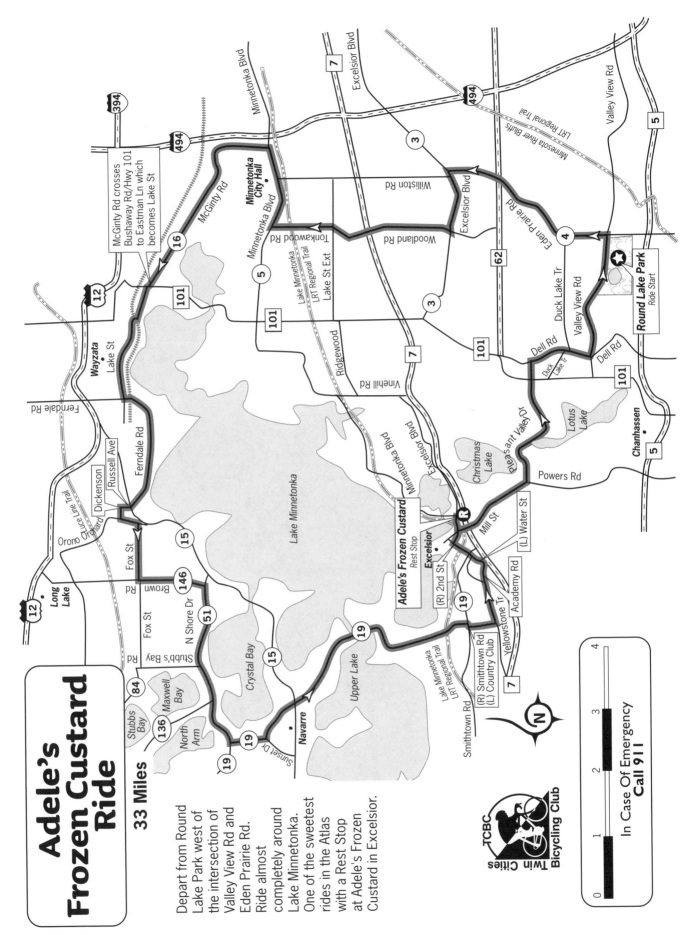

Adele's Frozen Custard Ride

33 Miles

Depart from Round Lake Park west of the intersection of Valley View Rd and Eden Prairie Rd. Ride almost completely around Lake Minnetonka. One of the sweetest rides in the Atlas with a Rest Stop at Adele's Frozen Custard in Excelsior.

In Case Of Emergency
Call 911

Twin Cities
Bicycling Club
TCBC

McGinty Rd crosses Bushaway Rd/Hwy 101 to Eastman Ln which becomes Lake St

Round Lake Park
Ride Start

Adele's Frozen Custard
Rest Stop

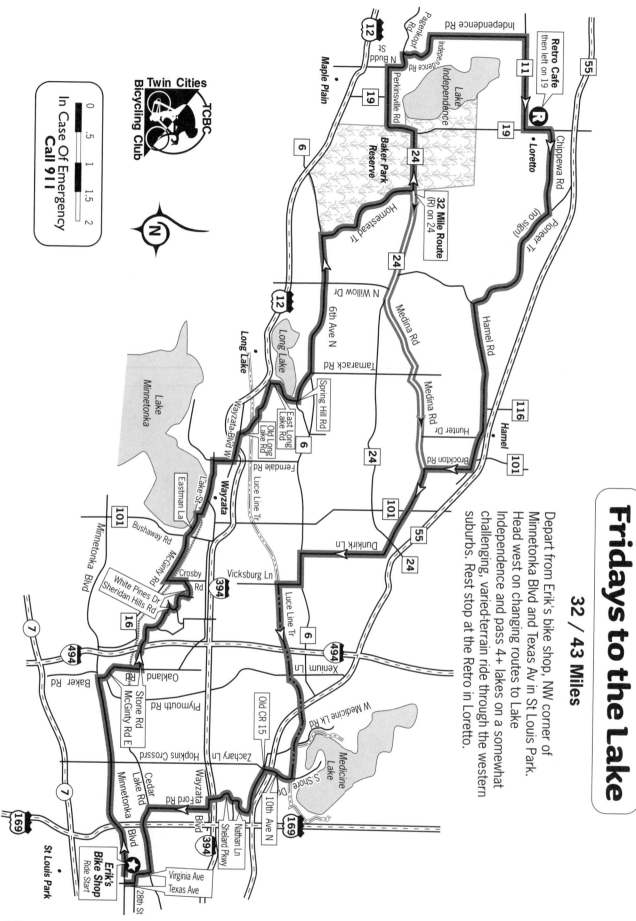

Fridays to the Lake

32 / 43 Miles

Depart from Erik's bike shop, NW corner of Minnetonka Blvd and Texas Av in St Louis Park. Head west on changing routes to Lake Independence and pass 4+ lakes on a somewhat challenging, varied-terrain ride through the western suburbs. Rest stop at the Retro in Loretto.

Twin Cities
Bicycling Club
TCBC

In Case Of Emergency
Call 911

0 .5 1 1.5 2

N

Dunn Bros & Back

33 Miles

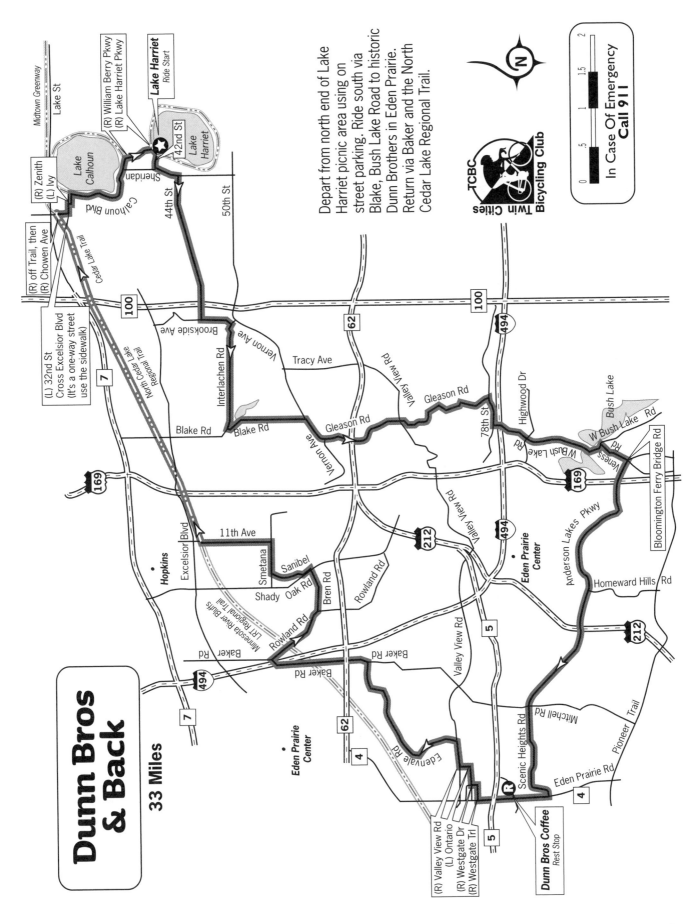

Depart from north end of Lake Harriet picnic area using on street parking. Ride south via Blake, Bush Lake Road to historic Dunn Brothers in Eden Prairie. Return via Baker and the North Cedar Lake Regional Trail.

TCBC
Twin Cities
Bicycling Club

In Case Of Emergency
Call 9 1 1

0   .5   1   1.5   2

N

Lake Harriet Ride Start

(R) William Berry Pkwy
(R) Lake Harriet Pkwy

Midtown Greenway

Lake St

42nd St

Lake Harriet

Lake Calhoun

Sheridan

44th St

50th St

(R) Zenith
(L) Ivy

Calhoun Blvd

(R) off Trail, then
(R) Chowen Ave

(L) 32nd St
Cross Excelsior Blvd
(It's a one-way street use the sidewalk)

Cedar Lake Trail

North Cedar Lake Regional Trail

7

100

100

62

494

Brookside Ave

Interlachen Rd

Vernon Ave

Tracy Ave

Valley View Rd

Gleason Rd

Gleason Rd

Highwood Dr

Bush Lake

W Bush Lake Rd

W Bush Lake Rd

78th St

Veness Rd

169

Bloomington Ferry Bridge Rd

Blake Rd

Blake Rd

Vernon Ave

169

11th Ave

Excelsior Blvd

Hopkins

Smetana

Sanibel

Shady   Oak Rd

Bren Rd

Rowland Rd

Rowland Rd

Minnesota River Bluffs LRT Regional Trail

Baker Rd

Baker Rd

Baker Rd

212

Eden Prairie Center

Valley View Rd

494

5

Anderson Lakes Pkwy

Homeward Hills Rd

212

7

494

Eden Prairie Center

62

4

Edenvale Rd

Valley View Rd

Scenic Heights Rd

Mitchell Rd

5

R

Eden Prairie Rd

Pioneer Trail

4

(R) Valley View Rd
(L) Ontario
(R) Westgate Dr
(R) Westgate Trl

Dunn Bros Coffee Rest Stop

5

Excelsior Sampler

35 Miles

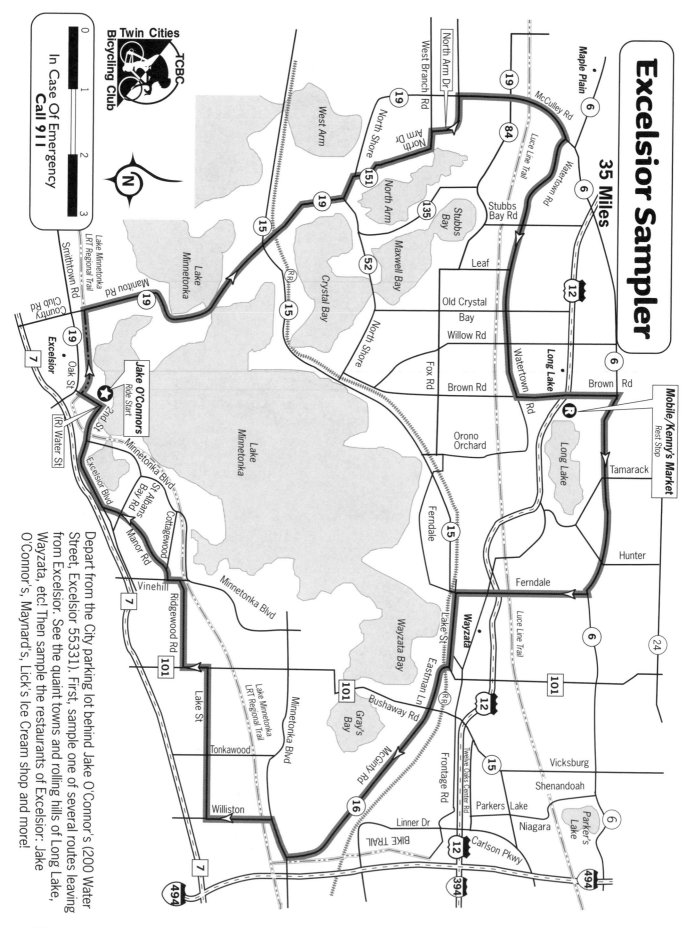

Twin Cities Bicycling Club TCBC

In Case Of Emergency Call 911

0 1 2 3

'N'

Jake O'Connors
Ride Start

Mobile/Kenny's Market
Rest Stop

Depart from the City parking lot behind Jake O'Connor's (200 Water Street, Excelsior 55331). First, sample one of several routes leaving from Excelsior. See the quaint towns and rolling hills of Long Lake, Wayzata, etc! Then sample the restaurants of Excelsior: Jake O'Connor's, Maynard's, Lick's Ice Cream shop and more!

West Arm

West Branch Rd
North Arm Dr
West Arm Dr
North Shore

North Arm Dr

Maple Plain
McCulley Rd
Watertown Rd

North Arm

Stubbs Bay
Maxwell Bay

Stubbs Bay Rd
Leaf

Old Crystal Bay
Willow Rd
Fox Rd
Brown Rd

Crystal Bay
North Shore

Lake Minnetonka

Long Lake
Brown Rd

Tamarack

Hunter

Watertown Rd

Orono Orchard

Ferndale

Ferndale

Wayzata Bay

Wayzata

Luce Line Trail

Lake St
Eastman Ln
Bushaway Rd
McGinty Rd
Gray's Bay
Frontage Rd
Twelve Oaks Center Rd

Vicksburg
Shenandoah
Parkers Lake
Niagara
Parker's Lake

Linner Dr
Carlson Pkwy
BIKE TRAIL

Smithtown Rd
Lake Minnetonka LRT Regional Trail
Country Club Rd
Manitou Rd

Excelsior
Oak St
2nd St
(R) Water St
Minnetonka Blvd
Excelsior Blvd
St Albans Bay Rd
Manor Rd
Cottagewood
Vinehill

Minnetonka Blvd

Ridgewood Rd
Lake St
Tonkawood
Williston

Lake Minnetonka LRT Regional Trail
Minnetonka Blvd

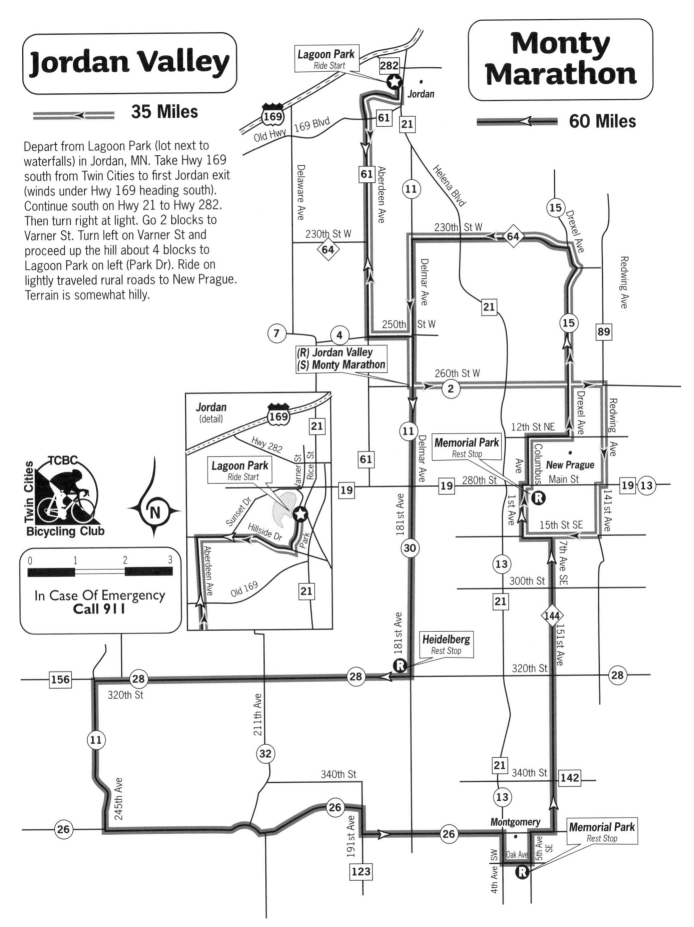

Jordan Valley

← 35 Miles

Depart from Lagoon Park (lot next to waterfalls) in Jordan, MN. Take Hwy 169 south from Twin Cities to first Jordan exit (winds under Hwy 169 heading south). Continue south on Hwy 21 to Hwy 282. Then turn right at light. Go 2 blocks to Varner St. Turn left on Varner St and proceed up the hill about 4 blocks to Lagoon Park on left (Park Dr). Ride on lightly traveled rural roads to New Prague. Terrain is somewhat hilly.

TCBC
Twin Cities
Bicycling Club

0 1 2 3

In Case Of Emergency
Call 911

Monty Marathon

← 60 Miles

Lagoon Park
Ride Start

Jordan

169 Old Hwy
169 Blvd

Delaware Ave

230th St W

64

7 4

(R) Jordan Valley
(S) Monty Marathon

Jordan
(detail)

169

Hwy 282

Lagoon Park
Ride Start

Sunset Dr

Hillside Dr

Aberdeen Ave

Old 169

Varner St
Rice St
Park

21

N

282

61
21

61

Aberdeen Ave

11

Helena Blvd

230th St W

64

15

Drexel Ave

Redwing Ave

Delmar Ave

250th St W

21

15

89

260th St W

2

11

Delmar Ave

Memorial Park
Rest Stop

12th St NE

Drexel Ave

Redwing Ave

61

19

19

280th St

Columbus Ave

1st Ave

New Prague
Main St

19 13

141st Ave

15th St SE

181st Ave

30

R

13

300th St

21

7th Ave SE

144

151st Ave

Heidelberg
Rest Stop

R

156

28

320th St

28

320th St

28

11

211th Ave

32

245th Ave

340th St

26

191st Ave

26

123

26

26

21

340th St

142

13

Montgomery

4th Ave SW

Oak Ave

5th Ave SE

Memorial Park
Rest Stop

R

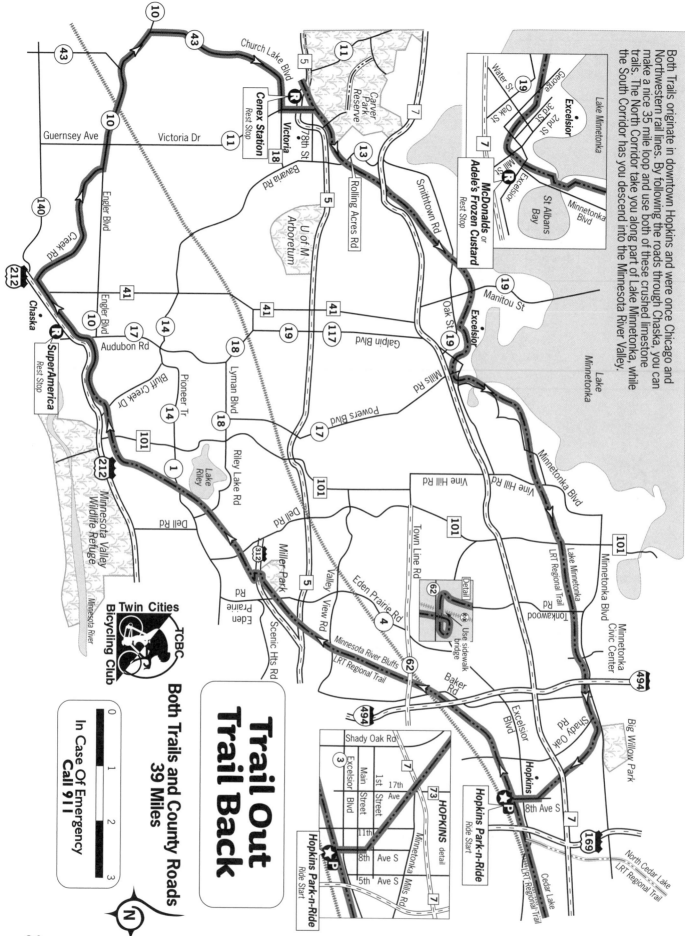

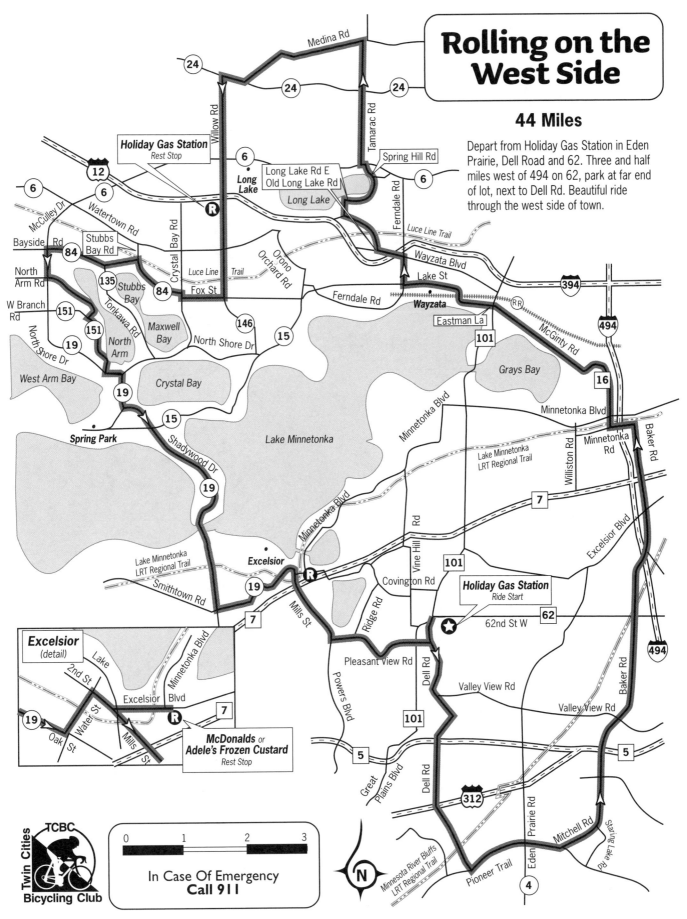

Rolling on the West Side

44 Miles

Depart from Holiday Gas Station in Eden Prairie, Dell Road and 62. Three and half miles west of 494 on 62, park at far end of lot, next to Dell Rd. Beautiful ride through the west side of town.

Holiday Gas Station — *Rest Stop*

Long Lake Rd E / Old Long Lake Rd

Long Lake

Spring Hill Rd

Stubbs Bay Rd

Wayzata

Eastman La

Grays Bay

Spring Park

Lake Minnetonka

Lake Minnetonka LRT Regional Trail

Holiday Gas Station — *Ride Start*

Excelsior

Excelsior (detail)

McDonalds or Adele's Frozen Custard — *Rest Stop*

Twin Cities Bicycling Club — TCBC

0 1 2 3

In Case Of Emergency Call 911

N

Minnesota River Bluffs LRT Regional Trail

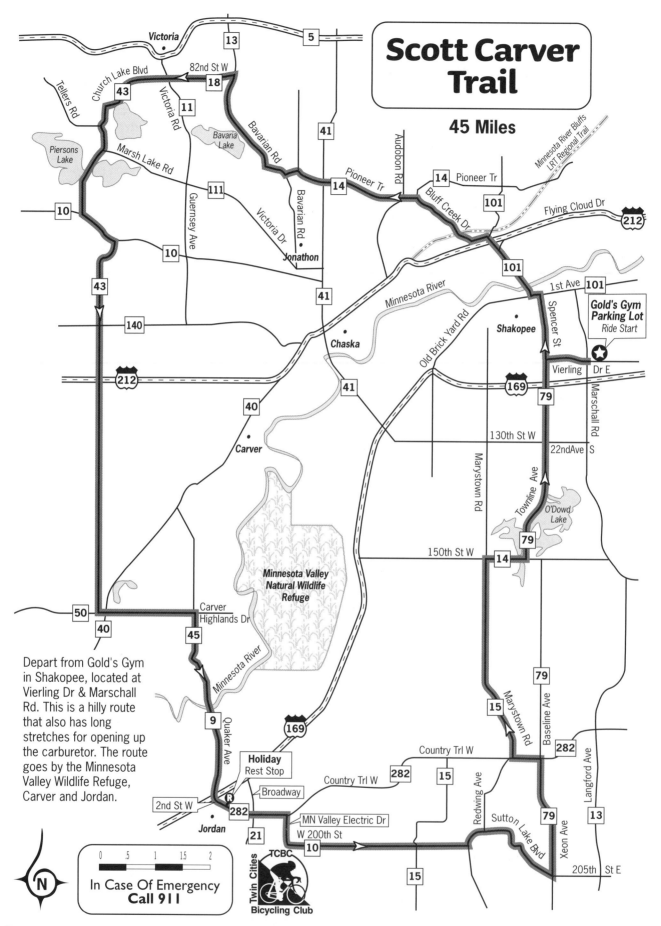

Scott Carver Trail

45 Miles

Victoria

Church Lake Blvd
82nd St W
Tellers Rd
Victoria Rd
Bavaria Lake
Piersons Lake
Marsh Lake Rd
Guernsey Ave
Victoria Dr
Bavarian Rd
Bavarian Rd
Jonathon

Minnesota River Bluffs LRT Regional Trail

Audobon Rd
Pioneer Tr
Pioneer Trl
Bluff Creek Dr
Flying Cloud Dr

1st Ave
Gold's Gym Parking Lot
Ride Start

Minnesota River
Old Brick Yard Rd
Shakopee
Spencer St
Vierling Dr E
Marschall Rd

Chaska

130th St W
22nd Ave S

Carver
Marystown Rd
Townline Ave
O'Dowd Lake

150th St W

Minnesota Valley Natural Wildlife Refuge

Carver Highlands Dr

Marystown Rd
Baseline Ave
Langford Ave

Minnesota River
Quaker Ave
Redwing Ave
Sutton Lake Blvd
Xeon Ave

Holiday Rest Stop
Broadway
2nd St W
Country Trl W
Country Trl W
MN Valley Electric Dr
W 200th St
205th St E

Jordan

Depart from Gold's Gym in Shakopee, located at Vierling Dr & Marschall Rd. This is a hilly route that also has long stretches for opening up the carburetor. The route goes by the Minnesota Valley Wildlife Refuge, Carver and Jordan.

N

0 .5 1 1.5 2

In Case Of Emergency
Call 911

TCBC
Twin Cities
Bicycling Club

Southwest Ride Journal

Date _____ Mileage _____
Route _____
Notes _____
_____
_____

Date _____ Mileage _____
Route _____
Notes _____
_____
_____

Date _____ Mileage _____
Route _____
Notes _____
_____
_____

Date _____ Mileage _____
Route _____
Notes _____
_____
_____

Date _____ Mileage _____
Route _____
Notes _____
_____
_____

Date _____ Mileage _____
Route _____
Notes _____
_____
_____

Date _____ Mileage _____
Route _____
Notes _____
_____
_____

Date _____ Mileage _____
Route _____
Notes _____
_____
_____

Date _____ Mileage _____
Route _____
Notes _____
_____
_____

Date _____ Mileage _____
Route _____
Notes _____
_____
_____

Northwest

CAUTION
HOME OF
10,000 BIKES
DONATED BY
COON RAPIDS LIONS CLUB

Welcome To
LORETTO
Gateway to West Hennepin Lakes
Est. 1886   Inc. 1940
TURN LEFT AT RAILWAY STREET

REST STOP AT THE RETRO CAFE
IN LORETTO - RETRO RIDE PAGE 109

WILLOW DRIVE IN THE FALL - A DUTCH TREAT - PAGE 104

OX YOKE
INN
CASUAL DINING
ON-OFF SALE
1 BLOCK NORTH

RIDING THE LUCE LINE OUT TO WATERTOWN - REST STOP AT THE OX YOKE IN LYNDALE

Legend: Food · Water · Toilet · Flat · Rolling · Hilly · Climbs · Roads · Trails · Lt Traffic · Traffic · Scenic · Treats

Page	Ride	Miles	At Ride Start	Terrain	Highlights
100	Saddle Up Shorty	11/18	Food, Water, Toilet	Flat, Roads, Traffic	Treats
101	Tater Tour	15/25	Water, Toilet	Flat, Roads, Trails, Lt Traffic	Scenic
102	Side Saddle	18 27/31	Food, Water, Toilet	Flat, Roads, Lt Traffic, Traffic	
103	Trailhead Trekking	20	Food, Water, Toilet	Flat, Roads, Trails, Lt Traffic	
104	A Dutch Treat	22/24	Food, Water, Toilet	Rolling, Hilly, Climbs, Roads, Trails, Lt Traffic	Scenic, Treats
105	Trailhead Trekking Twice	23/27	Food, Water, Toilet	Flat, Roads, Lt Traffic	
106	Spring Around the Corner	24	Food, Water, Toilet	Flat, Roads, Trails, Lt Traffic	
107	Saddle Up	25 32/42	Food, Water, Toilet	Flat, Roads, Traffic	
108	North Hennepin Tour	31	Water, Toilet	Flat, Roads, Trails, Lt Traffic	Scenic
109	Retro Ride	32/40	Food, Water, Toilet	Rolling, Hilly, Roads, Lt Traffic	Scenic, Treats
110	Trailhead North & South	33	Food, Water, Toilet	Flat, Roads, Trails, Lt Traffic	Treats
111	Weaver Express	34		Rolling, Hilly, Roads, Lt Traffic	
112	Golden Foliage	42	Food, Water, Toilet	Rolling, Hilly, Roads, Lt Traffic	Scenic, Treats
113	Heights Out West	48/55	Food, Water, Toilet	Flat, Roads, Traffic	Treats
114	Town Hall Meeting	51	Food, Water, Toilet	Flat, Roads, Lt Traffic	
115	Coon Rapids River Ride	52/64	Food, Water, Toilet	Flat, Roads, Lt Traffic	Scenic
116	Rolling to Rockford	60/80	Food, Water, Toilet	Rolling, Roads, Lt Traffic	Scenic

Saddle Up Shorty

11 / 18 Miles

Depart from Erik's Cycle in Coon Rapids, next to Lifetime Fitness at Hanson Blvd and Hwy 10.

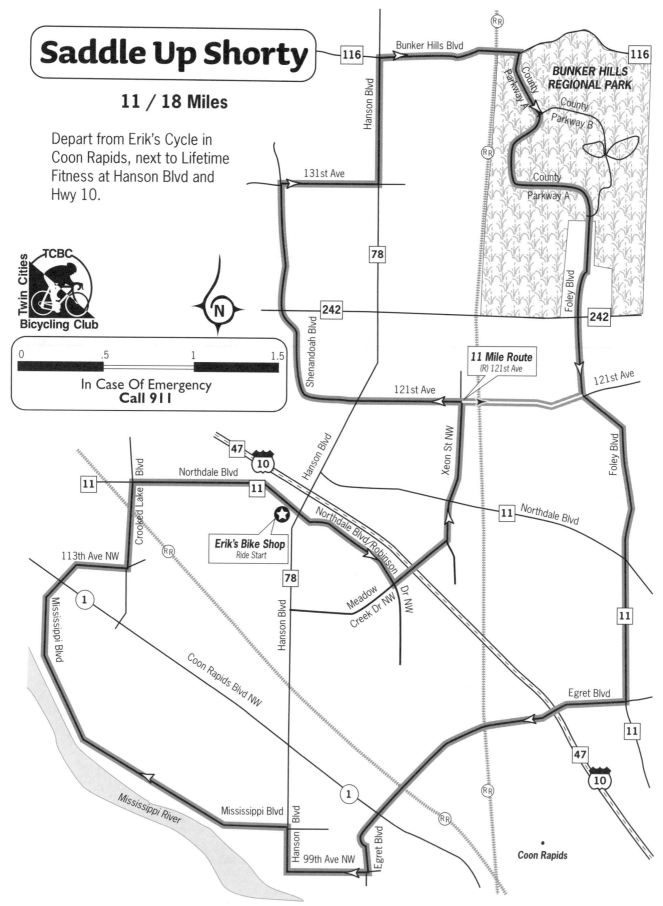

TCBC
Twin Cities
Bicycling Club

In Case Of Emergency
Call 911

Erik's Bike Shop
Ride Start

11 Mile Route
(R) 121st Ave

BUNKER HILLS REGIONAL PARK

Coon Rapids

Mississippi River

Tater Tour

15 / 25 Miles

The mostly flat 15-mile route travels roads and trails (including the North Hennepin Regional Trail) to Coon Rapids Dam and back. The 25-mile route includes the features of the 15-mile route as well as the rolling trails of Elm Creek Park Reserve.

NOTE: The 15- and 25-mile routes require the rider to cross four lanes of traffic at the beginning and end of the route.

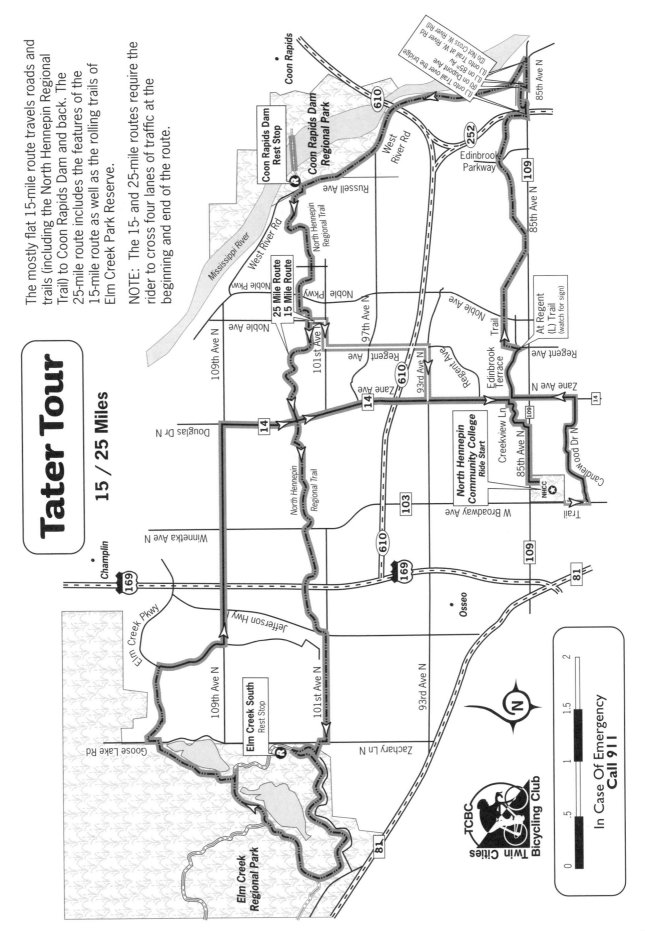

In Case Of Emergency
Call 911

Twin Cities
Bicycling Club

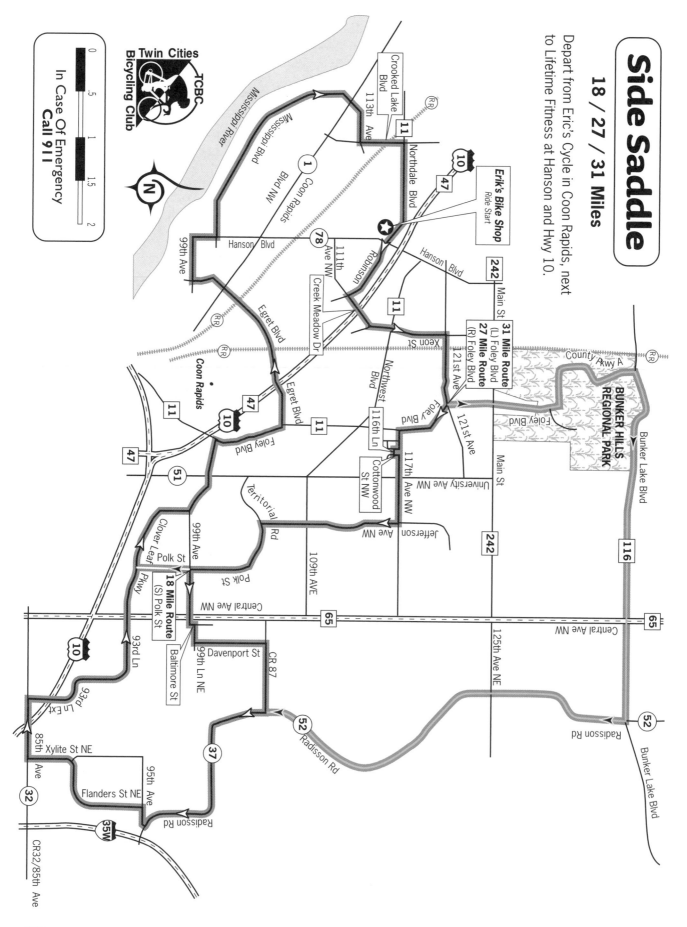

Side Saddle

18 / 27 / 31 Miles

Depart from Eric's Cycle in Coon Rapids, next to Lifetime Fitness at Hanson and Hwy 10.

Erik's Bike Shop
Ride Start

31 Mile Route
(L) Foley Blvd
27 Mile Route
(R) Foley Blvd

18 Mile Route
(S) Polk St

Twin Cities Bicycling Club
TCBC

In Case Of Emergency
Call 911

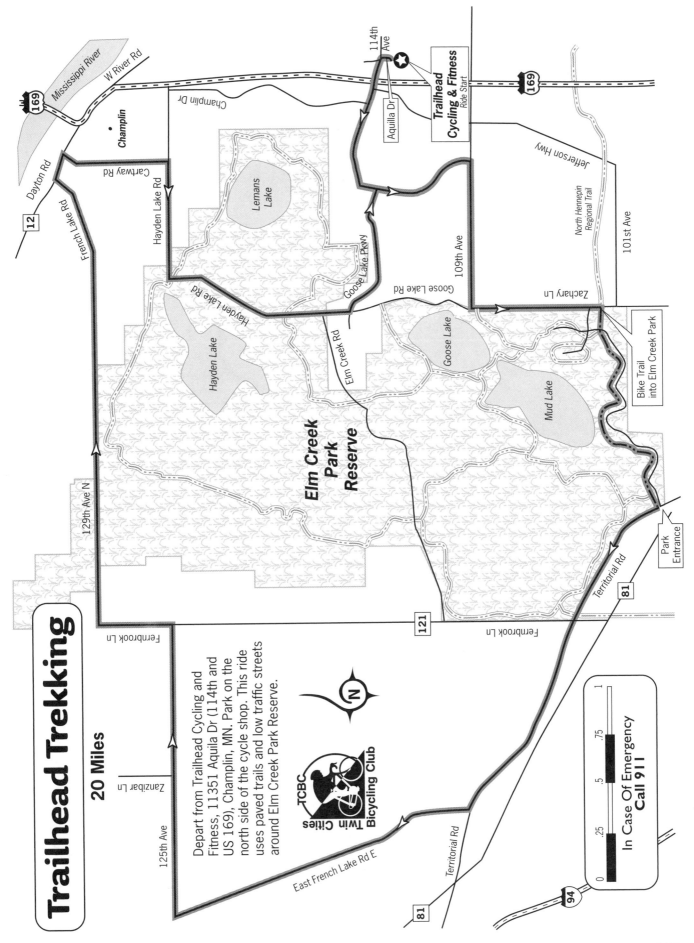

Trailhead Trekking

20 Miles

Depart from Trailhead Cycling and Fitness, 11351 Aquila Dr (114th and US 169), Champlin, MN. Park on the north side of the cycle shop. This ride uses paved trails and low traffic streets around Elm Creek Park Reserve.

Twin Cities Bicycling Club
TCBC

N

In Case Of Emergency
Call 911

0 .25 .5 .75 1

Mississippi River

W River Rd

169

Champlin

Dayton Rd

12

French Lake Rd

Cartway Rd

Champlin Dr

Hayden Lake Rd

Lemans Lake

Hayden Lake Rd

Hayden Lake

129th Ave N

Fernbrook Ln

125th Ave

Zanzibar Ln

East French Lake Rd E

Elm Creek Park Reserve

Elm Creek Rd

Goose Lake Pkwy

Goose Lake Rd

Goose Lake

Mud Lake

Fernbrook Ln

121

81

Territorial Rd

81

Territorial Rd

94

Park Entrance

Bike Trail into Elm Creek Park

Zachary Ln

109th Ave

North Hennepin Regional Trail

Jefferson Hwy

101st Ave

Trailhead Cycling & Fitness
Ride Start

114th Ave

Aquilla Dr

169

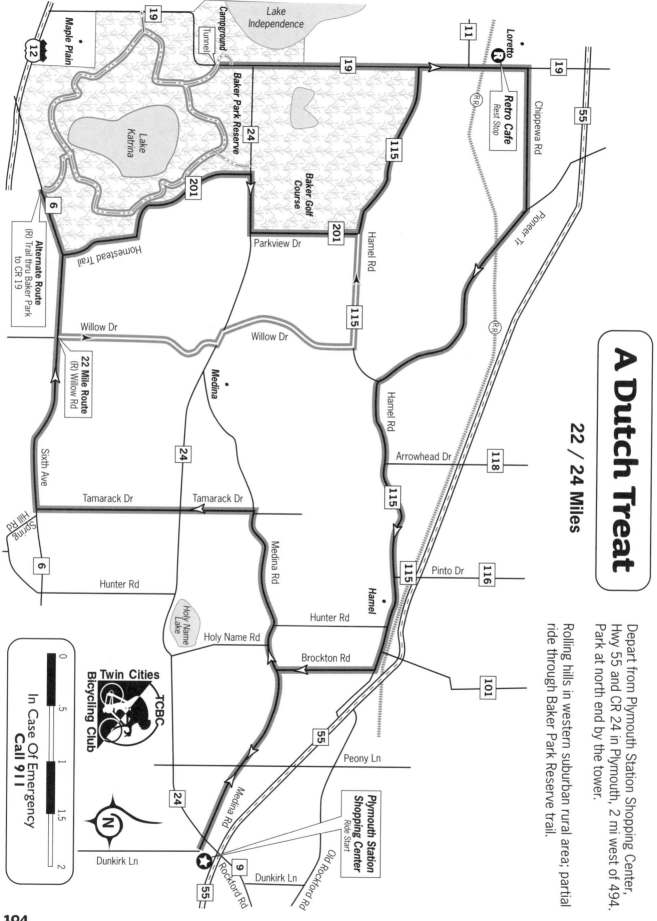

A Dutch Treat

22 / 24 Miles

Depart from Plymouth Station Shopping Center, Hwy 55 and CR 24 in Plymouth, 2 mi west of 494. Park at north end by the tower.

Rolling hills in western suburban rural area; partial ride through Baker Park Reserve trail.

Twin Cities Bicycling Club TCBC

In Case Of Emergency
Call 911

Lake Independence

Maple Plain

Baker Park Reserve

Lake Katrina

Baker Golf Course

Loretto

Retro Cafe
Rest Stop

Campground

Tunnel

Homestead Trail

Alternate Route
(R) Trail thru Baker Park to CR 19

Parkview Dr

Willow Dr

Willow Dr

Hamel Rd

Pioneer Tr

Chippewa Rd

22 Mile Route
(R) Willow Rd

Medina

Sixth Ave

Spring Hill Rd

Tamarack Dr

Tamarack Dr

Medina Rd

Hunter Rd

Arrowhead Dr

Hamel Rd

Holy Name Lake

Holy Name Rd

Hunter Rd

Hamel

Pinto Dr

Brockton Rd

Peony Ln

Plymouth Station Shopping Center
Ride Start

Dunkirk Ln

Rockford Rd

Old Rockford Rd

Dunkirk Ln

Medina Rd

19 12 11 19 55 115 24 201 6 201 115 118 116 115 101 24 6 9 55

104

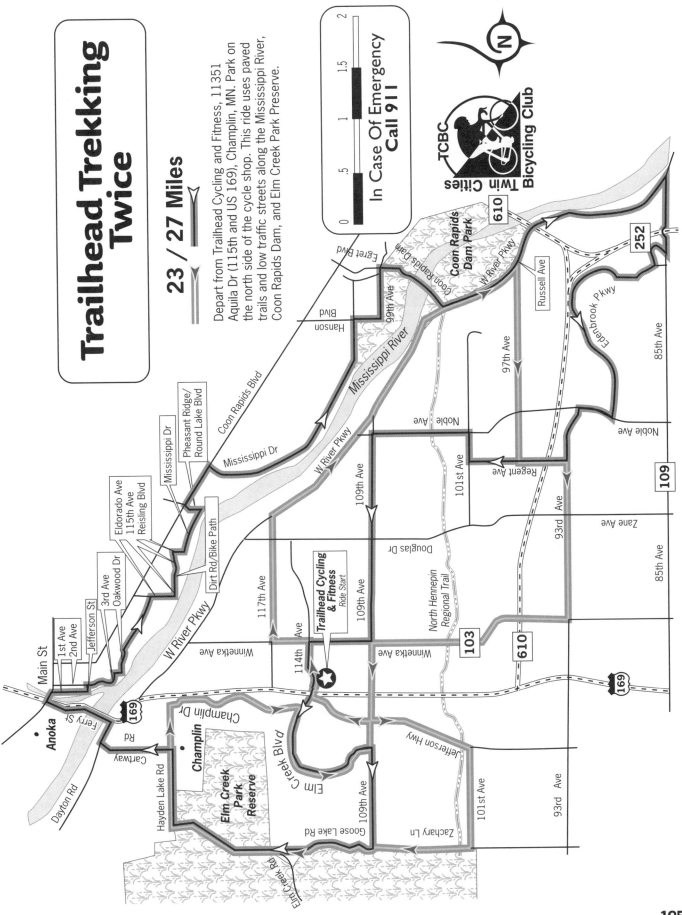

Trailhead Trekking Twice

23 / 27 Miles

Depart from Trailhead Cycling and Fitness, 11351 Aquila Dr (115th and US 169), Champlin, MN. Park on the north side of the cycle shop. This ride uses paved trails and low traffic streets along the Mississippi River, Coon Rapids Dam, and Elm Creek Park Preserve.

In Case Of Emergency
Call 9 1 1

0   .5   1   1.5   2

N

TCBC
Twin Cities Bicycling Club

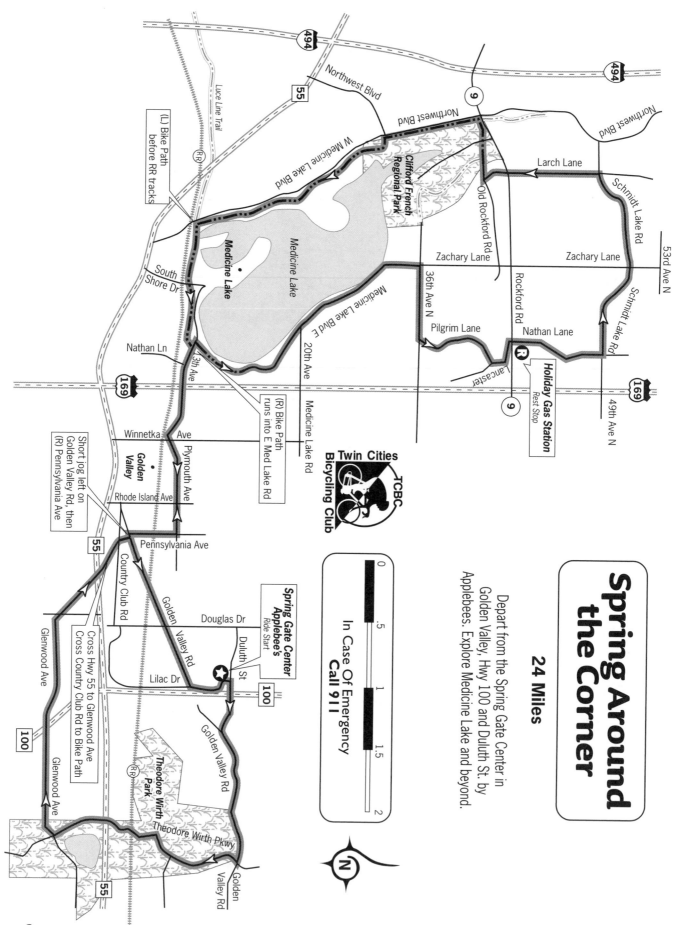

Spring Around the Corner

24 Miles

Depart from the Spring Gate Center in Golden Valley, Hwy 100 and Duluth St. by Applebees. Explore Medicine Lake and beyond.

In Case Of Emergency
Call 9 1 1

0 .5 1 1.5 2

Twin Cities Bicycling Club TCBC

Spring Gate Center
Applebee's
Ride Start

Holiday Gas Station
Rest Stop

(L) Bike Path before RR tracks

(R) Bike Path runs into E Med Lake Rd

Short jog left on Golden Valley Rd, then (R) Pennsylvania Ave

Cross Hwy 55 to Glenwood Ave
Cross Country Club Rd to Bike Path

Street and place labels

494 55 9 494 169 169 55 100 100 55 9

Northwest Blvd
Luce Line Trail
W Medicine Lake Blvd
Clifford French Regional Park
Medicine Lake
South Shore Dr
Nathan Ln
13th Ave
20th Ave
Medicine Lake Rd
Medicine Lake Blvd E
36th Ave N
Pilgrim Lane
Lancaster
Zachary Lane
Zachary Lane
Larch Lane
Schmidt Lake Rd
Schmidt Lake Rd
53rd Ave N
49th Ave N
Old Rockford Rd
Rockford Rd
Nathan Lane
Winnetka Ave
Golden Valley
Plymouth Ave
Rhode Island Ave
Pennsylvania Ave
Country Club Rd
Glenwood Ave
Glenwood Ave
Golden Valley Rd
Douglas Dr
Duluth St
Lilac Dr
Theodore Wirth Park
Theodore Wirth Pkwy
Golden Valley Rd

N

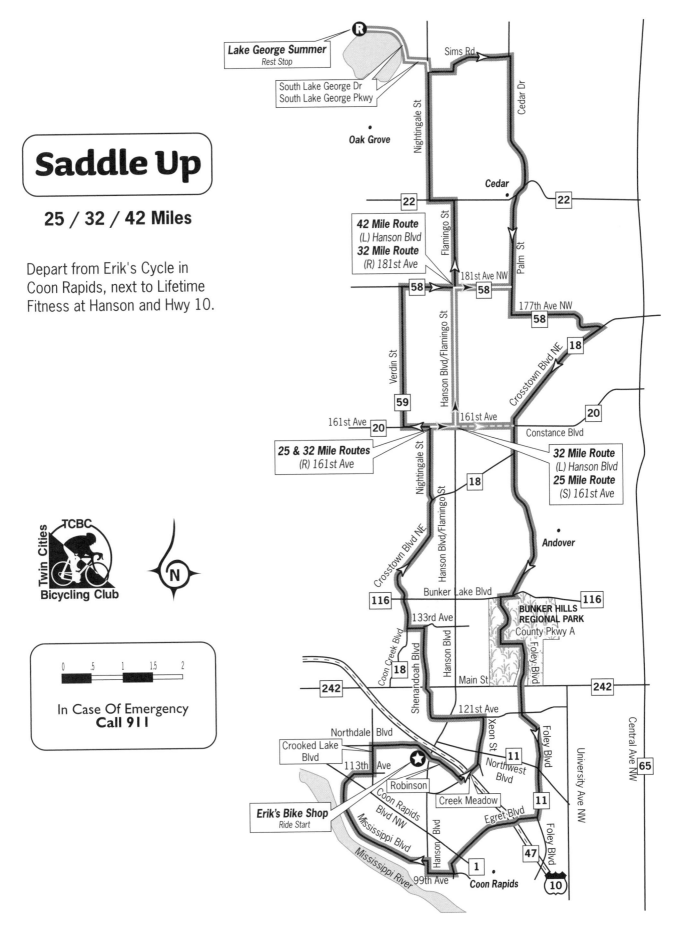

Saddle Up

25 / 32 / 42 Miles

Depart from Erik's Cycle in
Coon Rapids, next to Lifetime
Fitness at Hanson and Hwy 10.

Lake George Summer
Rest Stop

South Lake George Dr
South Lake George Pkwy

Oak Grove

Sims Rd

Cedar Dr

Cedar

Nightingale St

22

22

Flamingo St

42 Mile Route
(L) Hanson Blvd
32 Mile Route
(R) 181st Ave

Palm St

181st Ave NW

58

58

58

177th Ave NW

Verdin St

Hanson Blvd/Flamingo St

Crosstown Blvd NE

18

59

161st Ave

20

161st Ave

20

25 & 32 Mile Routes
(R) 161st Ave

Constance Blvd

32 Mile Route
(L) Hanson Blvd
25 Mile Route
(S) 161st Ave

Andover

TCBC
Twin Cities
Bicycling Club

N

Nightingale St

Hanson Blvd/Flamingo St

18

Crosstown Blvd NE

116

Bunker Lake Blvd

116

**BUNKER HILLS
REGIONAL PARK**
County Pkwy A

133rd Ave

Coon Creek Blvd

Shenandoah Blvd

Hanson Blvd

Foley Blvd

18

Main St

242

242

Central Ave NW

65

121st Ave

Northdale Blvd

Crooked Lake
Blvd

Xeon St

Foley Blvd

University Ave NW

113th Ave

11
Northwest
Blvd

Robinson

Creek Meadow

11

Erik's Bike Shop
Ride Start

Coon Rapids
Blvd NW

Hanson Blvd

Egret Blvd

47

Foley Blvd

Mississippi Blvd

Mississippi River

99th Ave

1

Coon Rapids

10

0   .5   1   1.5   2

In Case Of Emergency
Call 911

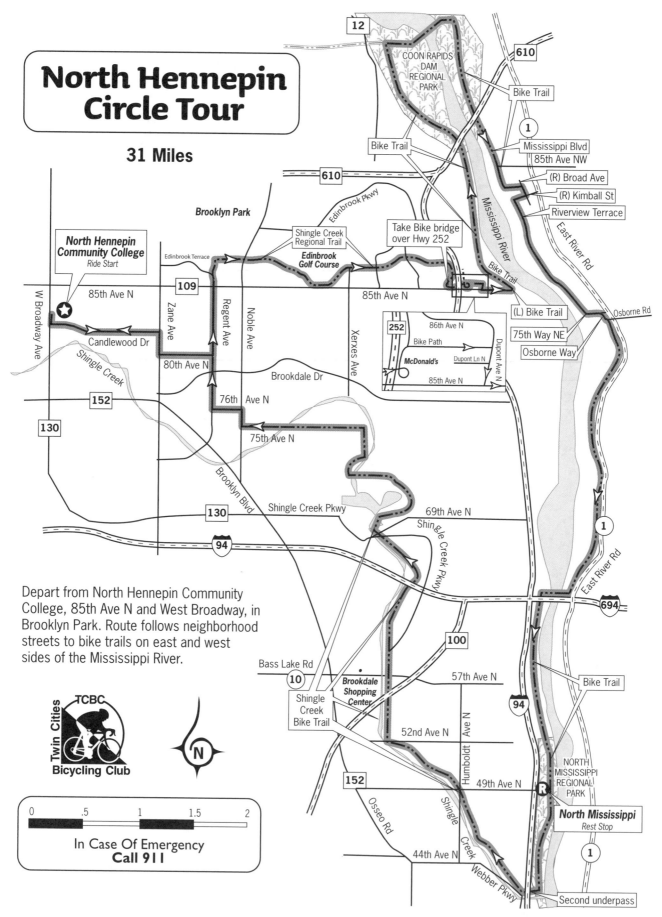

North Hennepin Circle Tour

31 Miles

12

COON RAPIDS DAM REGIONAL PARK

610

Bike Trail

1

Bike Trail

Mississippi Blvd
85th Ave NW

Edinbrook Pkwy

610

(R) Broad Ave

(R) Kimball St

Riverview Terrace

Brooklyn Park

Shingle Creek Regional Trail

Take Bike bridge over Hwy 252

Mississippi River

East River Rd

North Hennepin Community College *Ride Start*

Edinbrook Terrace

Edinbrook Golf Course

Bike Trail

85th Ave N

109

85th Ave N

(L) Bike Trail

Osborne Rd

75th Way NE

Osborne Way

W Broadway Ave

Zane Ave

Regent Ave

Noble Ave

Xerxes Ave

252

86th Ave N

Candlewood Dr

Bike Path

McDonald's

Dupont Ln N

Dupont Ave N

Shingle Creek

80th Ave N

Brookdale Dr

85th Ave N

152

76th Ave N

130

75th Ave N

Brooklyn Blvd

Shingle Creek Pkwy

69th Ave N

Shingle Creek Pkwy

130

94

Depart from North Hennepin Community College, 85th Ave N and West Broadway, in Brooklyn Park. Route follows neighborhood streets to bike trails on east and west sides of the Mississippi River.

East River Rd

694

Bass Lake Rd

100

57th Ave N

Bike Trail

TCBC

Twin Cities Bicycling Club

10

Brookdale Shopping Center

52nd Ave N

Humboldt Ave N

94

N

Shingle Creek Bike Trail

152

49th Ave N

NORTH MISSISSIPPI REGIONAL PARK

Osseo Rd

Shingle Creek

R

North Mississippi *Rest Stop*

| 0 | .5 | 1 | 1.5 | 2 |

44th Ave N

1

In Case Of Emergency
Call 911

Webber Pkwy

Second underpass

Retro Ride

32 / 40 Miles

Depart from Spring Gate Center by Applebees in Golden Valley, SW corner of Hwy 100 and Duluth St. Explore Medicine Lake, Plymouth, and beyond. Nicer weather, longer ride. Longer rides include a rest stop at the Retro Cafe in Loretto.

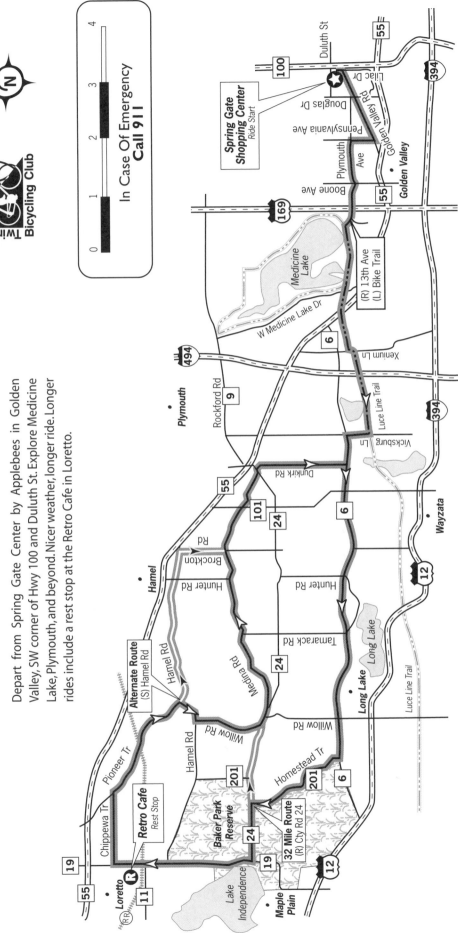

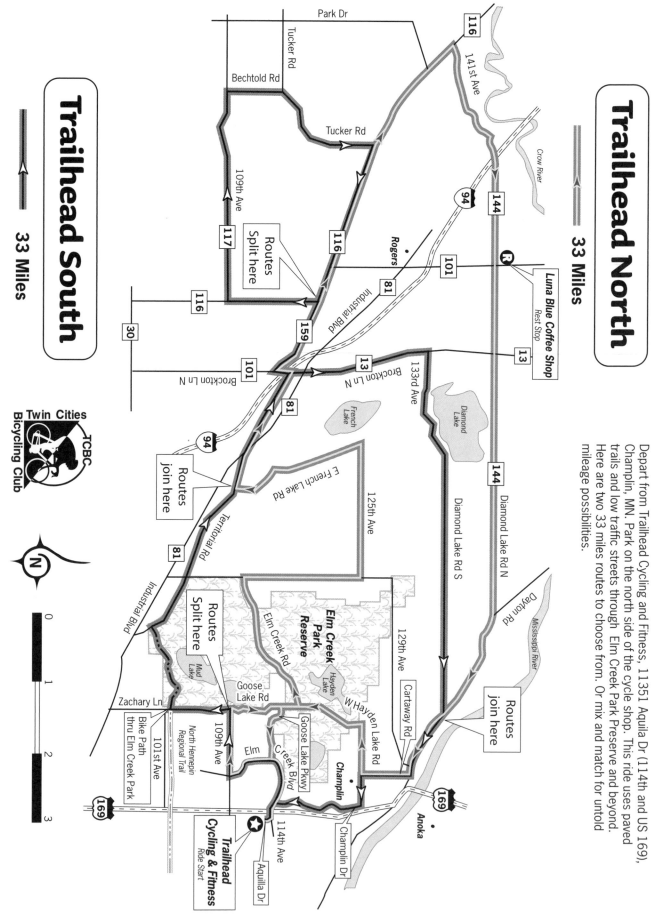

Trailhead North

33 Miles

Depart from Trailhead Cycling and Fitness, 11351 Aquila Dr (114th and US 169), Champlin, MN. Park on the north side of the cycle shop. This ride uses paved trails and low traffic streets through Elm Creek Park Preserve and beyond. Here are two 33 miles routes to choose from. Or mix and match for untold mileage possibilities.

Trailhead South

33 Miles

Twin Cities Bicycling Club
TCBC

Park Dr

Tucker Rd

Bechtold Rd

Tucker Rd

141st Ave

Crow River

116

116

94

144

109th Ave

Routes Split here

117

116

116

30

Rogers

Industrial Blvd

101

81

159

101

81

Brockton Ln N

Luna Blue Coffee Shop
Rest Stop

13

13

Brockton Ln N

133rd Ave

French Lake

Diamond Lake

144

Routes join here

94

E French Lake Rd

Territorial Rd

81

81

125th Ave

Diamond Lake Rd S

Diamond Lake Rd N

Dayton Rd

Mississippi River

Routes join here

Industrial Blvd

Routes Split here

Mud Lake

Goose Lake Rd

Elm Creek Rd

Elm Creek Park Reserve

Hayden Lake

W Hayden Lake Rd

129th Ave

Cartaway Rd

Zachary Ln

Bike Path thru Elm Creek Park

North Hennepin Regional Trail

101st Ave

109th Ave

Elm

Goose Lake Pkwy

Creek Blvd

Champlin

169

Anoka

Champlin Dr

169

Trailhead Cycling & Fitness
Ride Start

114th Ave

Aquilla Dr

N

0 1 2 3

Weaver Express

34 Miles

Depart from the Weaver Lake Elementary school parking lot in Maple Grove at 15900 Weaver Lake Road (1.2 miles West of I-94). Scenic country roads. Most of the route is rolling, but don't be surprised to be wailing a few "Momma Mia's!" on some hills.

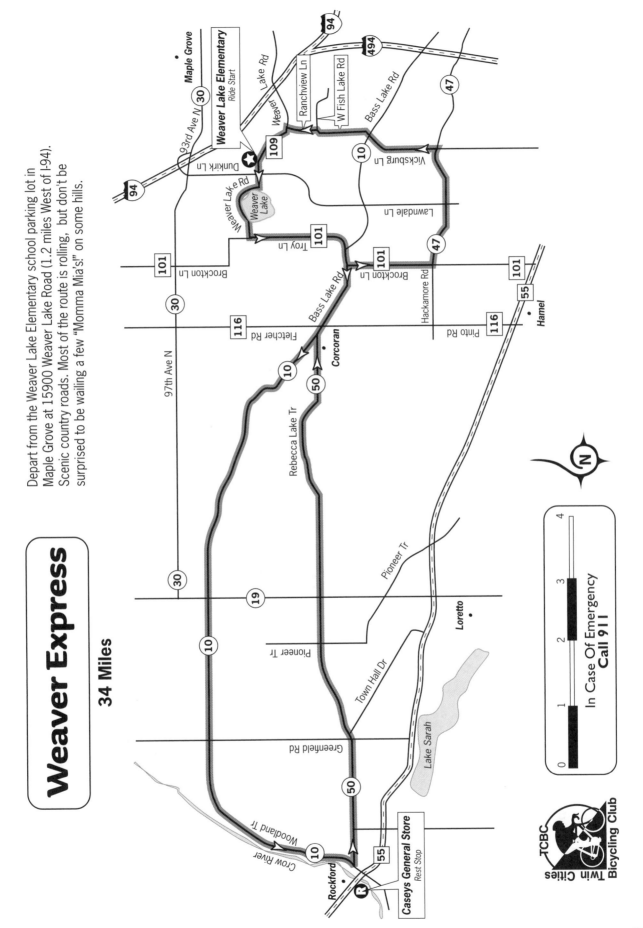

In Case Of Emergency
Call 9 1 1

Twin Cities Bicycling Club

Golden Foliage

42 Miles

An autumn romp through the western suburbs out to Delano. If ridden during early October the brilliant yellow leaves on Old Long Lake Road give this ride its name. Start at the Wayzata Bay Shopping Center; rest stops in Delano or Loretto.

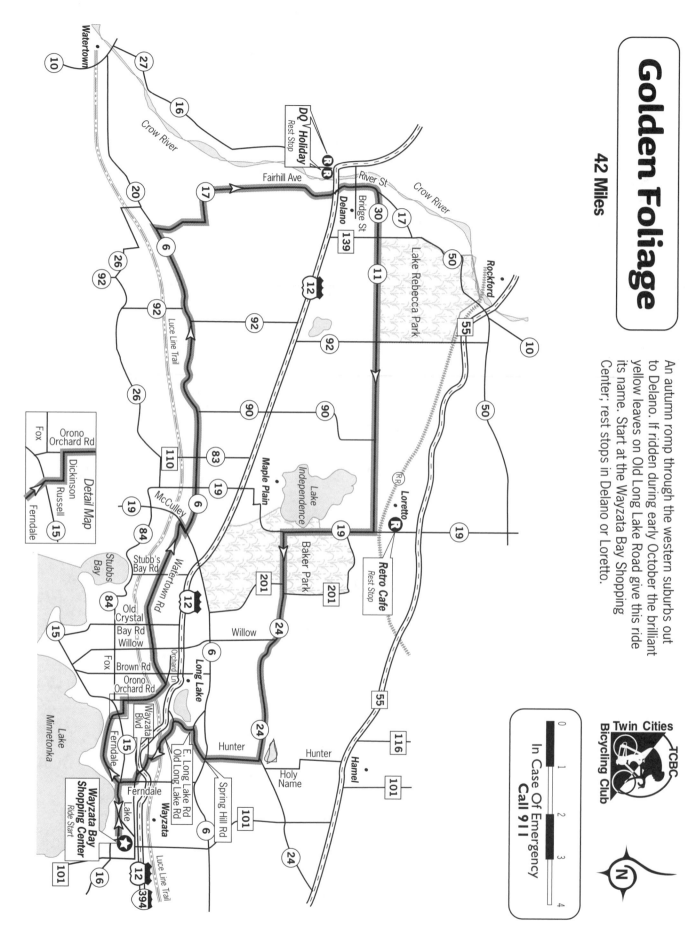

Twin Cities
Bicycling Club
TCBC

In Case Of Emergency
Call 911

0 1 2 3 4

Heights Out West

48 / 55 Miles

Enjoy this ride which will take you around Eagle Lake and Medicine Lake via a bike path. It's a moderately hilly route but doesn't have any difficult climbs. The return leg is quiet and scenic as you travel down Glenwood Ave. and Theodore Wirth Parkway.

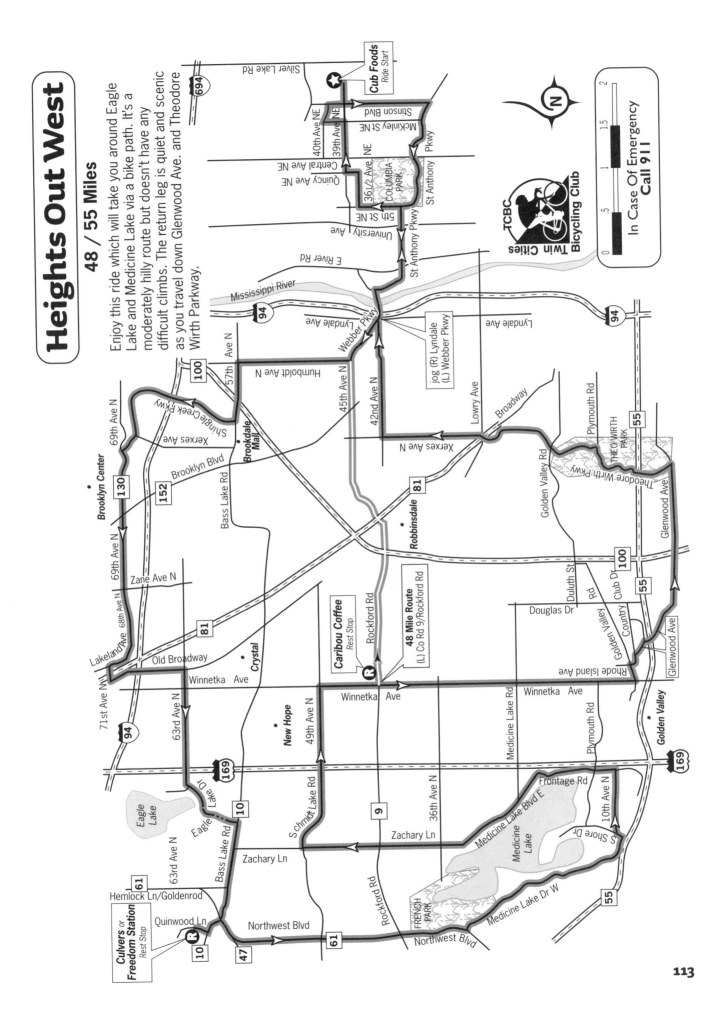

Cub Foods Ride Start

Caribou Coffee Rest Stop

48 Mile Route (L) Co Rd 9/Rockford Rd

Culvers or **Freedom Station** Rest Stop

jog (R) Lyndale (L) Webber Pkwy

In Case Of Emergency Call 911

Twin Cities Bicycling Club

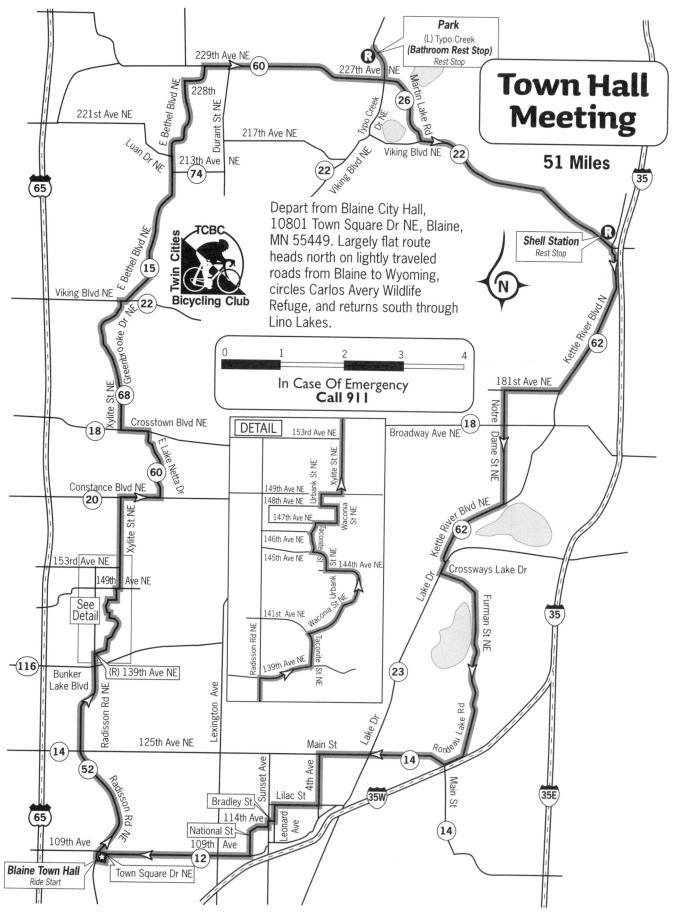

Town Hall Meeting

51 Miles

Depart from Blaine City Hall, 10801 Town Square Dr NE, Blaine, MN 55449. Largely flat route heads north on lightly traveled roads from Blaine to Wyoming, circles Carlos Avery Wildlife Refuge, and returns south through Lino Lakes.

Park
(L) Typo Creek
(Bathroom Rest Stop)
Rest Stop

Shell Station
Rest Stop

TCBC
Twin Cities
Bicycling Club

In Case Of Emergency
Call 911

DETAIL

See Detail

(R) 139th Ave NE

Blaine Town Hall
Ride Start

Coon Rapids River Ride

52 / 64 Miles

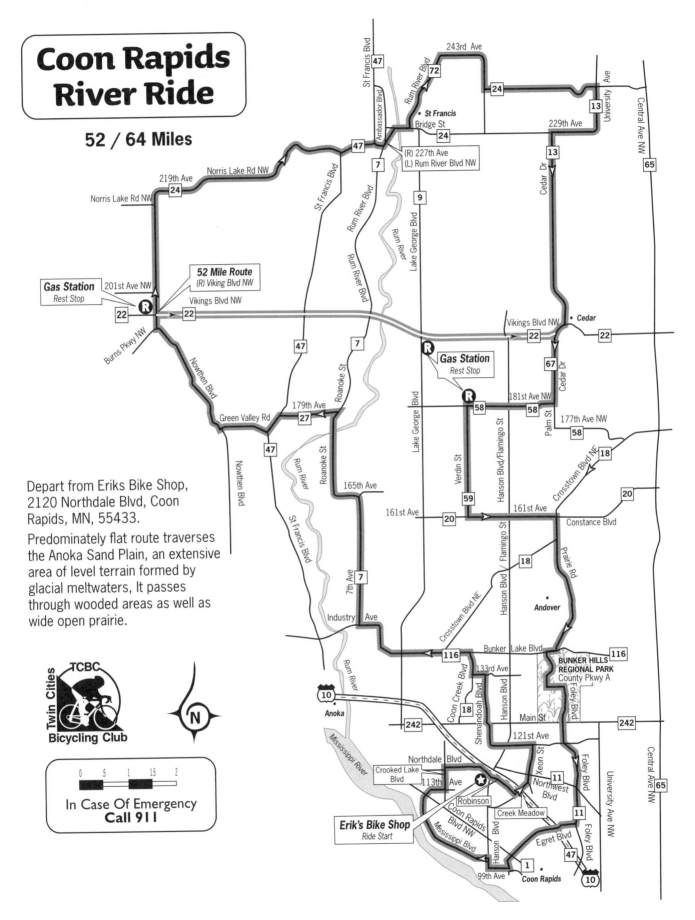

Depart from Eriks Bike Shop, 2120 Northdale Blvd, Coon Rapids, MN, 55433.

Predominately flat route traverses the Anoka Sand Plain, an extensive area of level terrain formed by glacial meltwaters, It passes through wooded areas as well as wide open prairie.

TCBC
Twin Cities Bicycling Club

0 .5 1 1.5 2

In Case Of Emergency Call 911

Gas Station
Rest Stop

201st Ave NW

52 Mile Route
(R) Viking Blvd NW

Vikings Blvd NW

Norris Lake Rd NW

219th Ave

Norris Lake Rd NW

243rd Ave

St Francis Blvd

Rum River Blvd

St Francis

Bridge St

229th Ave

University Ave

Central Ave NW

(R) 227th Ave
(L) Rum River Blvd NW

Ambassador Blvd

Lake George Blvd

Rum River

Cedar Dr

Burns Pkwy NW

Nowthen Blvd

Green Valley Rd

179th Ave

Roanoke St

165th Ave

Rum River

St Francis Blvd

7th Ave

Industry Ave

Nowthen Blvd

Vikings Blvd NW

Cedar

Cedar Dr

Gas Station
Rest Stop

181st Ave NW

Palm St

177th Ave NW

Crosstown Blvd NE

Verdin St

Hanson Blvd/Flamingo St

161st Ave

161st Ave

Constance Blvd

Lake George Blvd

Flamingo St

Prairie Rd

Andover

Crosstown Blvd NE

Hanson Blvd

Bunker Lake Blvd

BUNKER HILLS REGIONAL PARK
County Pkwy A

Coon Creek Blvd

133rd Ave

Hanson Blvd

Foley Blvd

Main St

Shenandoah Blvd

121st Ave

Rum River

Anoka

Mississippi River

Northdale Blvd

Crooked Lake Blvd

113th Ave

Robinson

Erik's Bike Shop
Ride Start

Coon Rapids Blvd NW

Mississippi Blvd

Hanson Blvd

Xeon St

Northwest Blvd

Creek Meadow

Egret Blvd

Foley Blvd

University Ave NW

Central Ave NW

99th Ave

Coon Rapids

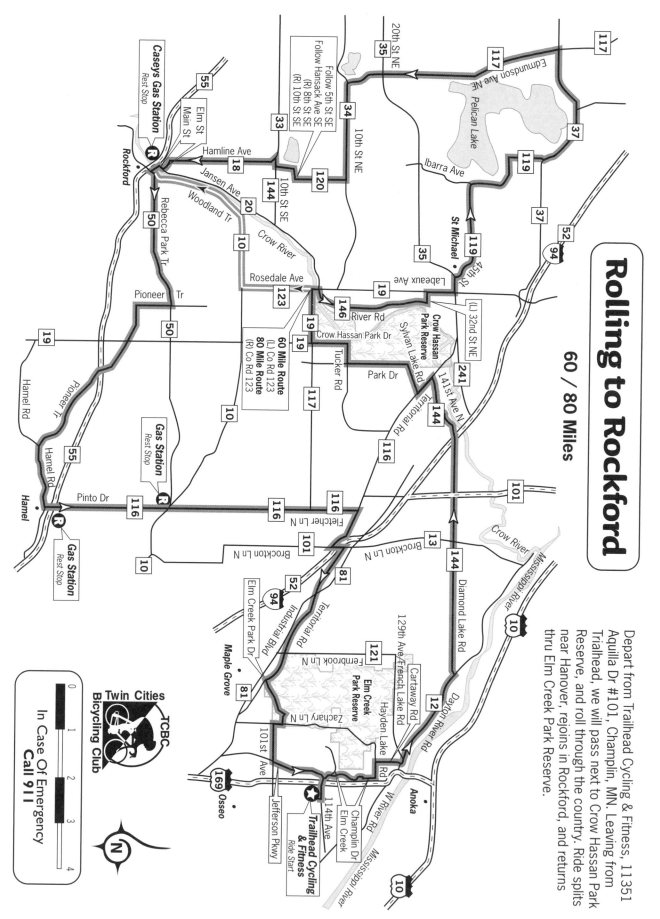

Rolling to Rockford

60 / 80 Miles

Depart from Trailhead Cycling & Fitness, 11351 Aquilla Dr #101, Champlin, MN. Leaving from Trialhead, we will pass next to Crow Hassan Park Reserve, and roll through the country. Ride splits near Hanover, rejoins in Rockford, and returns thru Elm Creek Park Reserve.

Caseys Gas Station Rest Stop

Rockford

Follow 5th St SE
Follow Hansack Ave SE
(R) 8th St SE
(R) 10th St SE

Elm St
Main St

Hamline Ave

Jansen Ave

Woodland Tr

Crow River

Rebecca Park Tr

Pioneer Tr

Rosedale Ave

60 Mile Route
(L) Co Rd 123
80 Mile Route
(R) Co Rd 123

Crow Hassan Park Reserve

Sylvan Lake Rd

River Rd
Crow Hassan Park Dr

Tucker Rd
Park Dr

Labeaux Ave

St Michael

Pelican Lake

Edmundson Ave NE

Ibarra Ave

20th St NE

10th St NE

45th St

(L) 32nd St NE

Territorial Rd

141st Ave N

Gas Station Rest Stop

Hamel Rd

Pioneer Tr

Pinto Dr

Gas Station Rest Stop

Hamel

Fletcher Ln N

Brockton Ln N

Brockton Ln N

Crow River

Mississippi River

Diamond Lake Rd

Dalton River Rd

W River Rd

Anoka

Mississippi River

Elm Creek Park Dr

Maple Grove

Industrial Blvd

Territorial Rd

Zachary Ln N

Fernbrook Ln N

Elm Creek Park Reserve

129th Ave/French Lake Rd

Cartaway Rd

Hayden Lake Rd

101st Ave

Osseo

Jefferson Pkwy

114th Ave

Champlin Dr Elm Creek

Trailhead Cycling & Fitness Ride Start

Twin Cities Bicycling Club
TCBC

In Case Of Emergency
Call 911

116

Northwest Ride Journal

Date _____ Mileage _____

Route _____

Notes _____

_____

_____

Date _____ Mileage _____

Route _____

Notes _____

_____

_____

Date _____ Mileage _____

Route _____

Notes _____

_____

_____

Date _____ Mileage _____

Route _____

Notes _____

_____

_____

Date _____ Mileage _____

Route _____

Notes _____

_____

_____

Date _____ Mileage _____

Route _____

Notes _____

_____

_____

Date _____ Mileage _____

Route _____

Notes _____

_____

_____

Date _____ Mileage _____

Route _____

Notes _____

_____

_____

Date _____ Mileage _____

Route _____

Notes _____

_____

_____

Date _____ Mileage _____

Route _____

Notes _____

_____

_____

Wisconsin

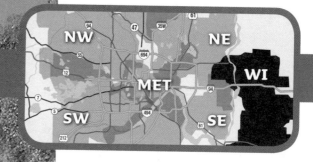

WISCONSIN HILLS PLUM CITY - PAGE 130

CHIPPEWA RIVER BRIDGE
ON THE RED CEDAR TRAIL

THE HILLS ARE ALIVE - PAGE 136

A TCBC FAVORITE - CRUISIN' THE COULEES 1 - PAGE 135

Legend

🍴	FOOD
⛲	WATER
🚻	TOILET
▭	FLAT
⌒	ROLLING
◠	HILLY
⛰	CLIMBS
🛣	ROADS
🗺	TRAILS
🚗	LT TRAFFIC
🚙	TRAFFIC
📷	SCENIC
🍦	TREATS

Page	Ride	Miles	At Ride Start	Terrain	Highlights
120	Diamond Bluff Express	26/37 40/49	Food, Water, Toilet	Rolling, Climbs, Roads, Lt Traffic	Scenic
121	Hudson Loops	28 33/40	Food, Water, Toilet	Rolling, Climbs, Roads, Lt Traffic	Scenic
122	WOW Menomonie South	29/38 58/60	Food, Water, Toilet	Rolling, Climbs, Roads, Lt Traffic	
123	WOW Menomonie North	31/48	Food, Water, Toilet	Flat, Roads, Lt Traffic	
124	Around the Badlands	32	Food, Water, Toilet	Rolling, Roads, Lt Traffic	Scenic, Treats
125	Rush Cady to Eau Galle	62/78	Food, Water, Toilet	Roads, Climbs, Lt Traffic	Scenic
126	Bass Lake Cheese Factory	34/45	Food, Water, Toilet	Flat, Roads, Traffic	Scenic, Treats
127	Cruisin' the Coulees 2	42/62	Food, Water, Toilet	Rolling, Climbs, Roads, Lt Traffic	Scenic
128	La Crosse Killer Hills Rev.	43/72	Food, Water, Toilet	Rolling, Climbs, Roads, Lt Traffic	
129	WOW Menomonie Sunday	45/66	Food, Water, Toilet	Rolling, Climbs, Roads, Lt Traffic	Scenic
130	WI Hills Plum City	46/52 61/70	Food, Water, Toilet	Rolling, Climbs, Roads, Lt Traffic	Scenic
131	WI Hills Maiden Rock	48 78/81	Food, Water, Toilet	Rolling, Climbs, Roads, Lt Traffic	Scenic
132	Hills out of Prescott	52/76	Food, Water, Toilet	Rolling, Climbs, Roads, Lt Traffic	
133	Knapping in Glen Hills	55/71	Food, Water, Toilet	Rolling, Roads, Lt Traffic	
134	WI Hills to Downsville	56 73/89	Food, Water, Toilet	Rolling, Climbs, Roads, Lt Traffic	Scenic
135	Cruisin' the Coulees 1	60	Food, Water, Toilet	Rolling, Climbs, Roads, Lt Traffic	Scenic
136	The Hills are Alive	68	Food, Water, Toilet	Climbs, Roads, Lt Traffic	Scenic

Disclaimer: The Twin Cities Bicycling Club, Hostelling International USA – Minnesota Council, and their respective officers, employees, trip leaders and members, and those whose work appears in this Atlas, and those people and establishments who distribute this Atlas, cannot be held responsible for the future condition of any of these routes, or for any injuries or damages sustained or occuring while using these routes.

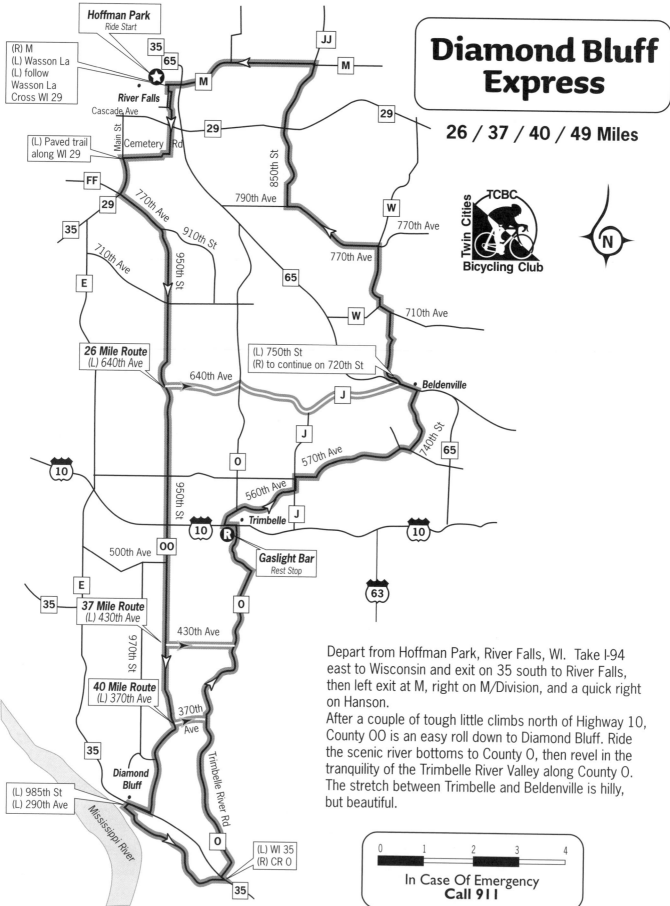

Diamond Bluff Express

26 / 37 / 40 / 49 Miles

TCBC Twin Cities Bicycling Club

N

Hoffman Park
Ride Start

(R) M
(L) Wasson La
(L) follow
Wasson La
Cross WI 29

River Falls

Cascade Ave

Main St

Cemetery Rd

(L) Paved trail
along WI 29

FF

29

35

E

710th Ave

770th Ave

910th St

950th St

850th St

790th Ave

JJ

M

29

W

770th Ave

770th Ave

710th Ave

W

65

26 Mile Route
(L) 640th Ave

640th Ave

(L) 750th St
(R) to continue on 720th St

J

J

J

O

570th Ave

740th St

Beldenville

65

10

950th St

560th Ave

J

Trimbelle

10

R

10

63

Gaslight Bar
Rest Stop

O

500th Ave

OO

E

35

37 Mile Route
(L) 430th Ave

970th St

430th Ave

40 Mile Route
(L) 370th Ave

370th
Ave

35

Trimbelle River Rd

Diamond Bluff

(L) 985th St
(L) 290th Ave

Mississippi River

O

(L) WI 35
(R) CR O

35

Depart from Hoffman Park, River Falls, WI. Take I-94
east to Wisconsin and exit on 35 south to River Falls,
then left exit at M, right on M/Division, and a quick right
on Hanson.
After a couple of tough little climbs north of Highway 10,
County OO is an easy roll down to Diamond Bluff. Ride
the scenic river bottoms to County O, then revel in the
tranquility of the Trimbelle River Valley along County O.
The stretch between Trimbelle and Beldenville is hilly,
but beautiful.

0 1 2 3 4

In Case Of Emergency
Call 911

120

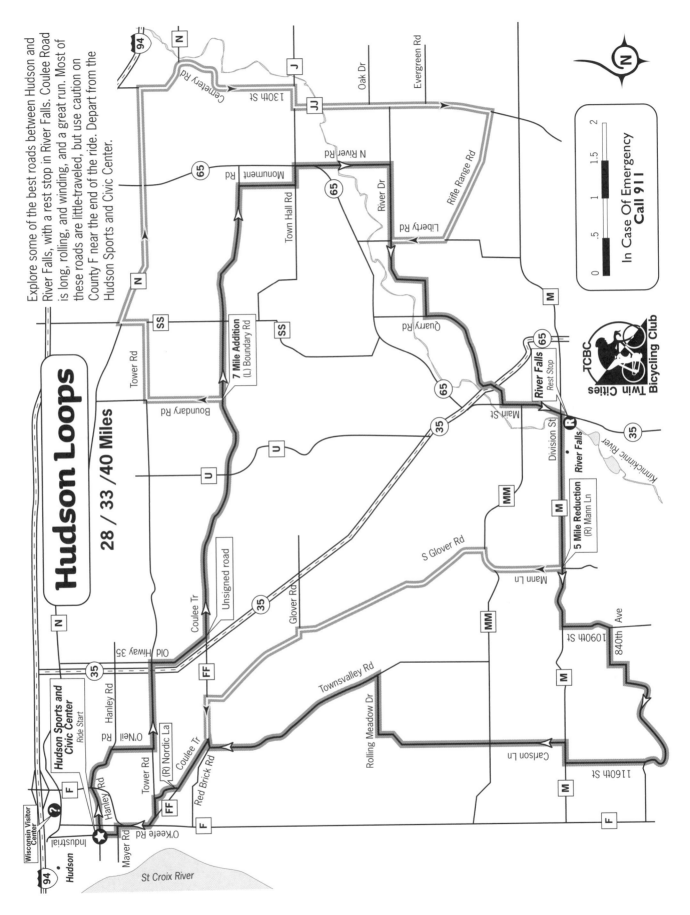

Hudson Loops

28 / 33 / 40 Miles

Explore some of the best roads between Hudson and River Falls, with a rest stop in River Falls. Coulee Road is long, rolling, and winding, and a great run. Most of these roads are little-traveled, but use caution on County F near the end of the ride. Depart from the Hudson Sports and Civic Center.

Hudson Sports and Civic Center
Ride Start

7 Mile Addition
(L) Boundary Rd

5 Mile Reduction
(R) Mann Ln

River Falls
Rest Stop

Wisconsin Visitor Center

In Case Of Emergency
Call 911

Twin Cities
Bicycling Club
TCBC

St Croix River

Kinnickinnic River

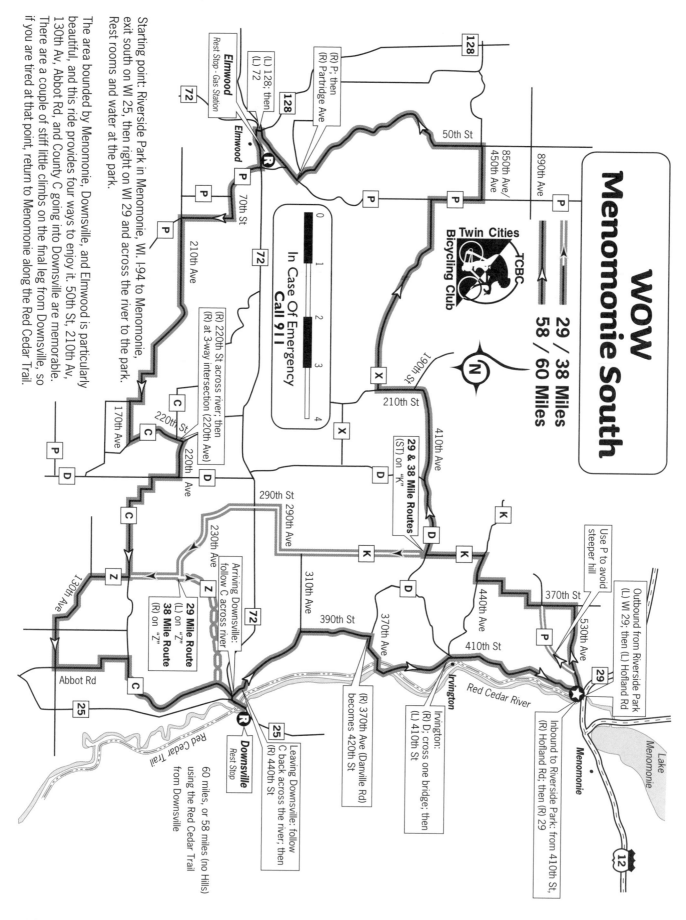

WOW
Menomonie South

Twin Cities Bicycling Club — TCBC

29 / 38 Miles
58 / 60 Miles

In Case Of Emergency Call 911

Starting point: Riverside Park in Menomonie, WI. I-94 to Menomonie, exit south on WI 25, then right on WI 29 and across the river to the park. Rest rooms and water at the park.

The area bounded by Menomonie, Downsville, and Elmwood is particularly beautiful, and this ride provides four ways to enjoy it. 50th St, 210th Av, 130th Av, Abbot Rd, and County C going into Downsville are memorable. There are a couple of stiff little climbs on the final leg from Downsville, so if you are tired at that point, return to Menomonie along the Red Cedar Trail.

Elmwood — Rest Stop - Gas Station

(L) 128; then
(L) 72

(R) P; then
(R) Partridge Ave

50th St

850th Ave/450th Ave

890th Ave

70th St

210th Ave

(R) 220th St across river; then
(R) at 3-way intersection (220th Ave)

220th St

290th St

290th Ave

230th Ave

Arriving Downsville: follow C across river

29 Mile Route
(L) on "Z"
38 Mile Route
(R) on "Z"

190th St

210th St

410th Ave

29 & 38 Mile Routes
(ST) on "K"

310th Ave

390th St

370th Ave

(R) 370th Ave (Danville Rd) becomes 420th St

Leaving Downsville: follow C back across the river; then (R) 440th St

60 miles, or 58 miles (no Hills) using the Red Cedar Trail from Downsville

Downsville — Rest Stop

Red Cedar Trail

Abbot Rd

130th Ave

440th Ave

410th St

370th St

530th Ave

Use P to avoid steeper hill

Irvington:
(R) D; cross one bridge; then
(L) 410th St

Irvington

Red Cedar River

Menomonie

Lake Menomonie

Outbound from Riverside Park:
(L) WI 29; then (L) Hofland Rd

Inbound to Riverside Park, from 410th St;
(R) Hofland Rd; then (R) 29

122

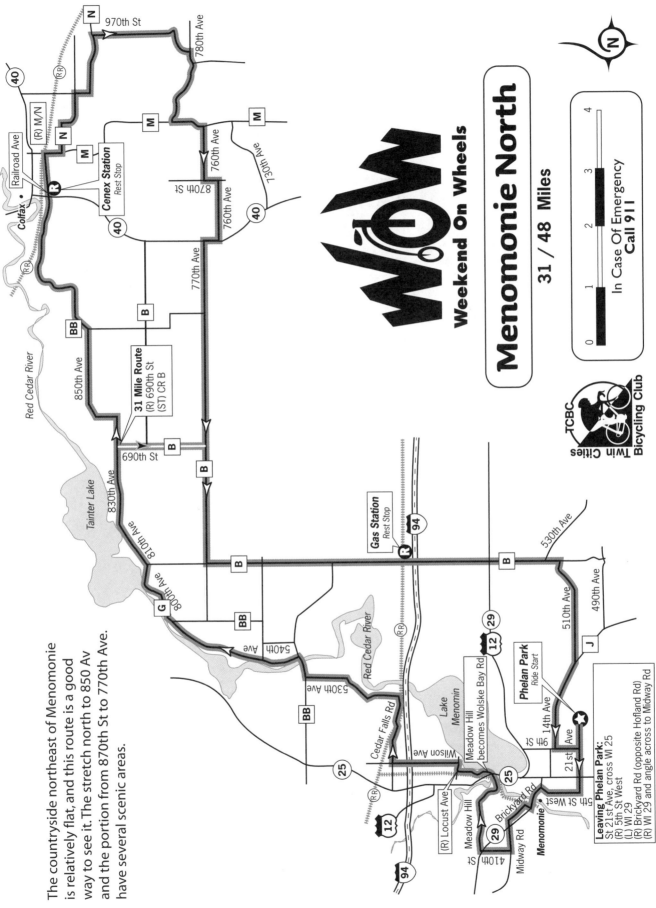

The countryside northeast of Menomonie is relatively flat, and this route is a good way to see it. The stretch north to 850 Av and the portion from 870th St to 770th Ave. have several scenic areas.

WOW
Weekend On Wheels

Menomonie North

31 / 48 Miles

TCBC
Twin Cities Bicycling Club

In Case Of Emergency
Call 911

Gas Station
Rest Stop

Cenex Station
Rest Stop

31 Mile Route
(R) 690th St
(ST) CR B

Phelan Park
Ride Start

Leaving Phelan Park:
St 21st Ave, cross WI 25
(R) 5th St West
(L) WI 29
(R) Brickyard Rd (opposite Hofland Rd)
(R) WI 29 and angle across to Midway Rd

Around the Badlands

38 Miles

Depart from Hudson Sports and Civic Center, 1820 Hanley Road, Hudson, WI 54016. This is a relatively flat route around the Hudson Badlands, which includes the Badlands Golf Course and Badlands Snopark. The route generally avoids the hills associated with badlands by going around them. The route will follow the quiet country roads through the farmland and around some lakes.

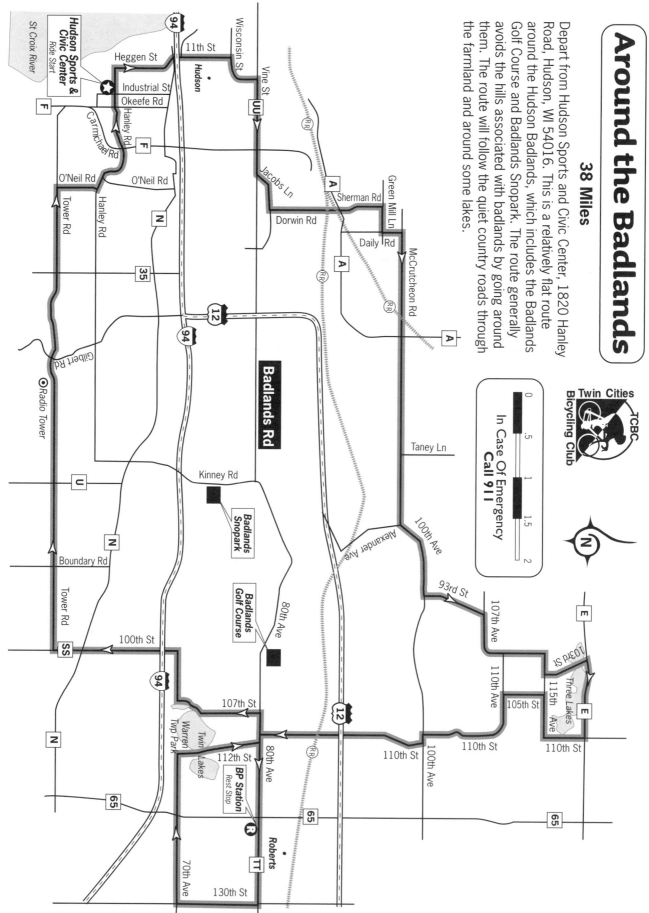

Twin Cities Bicycling Club TCBC

In Case Of Emergency Call 911

0   .5   1   1.5   2

N

Hudson Sports & Civic Center
Ride Start

St Croix River

94

Heggen St
Industrial St
Okeefe Rd
Hanley Rd
Carmichael Rd
11th St
Wisconsin St
Hudson
F
F
N
O'Neil Rd
O'Neil Rd
Tower Rd
Hanley Rd
35
Vine St
UU
Jacobs Ln
A
Sherman Rd
Dorwin Rd
Green Mill Ln
Daily Rd
McCrutcheon Rd
A
A
RR
12
94
Gilbert Rd
Radio Tower
Badlands Rd
U
N
Boundary Rd
Tower Rd
Taney Ln
Kinney Rd
Badlands Snopark
Badlands Golf Course
80th Ave
Alexander Ave
100th Ave
93rd St
107th Ave
110th Ave
105th St
115th Ave
103rd St
Three Lakes
E
E
110th St
SS
100th St
94
107th St
Warren Twp Park
Twin Lakes
112th St
80th Ave
BP Station
Rest Stop
R
65
110th St
100th Ave
110th St
65
65
N
70th Ave
130th St
Roberts
TT

124

Rush Cady to Eau Galle

→ 32 Miles
→ 78 Miles

Depart from Baldwin WI (Exit 19 on I-94). Park behind the Kwik Trip, just north of I-94. A ride through the river valleys of the Rush River, Cady Creek and Eau Galle River. Rest stops will be at 20-25 miles.

Baldwin

Park & Ride
Ride Start

Red Barn
Rest Stop

Spring Valley
Rest Stop (outside town)

Elmwood
Rest Stop

Spring Valley

Lake George

Eau Galle River

Cady Creek

Rush River

Cave Creek

Harmony Rd

55th Ave
50th Ave
30th Ave
27th Ave
25th Ave
10th Ave
890th Ave
730th Ave
690th Ave
610th Ave
710th Ave

233rd St
230th St
270th St
290th St
320th St
50th St
450th St
530th St
170th St
170th St
110th St

Exit 19

TCBC
Twin Cities
Bicycling Club

0 1 2 3

In Case Of Emergency
Call 911

N

Bass Lake Ride

34 / 45 Miles

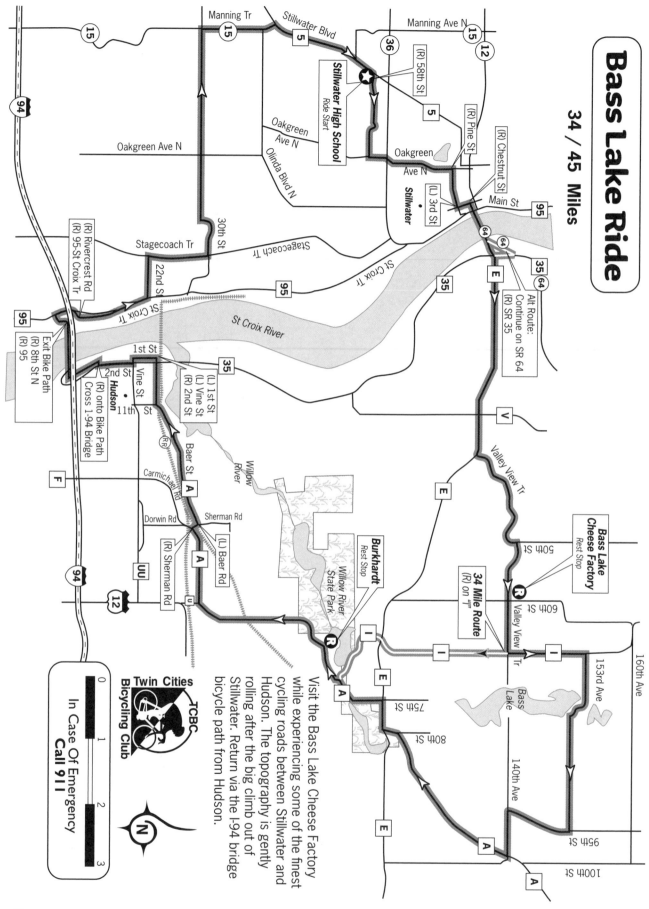

Manning Tr

Stillwater Blvd

Manning Ave N

15

15

15

12

5

94

36

(R) 58th St

5

Stillwater High School
Ride Start

(R) Pine St

(R) Chestnut St

Oakgreen Ave N

Oakgreen Ave N

Oakgreen Ave N

Olinda Blvd N

Main St

95

Stillwater

(L) 3rd St

64

64

35

64

E

35

Alt Route:
Continue on SR 64
(R) SR 35

Stagecoach Tr

Stagecoach Tr

Stagecoach Tr

30th St

22nd St

St Croix Tr

95

St Croix River

(R) Rivercrest Rd
(R) 95-St Croix Tr

95

V

St Croix Tr

95

Exit Bike Path
(R) 8th St N
(R) 95

1st St

35

(L) 1st St
(L) Vine St
(R) 2nd St

2nd St

Vine St

Hudson

11th St

(R)

Baer St

E

Valley View Tr

Willow River

Carmichael Rd

A

F

**Bass Lake
Cheese Factory**
Rest Stop

Dorwin Rd

Sherman Rd

50th St

UU

A

(L) Baer Rd

R

60th St

Valley View Tr

34 Mile Route
(R) on 4th

12

94

(R) Sherman Rd

U

Willow River
State Park

Burkhardt
Rest Stop

I

E

I

153rd Ave

160th Ave

I

A

Bass Lake

140th Ave

75th St

E

80th St

95th St

A

100th St

A

Visit the Bass Lake Cheese Factory
while experiencing some of the finest
cycling roads between Stillwater and
Hudson. The topography is gently
rolling after the big climb out of
Stillwater. Return via the I-94 bridge
bicycle path from Hudson.

(R) onto Bike Path
Cross I-94 Bridge

Twin Cities
Bicycling Club
TCBC

**In Case Of Emergency
Call 911**

0 1 2 3

N

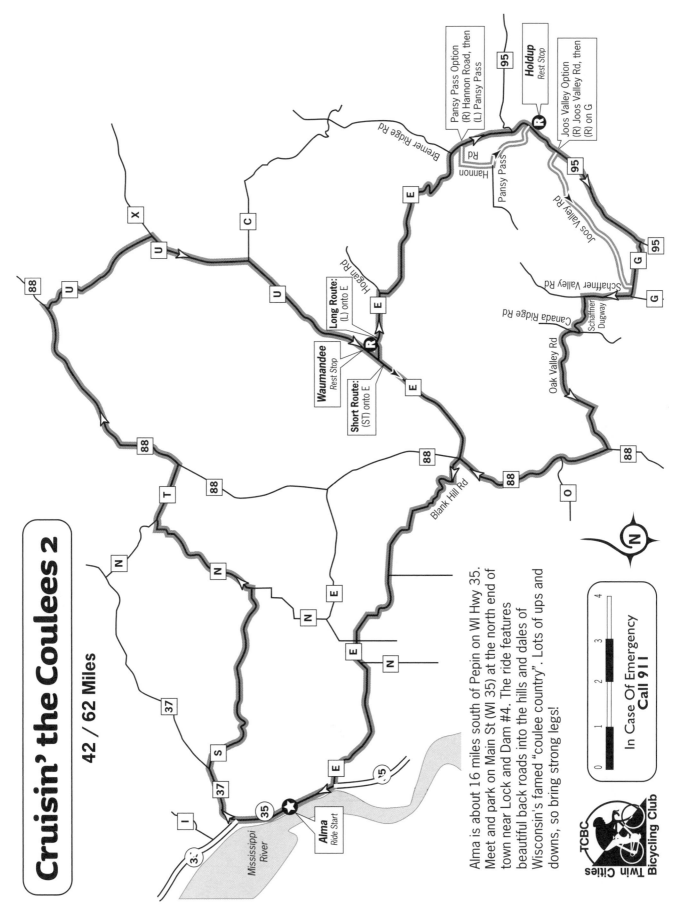

Cruisin' the Coulees 2

42 / 62 Miles

Pansy Pass Option
(R) Hannon Road, then
(L) Pansy Pass

Holdup
Rest Stop

Joos Valley Option
(R) Joos Valley Rd, then
(R) on G

Long Route:
(L) onto E

Waumandee
Rest Stop

Short Route:
(ST) onto E

Alma
Ride Start

Alma is about 16 miles south of Pepin on WI Hwy 35. Meet and park on Main St (WI 35) at the north end of town near Lock and Dam #4. The ride features beautiful back roads into the hills and dales of Wisconsin's famed "coulee country". Lots of ups and downs, so bring strong legs!

In Case Of Emergency
Call 911

Twin Cities
Bicycling Club
TCBC

127

La Crosse Killer Hill Revisited

43 / 72 Miles

This is a modified version of a classic SW Wisconsin hill ride, featuring the "killer hill" on County EE between Mindoro and Bangor. Enjoy the view from the Alpine Inn on County F, a few miles before the end of the ride.

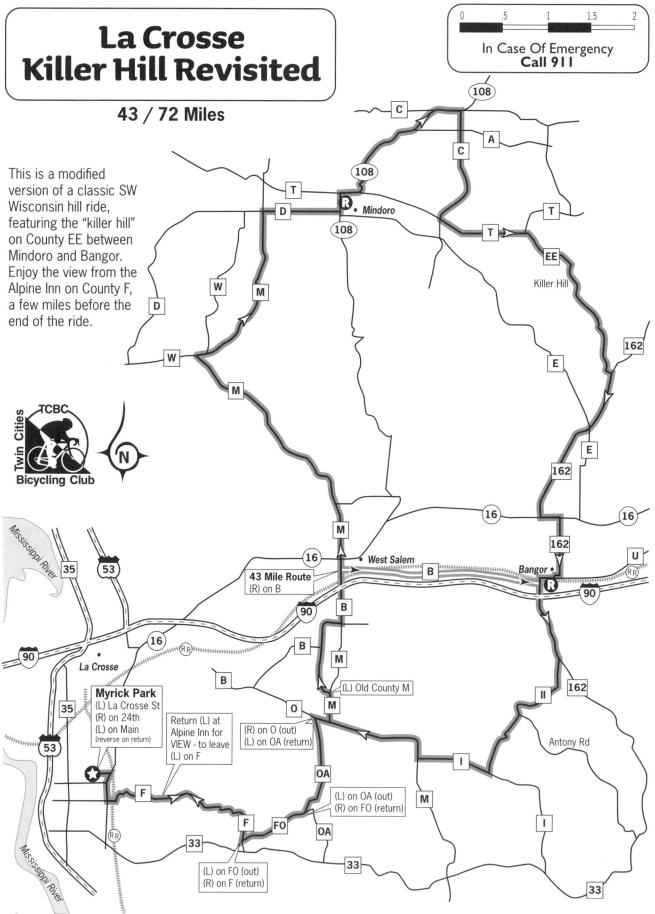

In Case Of Emergency
Call 911

TCBC
Twin Cities
Bicycling Club

N

Mississippi River

Killer Hill

Mindoro

West Salem

Bangor

La Crosse

Antony Rd

43 Mile Route
(R) on B

Myrick Park
(L) La Crosse St
(R) on 24th
(L) on Main
(reverse on return)

Return (L) at
Alpine Inn for
VIEW - to leave
(L) on F

(R) on O (out)
(L) on OA (return)

(L) Old County M

(L) on OA (out)
(R) on FO (return)

(L) on FO (out)
(R) on F (return)

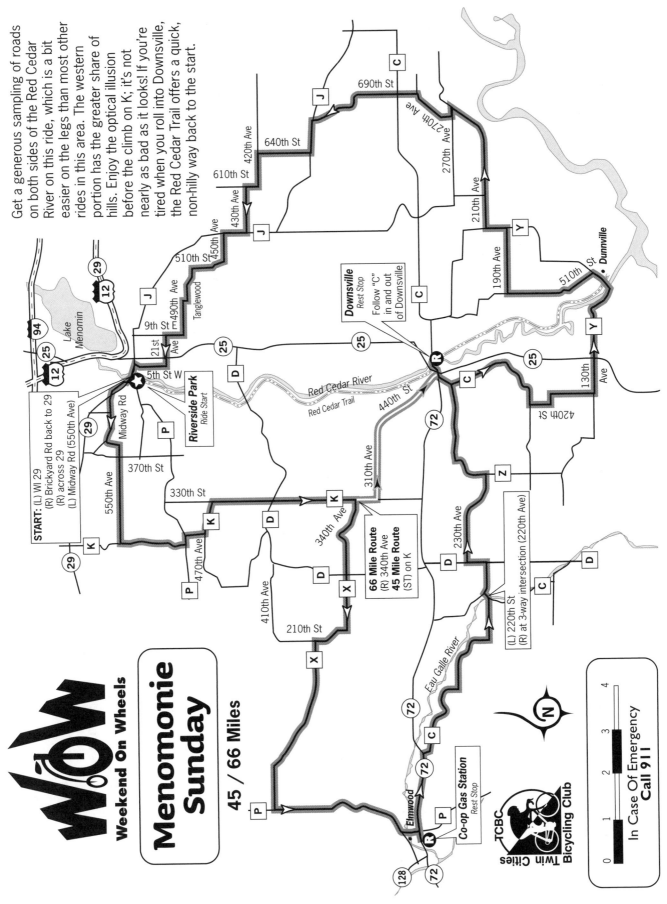

Get a generous sampling of roads on both sides of the Red Cedar River on this ride, which is a bit easier on the legs than most other rides in this area. The western portion has the greater share of hills. Enjoy the optical illusion before the climb on K; it's not nearly as bad as it looks! If you're tired when you roll into Downsville, the Red Cedar Trail offers a quick, non-hilly way back to the start.

Weekend On Wheels

Menomonie Sunday

45 / 66 Miles

START: (L) WI 29
(R) Brickyard Rd back to 29
(R) across 29
(L) Midway Rd (550th Ave)

Riverside Park
Ride Start

Downsville
Rest Stop
Follow "C" in and out of Downsville

66 Mile Route (R) 340th Ave
45 Mile Route (ST) on K

(L) 220th St
(R) at 3-way intersection (220th Ave)

Co-op Gas Station
Rest Stop

Twin Cities Bicycling Club

In Case Of Emergency
Call 911

Wisconsin Hills
Plum City

46 / 52 / 61 / 62 / 70 Miles

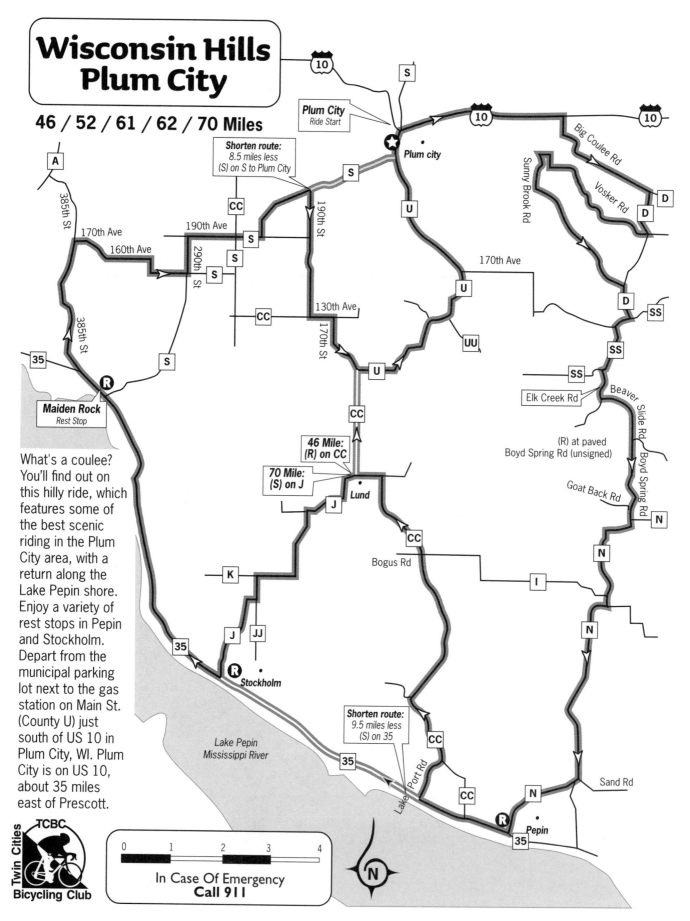

A

385th St

170th Ave

160th Ave

190th Ave

290th St

385th St

35

R

Maiden Rock
Rest Stop

What's a coulee?
You'll find out on
this hilly ride, which
features some of
the best scenic
riding in the Plum
City area, with a
return along the
Lake Pepin shore.
Enjoy a variety of
rest stops in Pepin
and Stockholm.
Depart from the
municipal parking
lot next to the gas
station on Main St.
(County U) just
south of US 10 in
Plum City, WI. Plum
City is on US 10,
about 35 miles
east of Prescott.

10

S

10

10

Plum City
Ride Start

★ Plum city

Big Coulee Rd

Vosker Rd

D

D

Shorten route:
*8.5 miles less
(S) on S to Plum City*

S

CC

S

190th St

S

S

CC

130th Ave

170th St

190th Ave

U

U

170th Ave

D

SS

SS

SS

U

UU

SS

Elk Creek Rd

U

Beaver

Slide Rd

Boyd Spring Rd

(R) at paved
Boyd Spring Rd (unsigned)

CC

Goat Back Rd

N

46 Mile:
(R) on CC

70 Mile:
(S) on J

• Lund

N

J

CC

Bogus Rd

I

N

K

J

JJ

35

R Stockholm

N

Sand Rd

Shorten route:
*9.5 miles less
(S) on 35*

Lake Port Rd

CC

CC

N

*Lake Pepin
Mississippi River*

35

R Pepin

35

Wisconsin Hills Maiden Rock

48 / 78 / 81 Miles

Start this ride from the park on the river in Maiden Rock, WI. Beginning with the green tranquility of the Rush River Valley, this route features some tough climbs (450th Av and Weber Rd) and thrilling descents (330th Av and Hartung Rd). Three mileage options are offered. The most reliable pre-ride food and restroom stop is the gas station in Bay City.

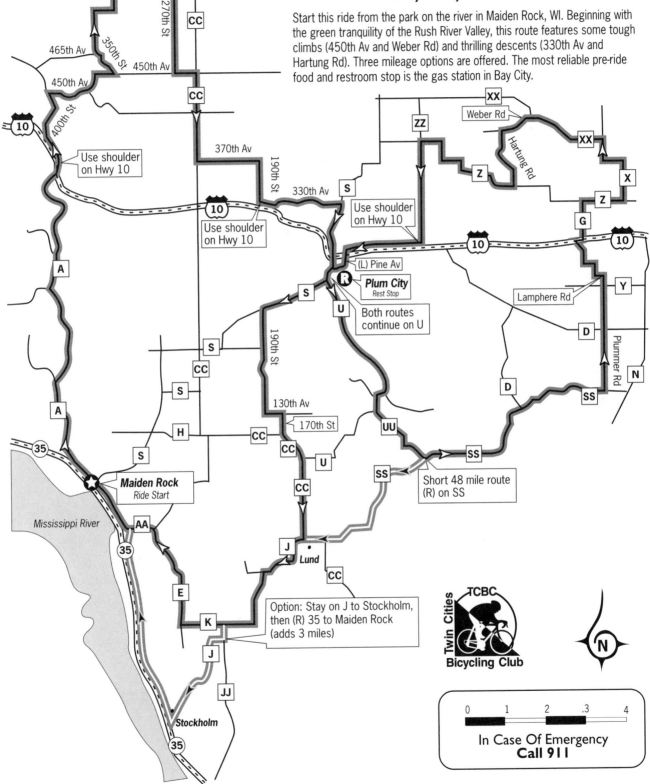

Use shoulder on Hwy 10

Use shoulder on Hwy 10

Use shoulder on Hwy 10

Weber Rd

Hartung Rd

(L) Pine Av

Plum City Rest Stop

Both routes continue on U

Lamphere Rd

Plummer Rd

Short 48 mile route (R) on SS

Maiden Rock Ride Start

Mississippi River

Lund

Option: Stay on J to Stockholm, then (R) 35 to Maiden Rock (adds 3 miles)

Stockholm

TCBC
Twin Cities Bicycling Club

0 1 2 3 4

In Case Of Emergency
Call 911

N

Hills Out of Prescott

52 / 76 Miles

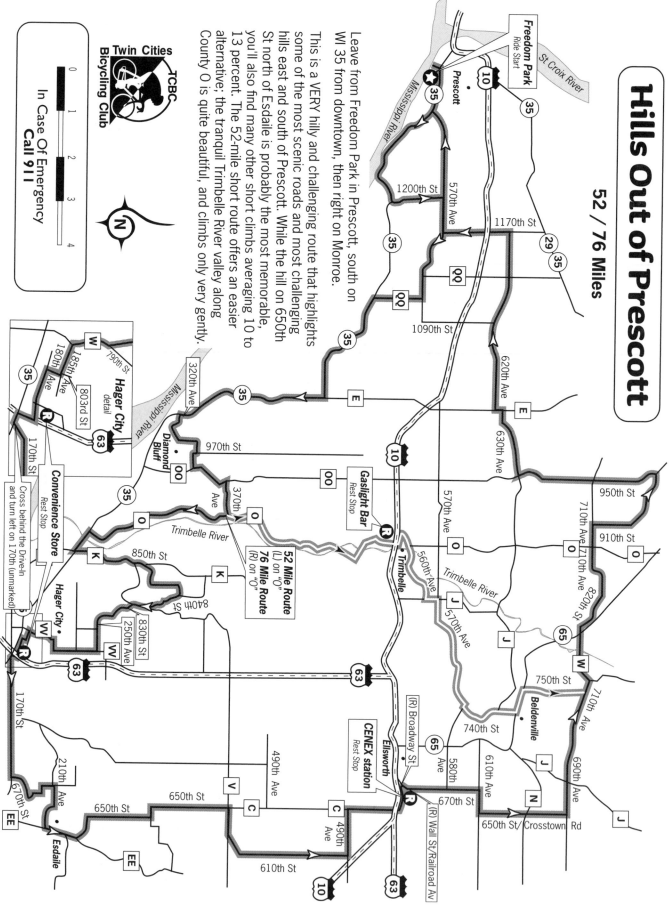

Leave from Freedom Park in Prescott, south on WI 35 from downtown, then right on Monroe.

This is a VERY hilly and challenging route that highlights some of the most scenic roads and most challenging hills east and south of Prescott. While the hill on 650th St north of Esdaile is probably the most memorable, you'll also find many other short climbs averaging 10 to 13 percent. The 52-mile short route offers an easier alternative; the tranquil Trimbelle River valley along County O is quite beautiful, and climbs only very gently.

Twin Cities Bicycling Club — TCBC

In Case Of Emergency
Call 911

Freedom Park
Ride Start

St Croix River

Mississippi River

Prescott

1200th St

570th Ave

1170th St

1090th St

620th Ave

630th Ave

950th St

910th St

710th Ave 710th Ave

820th St

E

570th Ave

570th Ave

Trimbelle River

Trimbelle

560th Ave

750th St

710th Ave

Beldenville

740th St

690th Ave

Gaslight Bar
Rest Stop

52 Mile Route
(L) on "O"
76 Mile Route
(R) on "O"

Trimbelle River

Hager City detail

790th St

180th Ave

185th Ave

803rd St

170th St

Convenience Store
Rest Stop

Diamond Bluff

Mississippi River

320th Ave

970th St

370th Ave

850th St

840th St

830th St

250th Ave

Hager City

Cross behind the Drive-In and turn left on 170th (unmarked)

170th St

490th Ave

650th St

650th St

610th St

210th Ave

670th St

EE

Esdaile

490th Ave

CENEX station
Rest Stop

Ellsworth

(R) Broadway St

670th St

650th St / Crosstown Rd

580th Ave

610th Ave

(R) Wall St/Railroad Av

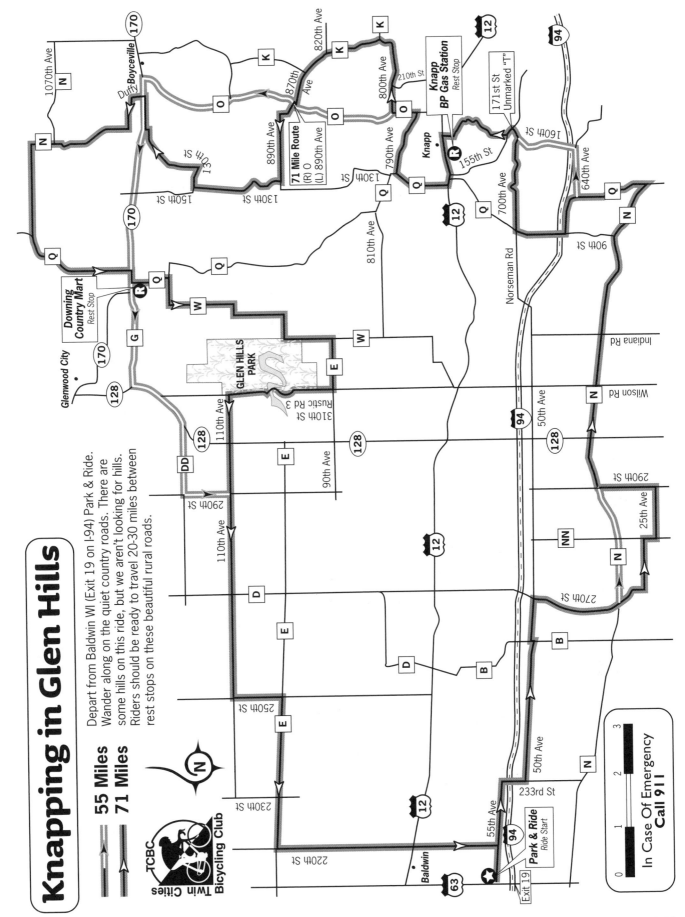

Knapping in Glen Hills

Depart from Baldwin WI (Exit 19 on I-94) Park & Ride. Wander along on the quiet country roads. There are some hills on this ride, but we aren't looking for hills. Riders should be ready to travel 20-30 miles between rest stops on these beautiful rural roads.

55 Miles
71 Miles

TCBC
Twin Cities Bicycling Club

In Case Of Emergency
Call 911

0   1   2   3

71 Mile Route
(R) O
(L) 890th Ave

Knapp
BP Gas Station
Rest Stop

*Downing
Country Mart*
Rest Stop

GLEN HILLS
PARK

310th St
Rustic Rd 3

Park & Ride
Ride Start

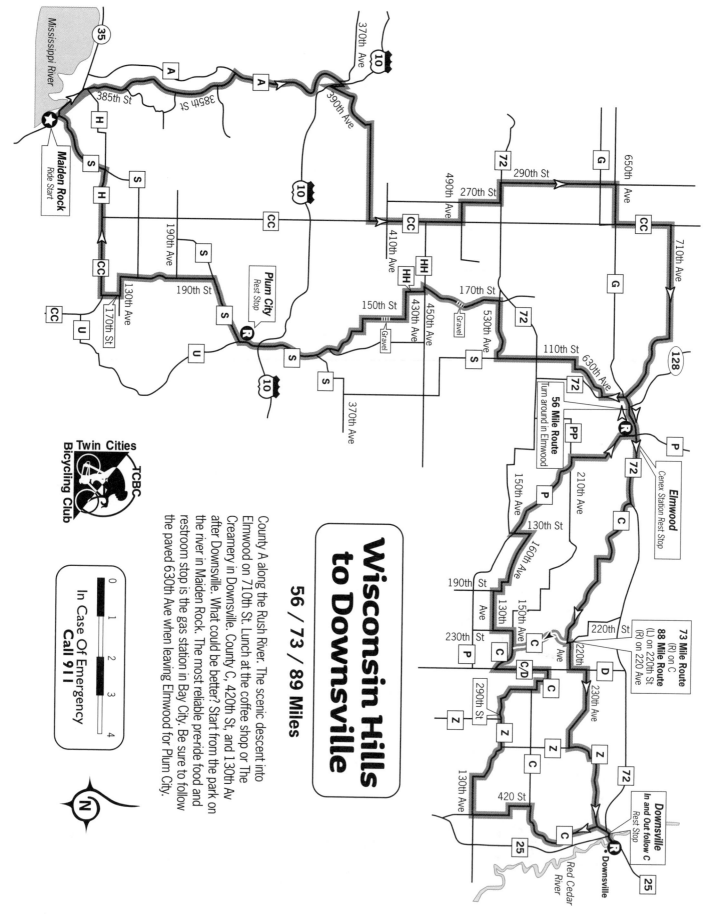

Wisconsin Hills to Downsville

56 / 73 / 89 Miles

County A along the Rush River. The scenic descent into Elmwood on 710th St. Lunch at the coffee shop or The Creamery in Downsville. County C, 420th St, and 130th Av after Downsville. What could be better? Start from the park on the river in Maiden Rock. The most reliable pre-ride food and restroom stop is the gas station in Bay City. Be sure to follow the paved 630th Ave when leaving Elmwood for Plum City.

Twin Cities Bicycling Club
TCBC

In Case Of Emergency
Call 911

0 1 2 3 4

N

Cruisin' the Coulees 1

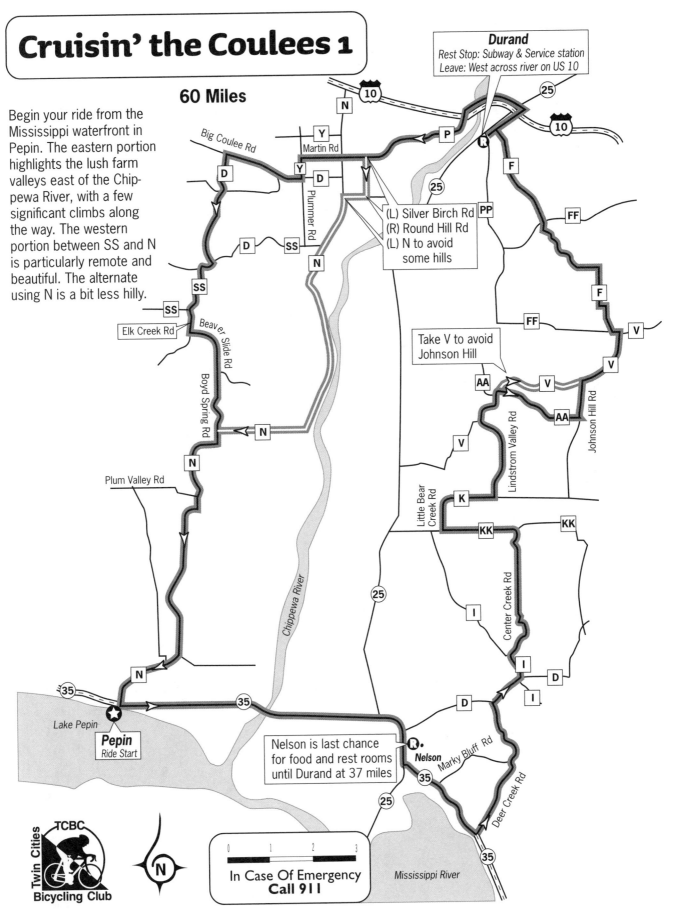

60 Miles

Begin your ride from the Mississippi waterfront in Pepin. The eastern portion highlights the lush farm valleys east of the Chippewa River, with a few significant climbs along the way. The western portion between SS and N is particularly remote and beautiful. The alternate using N is a bit less hilly.

Durand
Rest Stop: Subway & Service station
Leave: West across river on US 10

(L) Silver Birch Rd
(R) Round Hill Rd
(L) N to avoid some hills

Take V to avoid Johnson Hill

Big Coulee Rd
Martin Rd
Plummer Rd
Elk Creek Rd
Beaver Slide Rd
Boyd Spring Rd
Plum Valley Rd
Lindstrom Valley Rd
Johnson Hill Rd
Little Bear Creek Rd
Center Creek Rd
Marky Bluff Rd
Deer Creek Rd

Chippewa River

Lake Pepin

Pepin
Ride Start

Nelson is last chance for food and rest rooms until Durand at 37 miles

Nelson

Mississippi River

TCBC
Twin Cities
Bicycling Club

0 1 2 3

In Case Of Emergency
Call 911

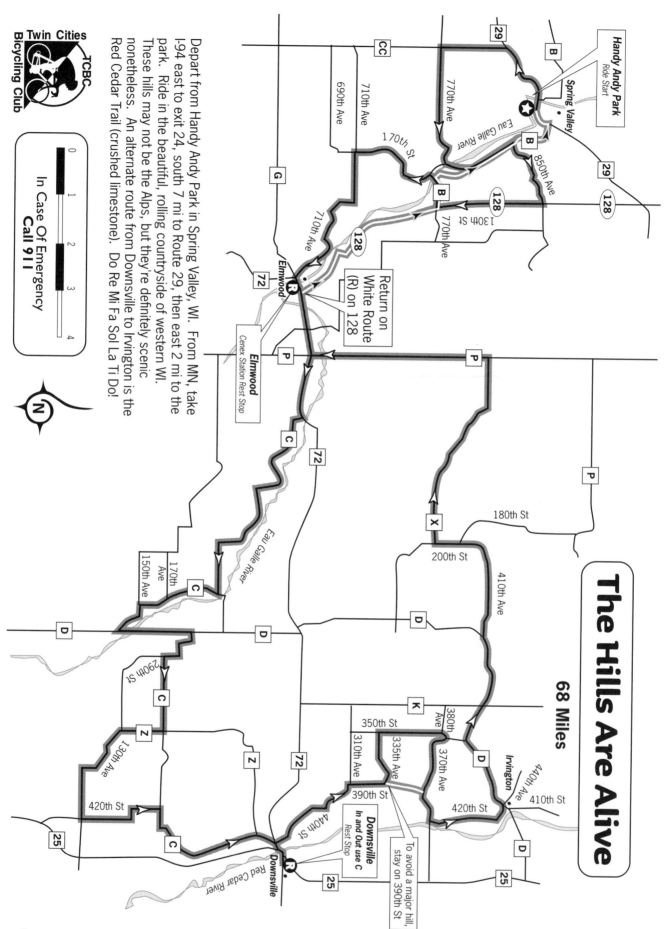

The Hills Are Alive

68 Miles

Depart from Handy Andy Park in Spring Valley, WI. From MN, take I-94 east to exit 24, south 7 mi to Route 29, then east 2 mi to the park. Ride in the beautiful, rolling countryside of western WI. These hills may not be the Alps, but they're definitely scenic nonetheless. An alternate route from Downsville to Irvington is the Red Cedar Trail (crushed limestone). Do Re Mi Fa Sol La Ti Do!

Twin Cities Bicycling Club
TCBC

In Case Of Emergency
Call 911

0 1 2 3 4

N

136

Handy Andy Park
Ride Start

Spring Valley

Eau Galle River

850th Ave

Return on White Route (R) on 128

Elmwood
Cenex Station Rest Stop

Eau Galle River

Red Cedar River

Downsville
In and Out use C
Rest Stop

Irvington

To avoid a major hill, stay on 390th St

Wisconsin Ride Journal

Date _____ Mileage _____

Route _____

Notes _____

_____

Date _____ Mileage _____

Route _____

Notes _____

_____

Date _____ Mileage _____

Route _____

Notes _____

_____

Date _____ Mileage _____

Route _____

Notes _____

_____

Date _____ Mileage _____

Route _____

Notes _____

_____

Date _____ Mileage _____

Route _____

Notes _____

_____

Date _____ Mileage _____

Route _____

Notes _____

_____

Date _____ Mileage _____

Route _____

Notes _____

_____

Date _____ Mileage _____

Route _____

Notes _____

_____

Date _____ Mileage _____

Route _____

Notes _____

_____

Minnesota Trail System Map

Asphalt

Crushed Limestone/Aggregate Crushed Aggregate

Natural Surface

Undeveloped

Tower • Ely
Grand Marais

Mesabi Trail

Grand Rapids

Gitchi-Gami

Bemidji
Cass Lake

Lake Itasca

Paul Bunyan

Heartland

Walker

Two Harbors

Park Rapids

Hackensack

Willard Munger Alex Leveau Segment

Duluth
Superior

Paul Bunyan

Cuyuna Lake

Aitkin

Carlton

Fergus Falls

Brainerd

Willard Munger

Central Lakes

Hinckley

Alexandria
Osakis

Willard Munger Boundary Segment

Avon

Lake Wobegon

Sunrise Prairie Hardwood Creek Trail

Richmond

St. Croix Falls

Glacial Lakes

Willard Munger Gateway Segment

Wilmar

Luce Line

Plymouth

St Paul

Hutchinson

Shakopee

Minnesota Valley

Cannon Valley

Red Wing

LeSueur

Mill Towns

Cannon Falls

Goodhue Pioneer

Mankato

Faribault
Pine Island

Great River Ridge

Onalaska

Walnut Grove

Douglas

Rochester

Pipestone

Casey Jones

Sakatah Singing Hills

Root River

La Crosse

Houston

Austin

Preston

Albert Lea

LeRoy

Harmony-Preston

Harmony

Blazing Star

Shooting Star

Minnesota has been blessed with a plethora of bike trails both in and outside of the metro area.

Metro Trails: Given that the number of trails is far too many to accurately depict within the contents of this Atlas, please visit www.dot.state.mn.us/bike/ and click on "Bicycle Maps".

Minnesota Trail Legend		TOTAL MILES	PAVED	NOT PAVED	Bicycling in Minnesota www.dot.state.mn.us/bike/
State Trail	**Segment**				**Links to Trail Maps**
Blazing Star Trail	Albert Lea - Big Island State Park	6	6		www.dnr.state.mn.us/state_trails/blazingstar/index.html
Casey Jones Trail	City of Pipestone - Murray Cty Line	12		12	www.dnr.state.mn.us/state_trails/casey_jones/index.html
	Lake Wilson	2		2	
	Currie-Lake Shetek State Park Loop	6	6		
Cannon Valley Trail	Red Wing _ Cannon Falls		42		www.mntrails.com/main.asp?SectionID=3&SubSectionID=85&TM=36774.91
Central Lakes Trail	Osakis - Fergus Falls	55	55		www.dnr.state.mn.us/state_trails/central_lakes/index.html
Cuyuna Lakes Trail	Crosby - Crow Wing County Road 128	5.1	5.1		http://cuyunalakestrail.org/index.cfm?pageid=105
Douglas Trail	Rochester - Pine Island	13	13		www.dnr.state.mn.us/state_trails/douglas/index.html
Gateway Trail	St. Paul - Duluth	88	88		www.dnr.state.mn.us/state_trails/gateway/index.html
Gitchi-Gami Trail	Silver Creek Cliff	1	1		www.dnr.state.mn.us/state_trails/gitchigami/index.html
	Gooseberry Falls State Park	1.2	1.2		
	Split Rock River - Beaver Bay	8.4	8.4		
	Schroeder - Tofte	3	3		
	Tofte - Onion River	2.5	2.5		
	Grand Marais	1	1		
Glacial Lakes Trail	Willmar - New London - Hawick	18	13.7	4.25	www.dnr.state.mn.us/state_trails/glacial_lakes/index.html
	Hawick - Richmond	22			
Goodhue- Pioneer Trail	Red Wing - Hay Creek Unit	4			http://cc.pineislandmn.com/naturalres0008.asp
	Zumbrota - 4 miles No. of Zumbrota	4		4	
Heartland Trail	Park Rapids - Cass Lake	47	47		http://files.dnr.state.mn.us/maps/state_trails/tra00718.pdf
Itasca Trail	Itasca State Park Loop				www.mntrails.com/main.asp?SectionID=49&SubSectionID=125&AdId=81
Lake Wobegon Trail	St. Joseph - Osakis				www.lakewobegontrails.com/
Luce Line Trail	Plymouth - Cedar Mills	53		53	www.dnr.state.mn.us/state_trails/luce_line/index.html
	Cedar Mills - Cosmos (Mowed grass)	10		10	
Mesabi Trail	International Falls - Tower	135		69	www.mesabitrail.com/
Mill Towns Trail	Dundas - Northfield	3	3		www.milltownstrail.org/
MN Valley State Recreation Area Trails	Ft. Snelling - Shakopee	19	6	13	www.dnr.state.mn.us/state_parks/minnesota_valley/index.html
	Shakopee - Chaska	5		5	
	Chaska - Belle Plaine	20		20	
North Shore Trail	Duluth - Grand Marais	146		146	www.dnr.state.mn.us/state_trails/north_shore/index.html
Paul Bunyan Trail	Brainerd / Baxter - Walker	71	70.5		www.dnr.state.mn.us/state_trails/paul_bunyan/index.html
	Walker - Lake Bemidji State Park	37	10	27	
Root River Trail	Root River Segment	42	42		www.dnr.state.mn.us/state_trails/blufflands/root_river.html
	Fountain - Houston Segment				
	Harmony - Preston Segment	18	18		
Sakatah Singing Hills	Mankato - Fairbault	39	39		www.dnr.state.mn.us/state_trails/sakatah/index.html
Shooting Star Trail	LeRoy - Taopi	8	8		www.dnr.state.mn.us/state_trails/shootingstar/index.html
Taconite Trail	Grand Rapids - Coleraine	4	4		www.dnr.state.mn.us/state_trails/taconite/index.html
	Coleraine - Ely	159		107	
Willard Munger Trail	Boundary Segment	80		80	www.dnr.state.mn.us/state_trails/willard_munger/index.html

Western Wisconsin Trail System Map

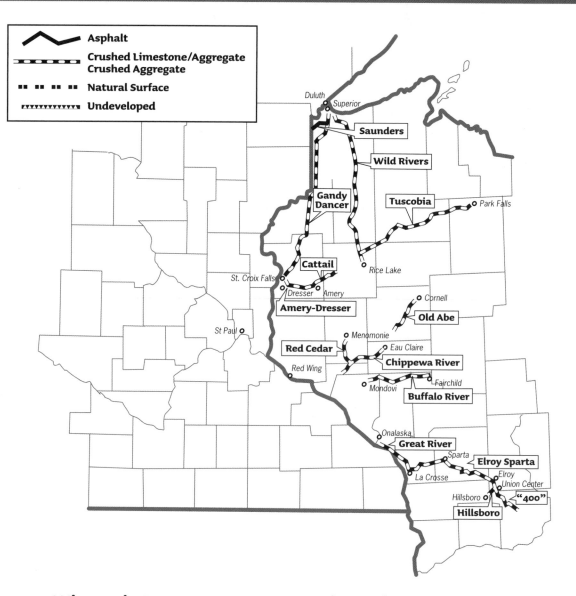

Legend:
- Asphalt
- Crushed Limestone/Aggregate Crushed Aggregate
- Natural Surface
- Undeveloped

Saunders
Wild Rivers
Gandy Dancer
Tuscobia
Cattail
Old Abe
Amery-Dresser
Red Cedar
Chippewa River
Buffalo River
Great River
Elroy Sparta
Hillsboro
"400"

Duluth, Superior, Park Falls, St. Croix Falls, Dresser, Amery, Rice Lake, Cornell, St Paul, Menomonie, Eau Claire, Red Wing, Fairchild, Mondovi, Onalaska, Sparta, La Crosse, Elroy, Union Center, Hillsboro

Wisconsin Department of Natural Resources

Touring Bike Trails
http://dnr.wi.gov/org/land/parks/trails/tbike.html

Find A Trail
http://dnr.wi.gov/org/land/parks/specific/findatrail.html

Wisconsin Department of Transportation

Wisconsin Bicycle Maps
www.dot.wisconsin.gov/travel/bike-foot/bike-maps.html

Downloadable County Bike Maps
www.dot.wisconsin.gov/travel/bike-foot/countymaps.html

Wisconsin Bike Trails
www.wisconline.com/attractions/biketrails.html

Wisconsin Trail Legend

State Trail	Segment	TOTAL MILES	PAVED	NOT PAVED	Trail Map Links
Amery - Dresser Trail	Amery - Dresser	14		14	www.dnr.state.wi.us/org/land/parks/specific/buffalo/index.html
Buffalo River Trail	Mondovi - Fairchild	36.4		36.4	www.dnr.state.wi.us/org/land/parks/specific/buffalo/index.html
Cattail Trail	Barron County	17.8		17.8	www.mntrails.com/main.asp?SectionID=3&SubSectionID=85&TM=36774.91
Chippewa River Trail	Eau Claire - Red Cedar Trail	26.5	5	21.5	www.dnr.state.wi.us/org/land/parks/specific/chiprivertrail/
400 Trail	Elroy - Reedsburg	22		22	www.dnr.state.wi.us/org/land/parks/specific/400/index.html
Gandy Dancer Trail	St. Croix Falls - Superior	98		98	http://cuyunalakestrail.org/index.cfm?pageid=105
Great River Trail	Onalaska - Trempealeau	24		24	www.dnr.state.wi.us/org/land/parks/specific/greatriver/index.html
Hillsboro Trail	Hillsboro - 400 Trail	4.2		4.2	www.dnr.state.wi.us/org/land/parks/specific/findatrail.html#map
Old Abe Trail	Lake Wissota Park - Brunet Island	19.5		19.5	www.dnr.state.wi.us/org/land/parks/specific/oldabe/index.html
Red Cedar Trail	Menomonie - Chippewa River Trail	14.5		14.5	www.dnr.state.wi.us/org/land/parks/specific/findatrail.html#map
Elroy Sparta Trails	Elroy - Sparta	32.5		32.5	www.dnr.state.wi.us/org/land/parks/specific/elroysparta/index.html
Saunders Trail	Connects Gandy Dancer to MN	8.4		8.4	www.dnr.state.wi.us/org/land/parks/specific/Saunders/index.html
Tuscobia Trail	Rice Lake to Park Falls	74		74	www.tuscobiatrail.com/
Wild Rivers Trail	Rice Lake to Superior	104		104	http://dnr.wi.gov/org/land/parks/specific/wildrivers/

ELROY-SPARTA STATE TRAIL

This 32 mile state trail was formerly the mainline of the Chicago and North Western Railway. The conversion from "rail to trail" represented a new concept in recreational development. Utilizing the abandoned railbed, it was the first trail of its kind in the United States to be designated a National Recreation Trail by the United States Department of Interior. The trail is primarily used for bicycling, hiking and snowmobiling. Passing through scenic areas, it links the communities of Elroy, Kendall, Wilton, Norwalk and Sparta. Added attractions are its three tunnels, the longest being 3,833 feet. Train service began in 1873 as steam locomotives hauled grain, livestock and passengers. Rail service ended in 1964. The trail was established by the Department of Natural Resources in 1965 and opened to the public in 1967.

Erected 1979

The Bike Atlas Committee

The Team

Front row L to R,

Steve Scott

Patt Seleen

Jim Dohogne

Scott Larson

Mary Derks

Mike Beadles

Cindy Hanson

Back row,

Pete May

Ben Wilson

Michael Mcnutt

Jim Pittenger

Charles Breer

Not shown:

Elroy Balgaard

Lee Thielman

Tony Wanschura

Jeremy Weizel

The 7th edition of the Minnesota Bike Atlas has come together - thanks to the countless hours of work put in by this volunteer committee. And what a team it was!

Meeting once a month since January 2007, ideas for the maps, cue sheets and CD and the look for the Atlas emerged. The shared talent and commitment from the group was unbelievable. We laughed, got creative, posed for pictures, and ate pizza. Then we went to work.

On every team, there are some key players who bring the project home. For this Atlas, it is only fair to give special credit to the following individuals:

Steve Scott, our Art Director with over 30 years in the business, guided us in every way and has designed this Atlas to be a professional publication.

Pete May, our Map Maker, has been involved with the last 6 Atlas editions. He took each map and gave it back to us with a consistent and friendly look.

Ben Wilson coordinated our section leaders (Mike Beadles, Charles Breer, Jim Dohogne, Scott Larson, Lee Thielman and Tony Wanschura) and Pete as they talked to the leaders, gathered the maps, checked the routes and completed the cue sheets.

Patt Seleen kept an eye on the entire project. Working closely with our content group (Mary Derks, Cindy Hanson, Michael McNutt, Jim Pittenger, Steve Scott and Jeremy Weizel), many great ideas were generated and incorporated.

Elroy Balgaard, a talented interactive CD designer, stepped forward when asked by his colleague, Steve Scott. Together with Pete's maps, they have put this Atlas on a CD, making it come alive for you as you begin to explore the rides.

Most of our committee members are also TCBC Ride Leaders. So, in addition to making this Atlas happen, we found time to collectively cycle tens of thousands of miles. We've ridden together on TCBC rides in Minnesota and Wisconsin, becoming good friends along the way. We've also taken on personal challenges such as riding across the United States, doing solo unsupported bike trips, and biking with our families in national parks.

We hope you will embrace the love of cycling as much as we all do. We have worked together this past year as a team and are proud to bring you this brand new edition of the Minnesota Bike Atlas!

JUST PLAIN
FANCY

To Justine Marie Arvold
and the plain fancy miracle
that brought her to us

Published by
Dragonfly Books®
an imprint of
Random House Children's Books
a division of Random House, Inc.
1540 Broadway
New York, New York 10036

Text and illustrations copyright © 1990 by Patricia Polacco

Visit us on the Web! www.randomhouse.com/kids

Educators and librarians, for a variety of teaching tools, visit us at
www.randomhouse.com/teachers

ISBN: 0-440-40937-3

Reprinted by arrangement with Bantam Books for Young Readers

Printed in the United States of America

April 1994

14 15 16 17 18 19 20 21 22 23

JUST PLAIN
FANCY

PATRICIA POLACCO

DRAGONFLY BOOKS®   NEW YORK

Kaleb and his two daughters hurried along Lancaster County Road in their buggy. Cars whizzed by them, but they paid no mind. *Clop, clop, clop* went the horse's hooves on the pavement.

"Papa," Naomi asked, "why don't we have a car like the English?"

"It is not our way, child. We are in no hurry," he said as he drew up the reins and slowly directed the horse into their farmyard.

PENNSTA
HATCH
EXOTIC & DOMESTIC BIRDS

While their father unharnessed and watered the horse, Naomi and Ruth skipped toward the henhouse. The chickens were Naomi's responsibility. She saw to their feeding and watering as well as the collecting of their eggs.

"Everything around here is so plain," Naomi complained. "Our clothes are plain, our houses are plain, even our chickens are plain. It would pleasure me—just once—to have something fancy."

"Shaw, Nomi, you aughtn't to be saying such things," little Ruth scolded.

As the days passed, Naomi and Ruth checked Henny's nest constantly. Every day they peered over the edge of the crib, watching for signs of cracks in the shells. Then, one day, the eggs hatched.

"Look at the little chick from the fancy egg, Nomi," Ruth squealed.

"That egg was fancy inside and out, wasn't it?" said Naomi. "Fancy. That's just what we'll name this chick."

"Fancy, Fancy, Fancy, Fancy," Ruth sang out as she jumped about. Naomi smiled and clapped her hands.

All that afternoon, the girls stayed with Henny, watching and studying their special little chick.

Weeks passed. Henny's chicks grew quickly and were soon scratching around in the dirt. They had all lost their yellow down feathers and had grown bright white ones. All of them, except Fancy. Fancy looked very different from the others. There was no doubt about it—this chick wasn't plain!

One afternoon in the washhouse, Naomi and Ruth overheard Aunt Sarai talking to cousin Hannah about a person in the neighboring Amish community.

"She dressed too fancy," Sarai said. "She had to be *shunned!*"

"Is it wrong to be fancy?" Naomi asked.

"Indeed, yes!" snapped Hannah. "We are plain folk. It is in our laws, the *Ordnung,* that we must be plain!"

"What does . . . 'shun' mean?" Ruth asked haltingly.

"Someone who is shunned is shamed in front of the elders. After that, friends and neighbors are instructed not to speak to that person. They are no longer one of us," Sarai answered with authority. Naomi and Ruth looked at each other and hurried outside to hang up the washing. Naomi felt botherment inside.

As soon as they were finished, the girls ran to the henhouse.

"What are we going to do?" Ruth asked. "Fancy is too fancy to be Amish!" Then Fancy ruffled up his feathers and did something that took their breath clean away.

"We'll have to hide him until we know what to do," Naomi said finally. "The elders will be here for the frolic tomorrow."

"He'll be shunned," Ruth whimpered. "Maybe we will be, too!"

They put Fancy into another part of the henhouse and locked the door.

The next morning, the neighboring Amish folk arrived for the frolic. The men and boys helped add a stable onto the Vleckes' barn. They worked hard in the sun while the womenfolk cooked and gossiped. Naomi and Ruth helped serve the food, pour lemonade, and thread needles for the women who were quilting. This should have been a happy day for them. But the girls were not pleasured because they were sad with worry about Fancy.

When she had served the last ladle of lemonade, Naomi started toward the henhouse. Just then she noticed the open door. But before she could get there to shut it, Fancy darted out and ran toward the gathering, flapping his wings.

"Oh, no!" Naomi called out. "This is all my fault. I wanted something fancy. I should have known better than to make that kind of wish!"

Tears ran down Ruth's cheeks when she saw what had happened. "Poooor Fancy," she cried. "Now he'll be shunned."

Over . . . Under . . . Around . . . Through. . . . Naomi ran after Fancy, trying to catch him before anyone noticed. And that's about the time that Fancy decided to head straight for the elders. He flew at Martha, the oldest member of the gathering. Adjusting her glasses, she gasped as he flew over her head just before landing on the clothesline where the quilts were airing.

"Please don't shun him," Naomi cried. "I did this! I made him fancy," she sobbed. At that moment, pleased with all the attention, Fancy ruffled his feathers and did for the guests what he had done for the girls in the henhouse the day before. Those who weren't speechless were stunned!

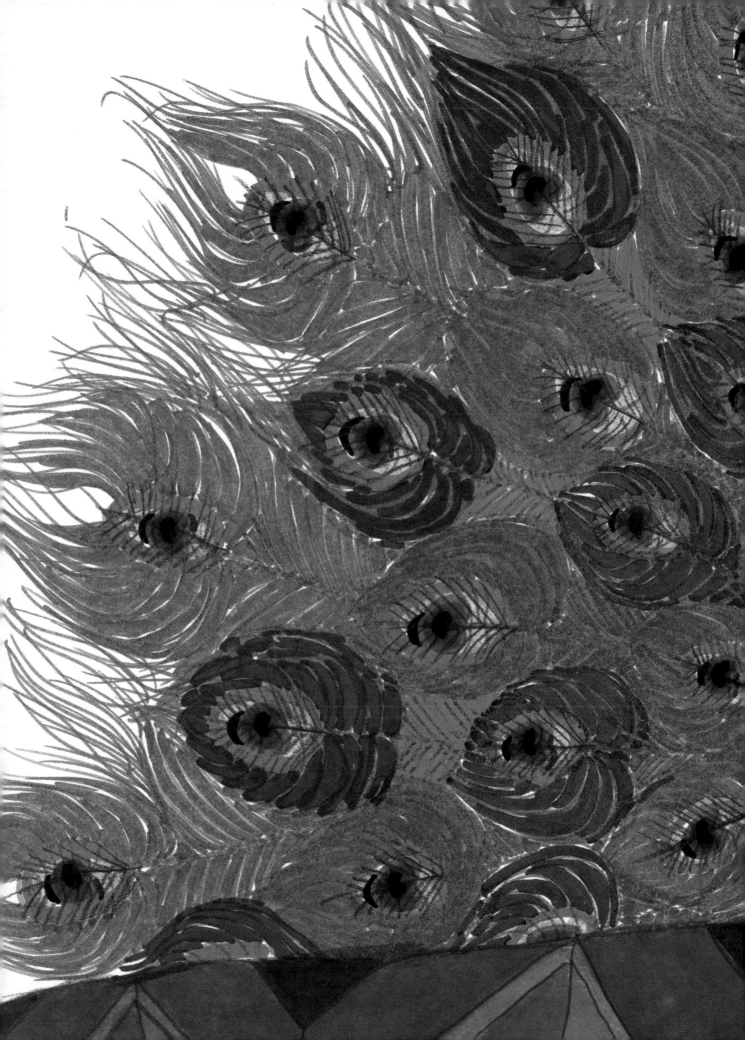

"Dry your tears, child." It was Martha who finally spoke. "This isn't your doing. This be God's handiwork. Only He could think up colors like that."

"You mean you aren't going to shun him?" Ruth asked.

"One can only be shunned for going against the ways of our people," Martha continued. "This is no plain old chicken. This be one of God's most beautiful creations. He is fancy, child, and that's the way of it."

All who were gathered there rejoiced in Fancy's beauty. "I believe you have this coming, child," old Martha said as she held out the new white organdy cap. "Your family believes you have earned this well. And I agree. Not only have you given good and faithful care to your flock of chickens, but you have also raised one of the finest peacocks I ever did see!"

Standing proudly amidst the gathering, Naomi held Fancy in her arms. She had learned many things that day.

And although no one ever quite knew how Fancy came to be hatched by Henny, it was never questioned. Plainly it was a miracle . . . and sometimes miracles are JUST PLAIN FANCY!